THE AIR TRAVELER'S HANDBOOK

CO-PILOT: HEATHROW GROUND FROM SILVERBIRD FIVE-O-ONE STAND JULIET ONE-FIVE
REQUESTING START-UP CLEARANCE.........TOWER: SILVERBIRD FIVE-O-ONE IS CLEARED
TO THE JOHN F. KENNEDY AIRPORT. YOUR INITIAL ROUTEING IS TO BRECON TWO-EIGHT......

......TOWER: CLEARED TO LINE UP AND HOLD ON RUNWAY TWO-EIGHT LEFT......................................

THE **AIR TRAVELER'S HANDBOOK**

THE COMPLETE GUIDE TO AIR TRAVEL, AIRPLANES, AND AIRPORTS

ST. MARTIN'S PRESS
New York

......SILVERBIRD FIVE-O-ONE IS CLEARED FOR TAKE OFF.....WIND TWO SIX-O AT ONE-TWO.........

Consultant Editor

Bill Gunston Associate compiler of *Jane's All The World's Aircraft*, formerly technical editor of *Flight International*, and author of more than 250 books on flight and flying.

Editor: Helen Varley
Revisions Editor: John O. E. Clark

Research: Helen Armstrong
Caroline Landeau
Jazz Wilson

Art Directors: Barry Moscrop
Eddie Poulton
Design: Paul Wilkinson
Hélène Morey

Artwork: Arka Graphics

Prelims Photographs: Arnold Desser

A Marshall Edition
Conceived, edited and designed by
Marshall Editions Ltd
170 Piccadilly
London W1V 9DD

Printed and bound in Singapore by Imago Productions (FE) PTE Limited

Library of Congress Cataloging-in-Publication Data
The air traveler's handbook
    1. Aeronautics, commercial   2. Transport planes   3. Airports. I. Marshall Editions Ltd.
TL552.A15   1988   387.7   88-18463
ISBN 0-312-02072–4

This edition first published in Great Britain by Pan Books Ltd under the title *The Flier's Handbook*.

First U.S. Edition

10 9 8 7 6 5 4 3 2 1

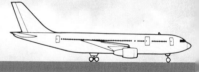

Contributors to original edition

Basil Arkell (Rotorcraft design consultant)

Gordon Bain (Civil Aviation Authority)

J. W. Birchall (Deputy Chief Air Traffic Controller, London Airport, Heathrow)

L. F. E. Coombs (Smiths Industries Ltd.)

Captain T. W. Cummings (Founder of Pan Am's "Fearful Fliers" seminars)

Captain Thomas G. Foxworth (727 pilot, Pan AM; ICAO Airworthiness Committee; author of *The Speed Seekers*)

Ian Goold (*Flight International*)

N. P. Harmse (KLM Royal Dutch Airlines)

Mike Hirst (Technical Editor, *Flight International*)

Bob Jackson (Flight engineer)

Judi Loach (University of Essex)

Alec Lumsden (Formerly of the British Aircraft Corporation, technical writer and Master Photographer)

Sir Peter Masefield (Chairman, Project Management Ltd., Deputy Chairman, British Caledonian Airways, Past President of the Royal Aeronautical Society and of the Chartered Institute of Transport)

Tony Osman (Science Editor, *The Sunday Times Magazine*)

Brian Tomkins (Managing Director, Airline Publications and Sales Ltd.)

Dr. Anthony Turner (Senior Overseas Medical Officer, British Airways Medical Service, Honorary Associate Physician, and Lecturer, Hospital of Tropical Diseases, London)

Ann Welch (Vice-President, Fédération Aéronautique Internationale; author of *Pilot's Weather*)

Mike Wilson (Technical Editor, *Flight International*)

David Woolley (Editor, *Airports International*)

Contents

"Rotate!"

The flight crew will be at the airport an hour before takeoff — earlier if the route is unfamiliar. Each member has to sign in, undertaking that he has read the flying regulations. Licences, vaccinations and passports must be up-to-date and all crew members must be "dry": no alcohol within eight hours of a flight, sometimes more, depending on airline rules or state laws.

Neither captains nor airlines like to deliver their customers late, so crews vie in the Flight Dispatch Office for the most favourable altitude on the shortest route. The dispatcher recommends a route; the captain may disagree. An unfavourable route may add half an hour of flying time. Over a year this could cost a large airline company as much as 2,500,000 tons of fuel on 500,000 flights in one year.

The captain settles on a fuel load allowing for a possible long wait before takeoff, and for fog or some other eventuality closing the destination airport, which would mean flying to an alternate.

About 40 minutes before departure time, the flight engineer begins a walk-round check. Rules for passing a plane to fly are laid down by the book: if an air-conditioning system is less than perfect the plane is still airworthy; a malfunctioning thrust-reverser would be acceptable on a short-haul flight to a fine-weather airport, but not for a trip to an ice-bound runway. But if one of the hydraulic systems is suspect, the plane will have to be grounded for repair.

A captain can close his doors on late passengers, but he may wait if the delay is justified commercially. He may call the control tower while the last passengers are boarding to request clearance for start-up. If several planes are scheduled to fly the same way at the same time, the first to be cleared gets the best route.

The co-pilot calculates the maximum allowable takeoff weight. This depends on ground conditions, outside air temperature, wind speed and direction, and runway length. Last-minute changes are possible; in the Persian Gulf air temperature can rise — and air density fall — within minutes. Freight, free-ticket passengers (often airline employees), fuel and sometimes even passengers may be offloaded. If the cargo has been unevenly loaded, it affects the plane's trim and has to be relocated.

Cleared for push-back, the aircraft is manoeuvred out of the parking bay by a tug. The tower gives the taxi-route to the runway over the radio.

In line for takeoff the crew checks the flying controls and instruments, and runs through the appropriate takeoff drills.

When takeoff clearance comes, the captain or co-pilot pushes the throttles forward with his right hand; the other pilot backs him up, watching the electronic engine displays. The captain, his left hand on the nose-wheel steering tiller by his left knee, steers the aircraft like a bus until the rudder becomes effective. The co-pilot holds the yoke steady, calling out the speed as the needle on his dial flickers: "Eighty knots." "Cross-check. I have the yoke," calls the captain, taking the wheel with his left hand. His right hand stays on the throttles, ready to chop power should a sudden need to stop arise. The white centreline markings rush at them, faster and faster. "Vee-one!" The co-pilot calls out the decision speed — Velocity one; if nothing untoward has happened the captain commits to takeoff. He puts his right hand on the wheel ... "Rotate!"

A gentle pull on the yoke and the nose rises. The ground falls away. "Vee-two — positive rate of climb." The plane is at the takeoff safety speed, calculated to produce the best

angle of climb for the weight. "Gear up," intones the captain. The landing-gears trundle into their wells.

The aircraft climbs steeply at first, at about 15 to 25 degrees, to gain height as quickly as possible and so reduce noise on the ground. The crew's attention is fixed on the flight instruments — the captain maintaining optimum speed, monitored by the co-pilot who calls out any discrepancies, the flight engineer watching the engine indicators. If speed drops too low alarms blare a warning.

Once clear of noise-sensitive zones, the aircraft is levelled off, speed increased, flaps retracted and the after takeoff checks carried out. The seat belt signs in the cabin are turned off, altimeters reset and systems checked. The autopilot may be engaged, relieving the pilot of much physical workload, but he still commands the automatics to fly the correct path.

An aircraft flies from radio beacon to radio beacon overland. Crossing the Atlantic from London to New York, the captain may follow a Standard Instrument Departure routeing (SID), initially heading for the Brecon radio beacon in South Wales while he calls up the Shanwick control centre for a route to Gander in Newfoundland.

The centre, or area, controllers may question the captain's route, and he may concede a reroute, argue or negotiate with another pilot on the "pilot's band". If he has to take a longer route than he planned, or is held down at an altitude uneconomical for his aircraft's engines, he may have to make a refuelling stop. Pilots and controllers usually give consideration to the flight with the longest haul and the heaviest load.

Once the plane is cruising, a rest roster is arranged. Some captains try to visit the cabin, a courtesy still appreciated by many passengers. On long flights, the crew keeps track of weather reports, checking winds regularly against the forecast, ready to request a rerouteing to gain a better flight time or a smoother ride.

The hard work begins again about 200 miles out from the destination. At busy terminals the plane may be cleared to descend to about 13,000 feet by a specific point on the map, and then guided by radar to within five miles of the runway. At airfields with little traffic the captain may be free to make his own approach, from cruise altitude. Tower controllers do not always know exactly who to expect, or when. Clearance to land is given as planes arrive.

There may be a long stay in a holding stack (where inbound traffic is directed to fly around an airport radio beacon) if there is a queue of traffic. Two minutes before touchdown, landing checks are made.

Some aircraft are equipped to land on the autopilot, but it is usually cut out at about 1,500 feet. Sometimes in bad weather one pilot will fly the approach and the other will take over when he sees the runway clearly.

With the flaps extended and the landing-gears down the plane needs more engine thrust and is noisier, so the pilot tries to keep it "clean" for as long as he can. It must be stabilized to land by 1,000 feet; if the gears are down five miles too early, the drag may cost an extra 80 gallons of fuel. To use minimum fuel, the plane should descend slowly, like a glider.

Thirty feet above the runway the pilot raises the plane's nose slightly in order to slow its rate of descent. He aims for a touchdown point — which disappears beneath the nose as he touches down at about 130 mph. Reverse thrust is engaged and wing lift-dumpers opened. As the rushing runway centreline slows in the pilots' vision to a series of separate markings, the series of after-landing checks begins.

Flight planning

The image of airline pilots poring over maps on long tables is archaic, and the old-style flight-planning room a relic of the past. These days flights are dispatched in a little under half an hour from an airline office filled with electronic equipment.

The crew checks in an hour or so before a flight. On some airlines crews work in teams, the same individuals always flying together, knowing each other well. Others may never have met before a brief handshake on signing in. If anyone fails to show up, a stand-in is called.

A computer, programmed by an army of personnel with data about the aircraft, its payload of passengers, freight, baggage and fuel, and updated with weather changes at high altitudes and at the destination, prints out several possible routes (minimum distance, minimum time, minimum cost) and selects the best. Several crews may want to fly the same airway at the same time; routes are allocated on a "first come, first served" basis.

The best route may ride a jet stream, a fast river of air which offers the most economical way of getting from A to B at high altitudes. It will be high above the weather, around the 250 millibar level at 34,000 feet.

Aircraft fly along designated airways. They are numbered like highways on the ground: J (for Jet) –80 is the "route 66" across the central tier of the USA. Airways do not necessarily link cities. They follow radio beams that radiate out from VOR navigation stations sited 200 to 300 miles apart. Pilots ply these tracks in the sky from station to station, but may deviate to avoid bad weather.

A captain planning a long-distance flight may take a great circle route, the shortest distance between departure point and destination, especially if no airway links the two. The latest

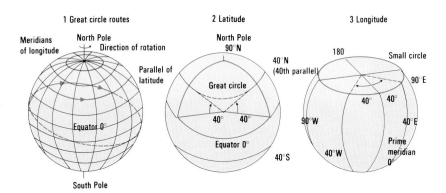

1 Great circle routes   **2 Latitude**   **3 Longitude**

The shortest distance between any two points on a sphere lies on a great circle which, marked on the surface of a globe, divides it into two equal halves. On a flight from A to B (**1**), since both A and B lie on the same parallel of latitude, the pilot could fly due east along it, but the shortest distance lies along the shorter of the two arcs that join the two points. If the path were continued round the Earth, along the dotted line, it would describe its diameter. Although the pilot leaves A initially heading north–east, by the time he arrives at B, he is flying south–east.

The Equator, the 0° latitude line, is the only parallel of latitude (**2**) that is a great circle; all other parallels are small circles. Latitude is measured north and south from the Equator through 90° in each direction. All meridians of longitude (**3**) are great circles. By international agreement the 0° or prime meridian passes through Greenwich, near London in the UK. Longitude is measured east and west from the prime meridian through 180° in each direction. Pilots calculate great circle distances using simple trigonometry. Long-range radio navigation waves also describe great circles.

navigation systems that do not depend on ground stations make this possible. To avoid annoying communities with sonic boom, Concorde's crew may have to pick a route that does not overfly land.

Fuel calculations follow choice of route. The heavier the plane the higher the rate of fuel consumption, so it costs fuel to carry fuel. The amount has to be correct to carry the payload to the destination, plus a contingency amount in case of unanticipated headwinds, and enough to divert to alternate airports.

A topped-up Boeing 747-400 carries about 387,000 pounds of fuel — enough for a big suburban swimming pool. It would be folly to haul so much on a short flight (New York to London is short, in modern aviation terms) or when the runway at departure or destination is short; planes must be light to take off and land safely on short runways.

But fuel prices vary from place to place and it may pay to load up with cheap fuel and burn extra to avoid filling up where fuel is costly.

Sheets of navigation and weather data, notices of conditions at destination airports and alternate routes, lists of VIPs and CIPs (a growing category: commercially important people), details of passengers' special requirements — and the flight plan — make a formidable document. When the captain has signed to accept the plan and the flight dispatch officer has confirmed it, it is filed, together with details of the aircraft's emergency equipment and procedures, with the national air traffic control service. Copies are teleprinted out to each of the control centres along the route.

Carrying briefcases laden with 12 pounds or so of charts and information, the crew leave for their aircraft.

One Jeppesen's high-altitude chart covers the entire USA. This section shows the area from El Paso to Albuquerque. The airways, numbered according to the degrees of the compass, converge on VOR navigation stations. They are marked with triangles and their latitude and longitude for insertion into aircraft navigation systems. The boxed numbers are nautical mileage distances between stations, and the upward-slanting lines show magnetic north. The shaded areas are military zones, forbidden to commercial and private planes. Established airways avoid them, but J-65-166 and J-108 that cross them are open at certain times.

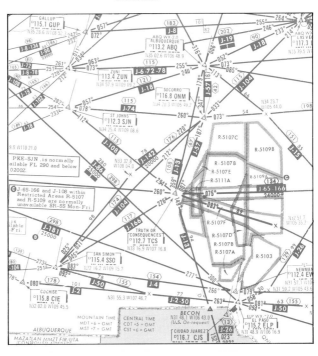

11

Predicting the weather

An airport weather office goes into high gear well before dawn, when the duty forecasters study data that has been flowing in all night from weather stations on land, at sea, in outer space, and from pilots in flight. Once fully digested by a computer, it is ready as coded hand-outs to give airline pilots the detailed information they need to satisfy themselves, as air regulations demand, that the weather is suitable for their flights.

Before takeoff pilots need to know the expected conditions for departure. Fog produces tedious delays, made more annoying when it is lying on the airport with gin-clear air only 1,000 feet up, and pilots need to know when it will clear and whether it may return. It often occurs on calm, cold nights, when warm air flows over cold sea, or during the passage of a cold front. Icing occurs in very moist air a little below freezing, and may mean that on takeoff hot air from jet en-

gines is needed for de-icing. This will reduce takeoff power, so loads may need adjustment.

Airline pilots must know surface conditions at airports within 30 minutes flying time. Should an engine fail after takeoff, the pilot may need a local alternative. Terminal area forecasts (TAFs) are made at major airport weather offices by meteorologists familiar with local weather patterns, and sent out by teleprinter.

Throughout the day forecasters produce synoptic weather charts giving the general weather picture for the surface and for high altitudes, and these are continuously updated. Synoptic charts warn about deep depressions and winds blowing around them. Over one side of a Low, planes encounter headwinds and use more fuel, but on the other, tailwinds shorten journey times and reduce fuel consumption. Jet streams, high-altitude tubes of air about 100 miles

Radio-sonde balloons, released at fixed intervals, provide local data on lapse rate (the fall of temperature with height) humidity, and wind velocity at different levels. Linked to a radio transmitter which emits a series of musical notes for interpretation by the ground station, the balloon takes about an hour to ascend to 60,000 ft, where it bursts. The apparatus descends by parachute and may be recovered.

Ceilometers enable airport meteorologists to establish the base height of low-lying cloud. A transmitter projects an angled light beam upwards. This bounces off the cloud base and is received by a recorder; from the angle of the beam meteorologists can calculate the cloud-base height.

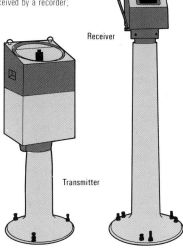

Receiver

Transmitter

wide and two miles deep which work to balance world temperatures, can produce 400-mph winds.

While fuel calculations are being made, the captain concentrates on any SIGs, significant weather reports, and may need to discuss these with the forecaster. They may warn of thunderstorms (grown from the hot, moist air and atmospheric instability which are common in warm climates) which may contain turbulence, lightning, heavy rain or hail.

Thunderstorms rumbling over a destination airport mean that aircraft have to land in the turbulence and sharp wind changes — windshear — beneath massive thunderheads. Forecasters keep a close watch for adverse windshear; it can reduce a jet's airspeed dangerously, sometimes by over 60 mph.

Sometimes, high in clear air, turbulence occurs with a peculiar "cobblestone" feel. Severe clear air turbulence (CAT) may cause a plane to shake noticeably and even alter altitude, but it does not last long if the captain can change flight level.

En route the crew tune into the continuous VHF Volmet radio transmission, and monitor the aircraft's weather radar (page 50), checking for storms, and endeavouring to fly above or around them. Storm lightning may not do structural damage but can burn off aerials (antennas) or affect radio-navigation equipment, particularly at lower levels. Hail, especially the giant variety, is dangerous. Millions of ice golf balls bombarding a wing may damage the skin. Crews also monitor inertial navigation equipment (page 52) for warning of windshear.

Because the weather knows no boundaries, meteorologists have developed an international language of data presentation, so airline pilots have no translation difficulties.

This tropopause/vertical windshear chart gives the altitude of the tropopause (the layer of atmosphere between the lower troposphere and the upper, almost weatherless, stratosphere) where most strong winds occur. It varies from 20,000 ft high over the Poles to more than 40,000 ft high above the Equator. For better engine performance, jet pilots fly in the cold air high above the relatively warm conditions near the tropopause. They avoid turbulent air in the high and low pressure contours where the tropopause penetrates the stratosphere, and around the jet streams, marked by arrows. The dotted lines, superimposed from a SIG (significant weather report) chart of the same date, mark areas of CAT (clear air turbulence).

The Earth's weather can be clearly seen from European Space Agency (ESA) satellites. Launched under the auspices of member countries of the World Meteorological Organization, five satellites have been sent up over the Equator to give an accurate global picture of prevailing weather conditions. The ESA satellites are geo-stationary: they move around the Earth in 24 hours, over fixed points on the surface. They transmit infra-red photographs of cloud formations over a large area of the Earth's surface.

The control tower

The control tower is the nerve centre of an airport. At the busiest international centres controllers may direct up to 2,000 aircraft movements a day, more than one a minute during the busiest hours.

The tower has to be tall enough to give controllers an unobstructed view across the airfield. It may be a small double-decker cabin at a club airfield, from which one controller directs aircraft along a single airstrip, or as large as the 260-foot monolith at Charles de Gaulle Airport, from where a team of seven or more command a view across a runway complex of 11 square miles.

Control towers in the largest airports have two control rooms. Controllers in the visual control room at the top are responsible for aircraft taking off, for aircraft taxiing, and for final landing instructions. Assistants log aircraft departure and arrival times, from which landing charges are prepared, and man the computer, which prints out the estimated times of arrival of each flight and scheduled times of departure. A ground movement planning controller books slots (available times) along the airways for departures.

An atmosphere of cool urgency prevails in the dimly-lit approach control room, usually located below. Here, approach controllers, working in the eerie glow from their radarscopes, guide inbound traffic to the runways. Should a runway inspection, or a change in landing direction caused by a wind change, or overloading at peak hours, cause a delay, aircraft are fed into holding stacks, flying around a radio beacon until given landing clearance. The approach controllers integrate the flow from two or more stacks, handing them over to a radar director, who weaves the streams into a single line stretching out along the approach path. A safe separation distance of three to four miles between incoming flights provides a landing interval of about one minute. Aircraft overflying the congested airport zone are controlled by a separate radar director.

The radar screens are ringed with concentric circles, called range marks, representing distances of two, five or ten miles from the antenna. With the aid of a compass rose superimposed on the radarscope, controllers can accurately calculate aircraft positions. Dotted and solid lines encircle radio-navigation reference points. The "blips" or "targets" pinpoint each moving aircraft. In modern alphanumeric displays, each target is labelled with the flight number, and the aircraft's altitude and routeing, for rapid identification. The blip continually fades, then brightens as a new position appears.

Intense concentration is needed to track dozens of aircraft moving at speed within a small area, and controllers take a 30-minute "winddown" break after a maximum of two hours' work on the radarscopes.

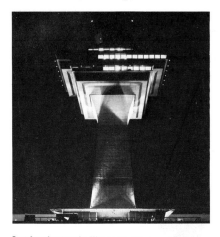

Saarinen's pagoda-like control tower at Dallas International Airport is 193 ft high. The glass-enclosed "cab" at the top is surmounted by obstruction lights as a warning to low-flying aircraft at night. A radome protects the short-range radar scanner and an FM radio antenna keeps controllers and pilots in contact.

The visual control room (the ''cab'') at the top of the tower at Chicago O'Hare Airport **above** is rounded to give the controllers an unobstructed view of the runway complex. The glass walls are angled outward so that reflections of the room's interior are not visible, and the glass is tinted to absorb solar heat, and reduce glare.

Radar controllers in approach control scan the skies for up to 50 miles around the airport on short-range radar **below**. Radarscopes can be adjusted to eliminate interference from rain or snow, and to give a close-up view of a small area. Computer-aided radar can be set to monitor airspace at different altitudes.

Runways

Although modern jet airliners are less affected by crosswinds than propeller airliners used to be, planning a new airport still includes a climatographical survey of a large area around the site. A wind rose, often drawn up by a computer, ensures that the runways are orientated to take advantage of prevailing winds.

Formerly, runways were laid out in a triangular pattern, like those at London's Heathrow Airport, so that one was always pointing roughly into the wind. Seen from the air it looks like the pattern made by a snowflake on black velvet.

Intersecting runways enable planes to take off from one and land on the other, but only alternately. Sets of parallel runways, the usual configuration at new airports, can be used simultaneously, even at busy times. A subsidiary runway may be built at an angle for use by small aircraft.

The hotter the climate and the higher the airfield above sea level, the longer the runways have to be. Air density decreases with altitude and heat, so aircraft need longer distances to generate the lift necessary for takeoff. The 15,000-foot long runway at Doha on the Persian Gulf is one of the longest at a civil airport.

Aircraft need a long takeoff run, too, to lift the heavy fuel loads needed to fly long distances. New York's John F. Kennedy Airport has one 14,572 feet long. But 6,000 feet or less may be enough for planes on short-haul services, and in remote places turboprop aircraft and even small jets use gravel, grass or even dirt strips.

An aircraft landing may weigh up to 300 tons and touch down at more than 140 mph. It takes some stopping. Surfaces must be strong and carefully graded for drainage, and scored with grooves to prevent aquaplaning, skidding on a film of water. Grooves are made two inches apart by a diamond-cutting wheel, or moulded during construction when still plastic, and have to be renewed every six to eight years at a cost of more than £50,000 ($100,000). In rain, ice and snow, friction meters towed at speed measure the runway's braking action and the information is relayed to pilots.

Runways cost up to £50 million ($90 million) to build and equip.

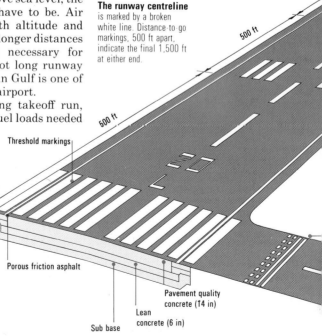

The runway centreline is marked by a broken white line. Distance-to-go markings, 500 ft apart, indicate the final 1,500 ft at either end.

Two-figure runway identification numbers, multiplied by ten, give centreline bearings to the nearest 10° measured from magnetic north. Parallel runways are marked "L" (left) or "R" (right). The letters are 30 ft long and 10 ft wide.

Threshold markings

Porous friction asphalt

Sub base

Lean concrete (6 in)

Pavement quality concrete (14 in)

500

500 ft

500 ft

500 ft

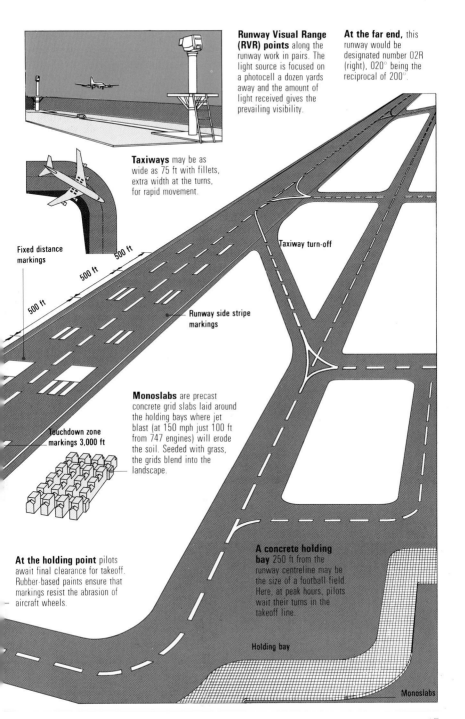

Runway Visual Range (RVR) points along the runway work in pairs. The light source is focused on a photocell a dozen yards away and the amount of light received gives the prevailing visibility.

At the far end, this runway would be designated number 02R (right), 020° being the reciprocal of 200°.

Taxiways may be as wide as 75 ft with fillets, extra width at the turns, for rapid movement.

Fixed distance markings

500 ft

500 ft

500 ft

500 ft

Taxiway turn-off

Runway side stripe markings

Monoslabs are precast concrete grid slabs laid around the holding bays where jet blast (at 150 mph just 100 ft from 747 engines) will erode the soil. Seeded with grass, the grids blend into the landscape.

Touchdown zone markings 3,000 ft

At the holding point pilots await final clearance for takeoff. Rubber-based paints ensure that markings resist the abrasion of aircraft wheels.

A concrete holding bay 250 ft from the runway centreline may be the size of a football field. Here, at peak hours, pilots wait their turns in the takeoff line.

Holding bay

Monoslabs

Ground control

The flight plan is put into operation from the moment the crew makes contact with air traffic control (ATC) by calling for permission to start up the engines using the appropriate radio frequency. Congestion along the route will mean a delay until there is space for the flight on the airways. The crew is given a "slot" time during which the aircraft must become airborne; if it misses a slot it has to request a new one, and this may mean further delay.

Changing radio frequency, the co-pilot calls the ground movement controller (GMC) to request taxi clearance. From a "nose-in" stand he asks for "push-back" clearance, but before issuing either, the controller must consider the effect of the manoeuvre on an airfield crowded with aircraft already taxiing, or about to begin. A simple push-back clearance may mean that another flight will have to be rerouted to a stand or runway, and one wrong decision can mean chaos.

On the taxiways, monitored by the GMC through binoculars — or perhaps on a ground radar screen — the captain is given airways clearance. At most airfields this is in the form of a Standard Instrument Departure (SID), and a "squawk". a SID is a routeing telling the crew which level and airways to take to start the jour-

ney. SIDs include noise abatement routeings to avoid annoyance to communities lying beneath the flightpath.

The squawk is a four-figure number code which the crew sets on a transponder, a radio receiver that can transmit an incoming signal in a different form. It is displayed as an identification number beside the flight's "blip" on the air traffic controller's radar screen.

At the holding point the aircraft is transferred to an air traffic controller whose job is to guide the aircraft into the air.

6
"Virgin one cleared for take off ... wind six-o at one-two"

5
"Virgin one cleared to line up and hold on runway two-six left"

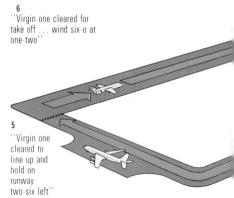

Using the ground movement monitor board **above** the GMC monitors and controls the runway lights. The airfield surface movement indicator, the ASMI **right,** depicts the airfield.

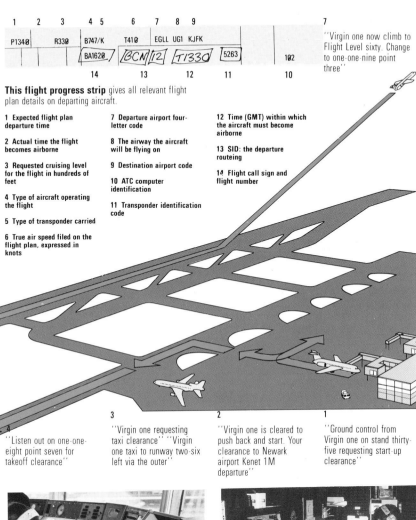

1	2	3	4 5	6	7	8	9
P1340	R330	B747/K	T410	EGLL UG1 KJFK

BA1620 / BCN 12 T1330 5263 102

14   13   12   11   10

7

"Virgin one now climb to Flight Level sixty. Change to one-one-nine point three"

This flight progress strip gives all relevant flight plan details on departing aircraft.

1 Expected flight plan departure time

2 Actual time the flight becomes airborne

3 Requested cruising level for the flight in hundreds of feet

4 Type of aircraft operating the flight

5 Type of transponder carried

6 True air speed filed on the flight plan, expressed in knots

7 Departure airport four-letter code

8 The airway the aircraft will be flying on

9 Destination airport code

10 ATC computer identification

11 Transponder identification code

12 Time (GMT) within which the aircraft must become airborne

13 SID: the departure routeing

14 Flight call sign and flight number

3
"Virgin one requesting taxi clearance" "Virgin one taxi to runway two-six left via the outer"

2
"Virgin one is cleared to push back and start. Your clearance to Newark airport Kenet 1M departure"

1
"Ground control from Virgin one on stand thirty-five requesting start-up clearance"

4
"Listen out on one-one-eight point seven for takeoff clearance"

Air traffic control assistants prepare a flight progress strip for every inbound and outbound aircraft **left**. Aircraft movements are monitored by air traffic controllers **above**.

Air traffic control

The sky over most countries is full of different kinds of aircraft flying at different speeds in different directions, crossing over each other at different heights. Keeping them separated is the main task of the air traffic (or tower) controller.

There is usually a minimum separation time of one minute between two aircraft of the same type taking off in different directions. If they are taking off in the same direction, the time gap is two minutes, and a light aircraft taking off behind a wide-bodied jet may be held back by ten minutes to avoid the turbulent air it leaves in its wake.

When a flight has been safely separated and is climbing away on its SID (Standard Instrument Departure) the air controller will transfer it to the care of the first radar sector (departure) controller for further climb clearance toward its cruising level.

Aircraft usually follow the airways, which are divided into three main altitude layers. The highest altitudes, from 45,000 to 75,000 feet (the limits of usable airspace) are used by supersonic and high-flying business jets; below them, subsonic airliners occupy the main jet airways and the levels below are generally used by slower turboprops and propeller-driven aircraft. Many sectors are re-stricted to military use, and civil airways are channelled into the often narrow gaps between them.

Along the lower airways, means to avoid bottlenecks are essential in busy areas above the VOR navigation beacons where airways intersect, and this is provided by area controllers, not necessarily operating from airport ATC centres, but in charge of vast sectors of airspace. One covers the whole of Belgium. Area (or centre) controllers watch dozens of aircraft at once on huge radarscopes. They tell pilots which altitudes and headings (called "vectors") they should fly to avoid aerial traffic jams.

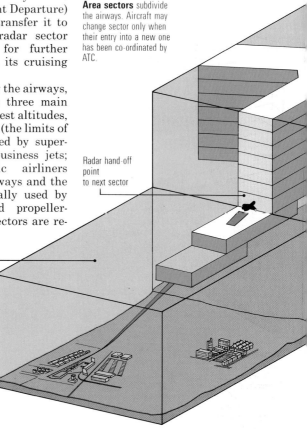

Area sectors subdivide the airways. Aircraft may change sector only when their entry into a new one has been co-ordinated by ATC.

Radar hand-off point to next sector

The airport control zone is the airspace around the airport. Its limits, and the degree of control, vary with the importance of the airport, but large airports may have a control zone extending up to 20 miles around them. All aircraft arriving and departing, and those crossing the zone, are subject to local controls and regulations.

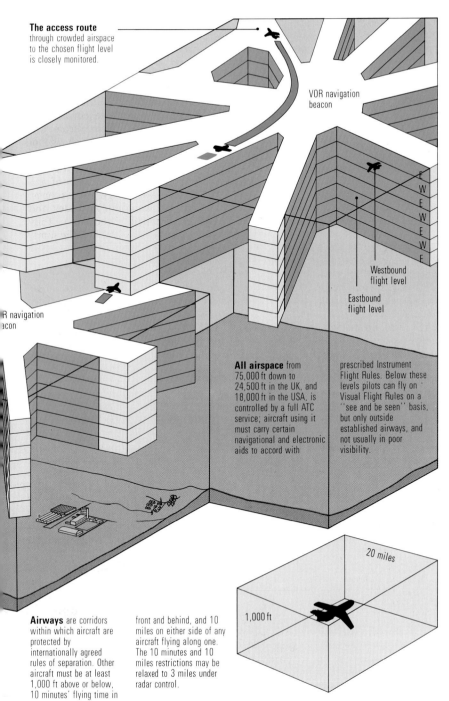

The access route through crowded airspace to the chosen flight level is closely monitored.

VOR navigation beacon

Westbound flight level

Eastbound flight level

R navigation acon

E
W
E
W
E
W
E
W
E

All airspace from 75,000 ft down to 24,500 ft in the UK, and 18,000 ft in the USA, is controlled by a full ATC service; aircraft using it must carry certain navigational and electronic aids to accord with prescribed Instrument Flight Rules. Below these levels pilots can fly on Visual Flight Rules on a "see and be seen" basis, but only outside established airways, and not usually in poor visibility.

Airways are corridors within which aircraft are protected by internationally agreed rules of separation. Other aircraft must be at least 1,000 ft above or below, 10 minutes' flying time in front and behind, and 10 miles on either side of any aircraft flying along one. The 10 minutes and 10 miles restrictions may be relaxed to 3 miles under radar control.

20 miles

1,000 ft

21

The rules and regulations of air travel

From the routes that an airline is permitted to fly to passengers' legroom, from fares to air crews' training standards, from noise levels around an airport to charges for in-flight movies — all may be subject to regulation by national and international organizations. In the long run these groups have the same aim: the good of civil aviation. In the short term, aims may conflict.

In 1944, 52 nations signed the Chicago Convention, which established the International Civil Aviation Organization, ICAO. This UN agency recommends international standards (usually to do with safety) on technical and operational matters. For example, many countries are currently applying Annexe 16 of the Chicago Convention, regulating takeoff and landing noise, even though this is forcing the retirement of elderly, but airworthy, aircraft.

Freedoms of the air
The Chicago Convention defined "freedoms of the air", which are put into practice as a result of bilateral agreements between pairs of countries. The first freedom is the privilege of overflying a territory without landing. The second freedom is the privilege of making a "technical" landing, to refuel or repair. Most air traffic is third-freedom or fourth-freedom; that is, carried between two countries by the airlines of those countries. Under fifth-freedom rights a US airline, for example, can carry passengers from Rome to Bahrain on a New York–Rome–Bahrain flight.

Most bilateral agreements have been modelled on the 1946 Bermuda Agreement between the UK and the USA. This classic agreement was ended by the British in 1977. Ten minutes after its expiry, hectic bargaining resulted in a new agreement. For example, the UK gained the right to fly the direct London–San Francisco routes, while the USA was permitted to open direct services from certain American cities to London. The USA also agreed to limit the routes on which it would allow two US airlines to compete, and agreed to control the growth in numbers of seats offered. Bermuda-style agreements aim to give "fair and equal" commercial opportunities to the countries involved regardless of the strength of their airline industries.

IATA, the International Air Transport Association, is the trade association of airlines offering scheduled services; charter operators have their own association, IACA. Traditionally, not only fares but such things as baggage allowances, service, seat space and travel agents' commissions are decided by IATA. All recommendations must have the unanimous approval of IATA's 100 or more members, but are binding only when they have been incorporated into the bilateral inter-governmental treaties.

The Warsaw Convention
IATA also sets conditions of carriage for passengers and baggage, stemming from the Warsaw Convention of 1929. For most journeys the Convention limits an airline's liability for loss of or damage to checked-in baggage to about £5 or $9 per pound, or to £200 (about $400) for unchecked hand baggage. Higher figures apply on US flights.

Compensation for injury or death is also set by the Warsaw Convention at about £5,000 or £10,000 ($10,000 or $20,000) on flights wholly outside the US. But for any flight involving a stop in the US, an airline has a maximum liability of $75,000 (about £40,000) including legal costs. These figures represent a "strict" liability: the claimant does not have to prove negligence by the airline. Agreements such as the Hague Protocol and the Montreal Agreement increase the maximum liability of airlines.

It is impossible to generalize about the contract a passenger enters into in buying a ticket. Passengers willing to brave a legal struggle might be able to prove in a US court that an American-built aircraft was unsafe. The manufacturer is not protected by the international insurance conventions. Record awards were made after one of the world's worst in-flight accidents, a crash in France of an American-built aircraft belonging to a Turkish airline. There were over 340 victims, of a score of nationalities. The dependants pursued a joint action in California against the aircraft manufacturers, one of their subcontractors and the airline. After nine months of preliminary hearings the defendants, while not admitting liability, decided not to contest it.

Price warfare

In 1977 the IATA system came under attack. Laker Airways, a non-IATA airline, started its Skytrain service between London and New York, offering minimal facilities and only a few hours' advance booking. It was licensed after years of opposition from the major airlines and after legal battles with the British government. Laker was driven out of business, but operators offering lower fares and a value for money service are here to stay — an example on the transatlantic route is Virgin Atlantic.

US airlines had other reasons to worry; their internal fares were set by the Civil Aeronautics Board, and they had been allowed to take part in IATA price-setting through a special exemption from the American antitrust laws. Under a new administration, the CAB threatened to lower internal fares and forbid the airlines to negotiate fares through IATA.

The "deregulation" of US airlines led to violent upheavals, takeovers, bankruptcies and the emergence of new carriers. Delays, cancellations and overbooking are now an accepted part of the American scene.

Air safety

The civil aviation board of the country in which an aircraft is registered (such as the Federal Aviation Administration (FAA) in the US and the Civil Aviation Authority (CAA) in the UK) fixes and enforces stringent air-safety standards for airlines and air crews. Manufacturers' tests are carried out to schedules laid down by the boards, and some may be repeated by them. The boards' pilots make tests in addition, to ensure that the aircraft operates safely in conditions well beyond normal limits.

When the aircraft type has been awarded a certificate of airworthiness, each model must be certified as complying with the type specification. Samples of newly delivered airliners are tested by the board, and in service they must be maintained by authorized procedures.

Consumer organizations, such as the Aviation Consumer Action Project in the US and the International Airline Passengers' Association, speak for the passenger. Governments fund groups such as the UK Air Transport Users' Committee. IATA supports their efforts to persuade authorities to streamline immigration and Customs controls and improve airport service. They can also press the airlines to, say, compensate passengers denied seats because the airlines have overbooked.

Many safety regulations are promoted by the professional associations of air crews and air traffic controllers. Lobbying by IFALPA, the International Federation of Airline Pilots' Associations, has contributed to the adoption of many procedures and devices that are now commonplace, such as improved runway lighting and flight recorders.

Takeoff

When he pushes the throttles forward to begin takeoff, the pilot of a big jet has 100,000 thrust horsepower at his fingertips — the power a heavily laden Boeing 747 needs to accelerate to 180 mph so that the wings can haul its mass free of the ground.

The amount of lift an aircraft needs to generate for takeoff depends on its weight — the more the wings have to lift, the higher takeoff speed must be. All aircraft have a maximum takeoff weight, determined by the manufacturer, but other factors may limit the allowable takeoff weight. These have to be considered at the planning stage of the flight.

Most major airports have runways two or even three miles long to provide room for the speed-gathering needed for flight. If the runway is shorter, the aircraft's capacity for passengers, freight and fuel will be limited. Because wing lift depends on air density, jets at airports in the tropics, or at high altitudes where the air is thin, have to generate higher speeds for takeoff, and runways need to be correspondingly longer.

A pilot's logical choice for takeoff is a long runway aligned into the wind. Since lift depends on air speed, the bonus of a 20-mph headwind means that an aircraft need only accelerate to 160 mph to achieve an airspeed of 180 mph. Sometimes, though, a short runway, or one aligned across or even downwind, has to be used to direct departing traffic away from noise-sensitive communities.

Before liftoff, the pilot has to make the commitment to take off. The point

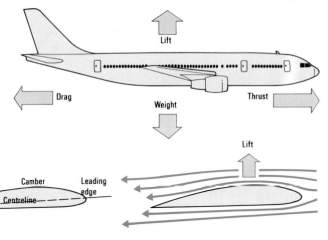

Four counterbalancing forces act on an aircraft in flight. *Lift*, generated by the airflow over the wings, overcomes *weight*; and *drag*, caused by the resistance of the air, opposes the *thrust* of the engines. When an aircraft is in straight and level flight thrust counterbalances drag, and lift counterbalances weight.

Lift

Drag

Weight

Thrust

Lift

Camber   Leading edge

Trailing edge   Centreline

The cross-section of a wing — the aerofoil — shows the curved shape that is the key to flight. A classic wing is cambered, or curved more sharply on the top than on the underside, and more strongly at the leading than at the trailing edge. Lift is generated only when the aerofoil moves forward, so a plane needs speed to fly. Its shape causes the streamlines, caused by its passage through the air, to be close together above the top surface, and farther apart below the bottom surface. The laws of physics state that fluid flow accelerates through a constriction, and where the velocity is high, the pressure is low. Above the wing there is constriction, high velocity and low pressure; below there is low velocity and high pressure. Low pressure above and high pressure below constitute an upward force, which is lift.

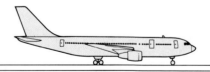

along the runway at which he makes this decision is determined by speed, and this is termed "decision speed" or "velocity one" (V_1). If an engine fails, or a warning sign or klaxon indicates a systems failure, he can abort the takeoff up to this point by applying maximum brakes, retarding throttles, raising wing spoilers and engaging reverse thrust. All rules governing takeoff performance are based on the assumption that an engine *will* fail at the worst possible moment; if this happens after V_1, he can still climb, fly a circuit and reroute to join the inbound traffic, and land again with one engine out.

At takeoff speed, the precalculated "velocity-rotate" (V_R) speed, he pulls back the control column, lifting the aircraft's nose until it rises to an angle of about 12 degrees. The plane lifts off and the landing-gears are retracted by moving a single lever on the flight-deck console. Aircraft climb out at "velocity two" (V_2), the speed that produces the best angle of climb for the weight. But if a steep climbout after takeoff is necessary to avoid high ground, that can limit takeoff weight.

The airborne plane climbs steeply, the nose 15 to 20 degrees up, speed at V_2 plus about 10 mph, to 1,000 feet or more, where the power may have to be cut back for noise suppression. Speed increases and the wing flaps are retracted, often in stages. By the time the flaps are finally retracted, a 747 will be flying at around 280 mph, about 250 knots, the unit in which aircraft speeds are usually measured.

Lift increases as the angle of attack (the angle at which the aerofoil meets the airstream) increases. The upper airflow is forced to make a longer detour and the downward acceleration of the airflow increases. but increasing lift by increasing the angle of the wing cannot be continued indefinitely. At an angle of about 17° the airflow suddenly breaks down. The wing stalls, and the aircraft drops like a stone.

A wing stalls when its angle of attack is too great: the airflow over its surface becomes turbulent, and lift is lost. The greater the load on the wing (this increases in a turn), the higher the speed necessary to avoid stalling.

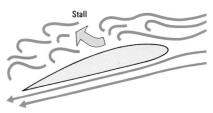

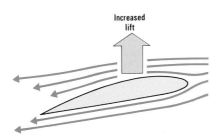

Increased lift

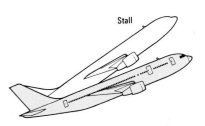

Stall

An airliner "rotates" to take off. When it has passed V_R, the optimum speed for takeoff, the pilot raises the nose; lift increases with angle of attack, overcoming the aircraft's weight.

The angle of climb is a compromise between conflicting requirements. The noise disturbance to nearby communities is least when an aircraft climbs steeply, but fuel consumption and the risk of a stall are least when the climb is shallow. The control column vibrates vigorously to alert the pilot if a stall is imminent.

Flight

A railway locomotive has one freedom of motion. Directed by its track, it can only go forward or backward. A car, under the direction of its driver, has two freedoms of motion, it can also turn left or right. But an aircraft has three freedoms of motion, it can be made to climb or dive.

Within each of the three freedoms of motion, an aircraft has two others. It can pitch nose-up or down about an imaginary line stretching from wingtip to wing-tip — its lateral axis. It can roll about a line from nose to tail — the longitudinal axis; and it can

yaw, left or right, about the vertical axis.

The fuselage and wings alone would, like a dart without flights, be too unstable to fly. An aircraft has to be stabilized about its three axes of rotation by adding a tailplane (horizontal stabilizer) for pitch, a fin (vertical stabilizer) for yaw, and by setting the wings at a positive dihedral angle (an angle raised from the horizontal plane) for roll.

Control about each axis is provided by manipulating hinged control surfaces on the aircraft. Elevators on the

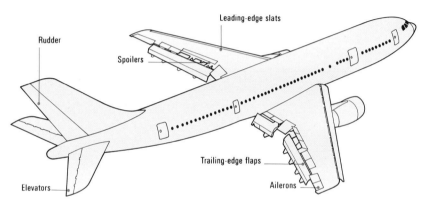

The elevators are lowered or raised by moving the control yoke forward or backward to dive or climb.

To move the rudder left or right, the pilot depresses corresponding left or right rudder pedals at his feet.

The ailerons are moved by turning the control yoke left to cause a roll to the left, and vice versa.

The area and camber of the wings increase when leading- and trailing-edge slats or flaps are deployed.

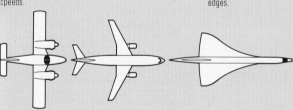

Straight wings give good lift at low speeds so the flaps and slats are simple, but they produce excessive drag at high speeds.

Sweptback wings cause minimum drag at high speeds, but they need complex flaps and slats for lift at low speeds.

Delta wings, streamlined for supersonic speeds, have elevons, combined elevators and ailerons, on the trailing edges.

When an aircraft changes speed, lift alters and the angle of attack must be changed to compensate, by adjusting the elevators. The pilot uses a ''trimming'' system to take the strain of holding them against the airflow. This is done by operating tabs on the elevators, which use the force of the airflow to hold the elevators in position.

tailplane control pitch. Raising them causes a down-load on the tailplane, which drops, and the nose pitches up; the reverse happens if they are lowered.

The rudder controls yaw exactly like the rudder on a boat. Swinging it to the right forces the tail left and the plane yaws to the right; swinging it left has the opposite effect.

The ailerons are moved in opposite senses to make the plane roll. Lift is lost on the wing when the aileron is raised, but it increases on the side where the lowered aileron increases the camber of the wing.

On modern jets almost the entire leading and trailing edges are taken up by lift-increasing flaps and slats for takeoff and landing. Ailerons are smaller than on the older jets, and they are aided by spoilers mounted on the tops of the wings. When a spoiler is raised, the wing on that side drops. When both are raised, overall lift falls and drag increases, so the aircraft descends.

Like a bicycle, an aircraft turns by banking. To turn left, the pilot deflects the ailerons so that the left aileron goes up to make the left wing incline downward, and the right aileron goes down to make the right wing tilt up. The lift force is pulled inward, away from the vertical. The elevator, tilted upward slightly, increases the down-load on the tail. Centrifugal force plays a counter-balancing role, pulling the aircraft outward, to the right; held in equilibrium, the aircraft turns smoothly.

The rudder plays a secondary role. During a turn it is used to prevent yawing. If a pilot tries to turn with the rudder alone, centrifugal force makes the aircraft skid out sideways. Often the rudder is controlled in flight by one or more automatic yaw dampers, robot devices which, together with many others, handle corrections on modern airliners.

As an aircraft approaches higher speeds, close to the speed of sound the trim will be changed automatically to keep the fuselage level. This compensates for a backward movement of the lift forces.

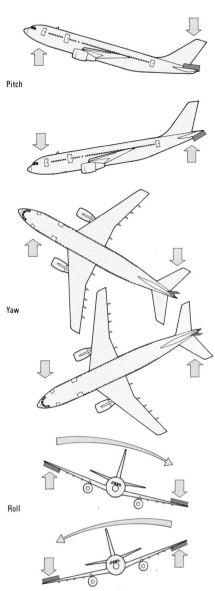

Pitch

Yaw

Roll

Aircraft design

Aircraft in a variety of shapes took to the air after World War I. Some were more efficient than others, but their speed, around 90 mph, was not too testing of their design and structure. Gradually, as cantilever monoplanes proved their efficiency, less economical designs were discarded, and aircraft took on a more stereotyped look. The last important piston-engined airliners, the Lockheed Constellation (1943) and the Douglas DC–6 (1946) were basically similar.

In 1954 the celebrated Boeing 707 established a basic configuration for the four-engined jetliner and serves to illustrate the classic shape. From a distance it looks just like its close rival, the Douglas DC–8.

The classic sweptback shape enables jets to fly up to a speed of Mach 0.8 (about 550 mph) and to slow down, using complex flaps and slats, to speeds safe for takeoff and landing. This cruising speed is unlikely to be surpassed by airliners designed for subsonic flight; the extra strength and weight a faster jet would need to resist the onset of shockwaves caused by flying close to the speed of sound — around 660 mph — would be reflected in its running costs.

The 707 needed four turbojets to travel intercontinental distances. If one or even two engines failed, the plane could still fly. But today's turbofan engines are so powerful and reliable that four may not be justified

Classic jet wings are swept back at an angle of around 35° so they can reach Mach 0.8 (about 550 mph) before drag becomes excessive. Much less sweepback would slow them down, and more may cause flutter at speed and reduce lift on landing and takeoff.

Wings as thin as 7% of their chord, or width from leading to trailing edge, bend noticeably up and down in flight. This is normal; their high elasticity smooths out the worst of the bumps in turbulent conditions.

The classic tricycle landing-gear, still the most common configuration, consists of a dual-wheel nose gear and two dual-tandem wheel main gears. To minimize drag each platform or bogie bearing four main landing-gear wheels is retracted inward after takeoff into an unpressurized well in the lower fuselage. The nose gear can be steered up to 60° to either side. It retracts forward into a well beneath the flight deck.

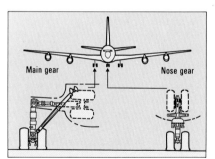

Main gear   Nose gear

The fuselage tube has a constant diameter over most of its length, making it cheap and easy to produce in quantity because all the frames are the same shape and size. A new fuselage can be made longer or shorter by adding or subtracting "plugs" — extra sections — as the customers and the traffic require. The cabins of high-flying jets are pressurized up to more than three times the pressure of the thin air outside.

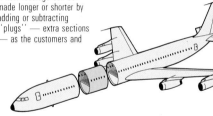

in future airliners. Some of the newest transoceanic aircraft, such as the A310 and B-767, have only two engines.

In 1955 the Caravelle appeared with two engines attached to the rear of the fuselage. This configuration became another classic formula. The Caravelle has its horizontal tail mounted fairly high to get it out of the way of the jets. Most later rear-engined aircraft have the even more extreme T-tail, in which the horizontal tail is on top of the fin. The latest rear-engined designs (in production) have propfans.

The most noticeable innovation in recent years has been in the size of subsonic jets, but the Boeing 747 looks like a scaled-up version of the trend-setting 707, and designers of other wide-bodied jets have not deviated from the classic norm.

The long narrow delta shape of supersonic aircraft is an example of aesthetic functionalism, an extreme form of streamlining that is essential to minimize drag. Experience in supersonic flight is modifying subsonic aircraft design. The Airbus, perhaps the most advanced subsonic airliner in use, has wings designed so that lift is spread along their breadths. They give a better performance, with less sweepback, at high and low speeds. But it is unlikely that the shape of subsonic aircraft will change radically in the near future.

The tailplane and fins (the stabilizers) are, in effect, miniature wings. They are swept back to minimize drag in flight.

Wings set low on the fuselage allow the wing-mounted landing-gears to be shorter than on high-wing aircraft, and relatively lightweight.

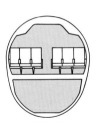

One cross-section is an egg-shape in which all interior space can be used both for seats and cargo. The floor beams in tension take the pressure loads.

Engines in pods help to improve the lift of the wings. Mounted on thin pylons ahead of and just below them, they are accessible for servicing from the ground, and a sudden fracture of part of an engine will not damage the vital wing structure. Together they act as a balance preventing flutter at high speeds, and so reduce the need for stiffening, whose weight would lower the payload or range.

The introduction of the Boeing 707 began a decade of intense competition among manufacturers. Boeing and McDonnell Douglas produced "families" of airliners of varying lengths, all designed to fly at around 35,000 ft high in the stratosphere (where the thin air offers less resistance, reducing fuel consumption). The McDonnell Douglas DC-9 had several "stretched" versions of the original model, the DC-9-10.

"Stretched" versions

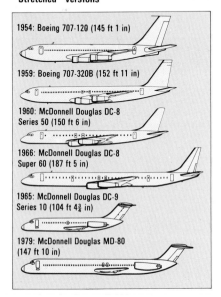

1954: Boeing 707-120 (145 ft 1 in)

1959: Boeing 707-320B (152 ft 11 in)

1960: McDonnell Douglas DC-8 Series 50 (150 ft 6 in)

1966: McDonnell Douglas DC-8 Super 60 (187 ft 5 in)

1965: McDonnell Douglas DC-9 Series 10 (104 ft 4¾ in)

1979: McDonnell Douglas MD-80 (147 ft 10 in)

Aircraft structure

A modern airliner flies more hours in one year than pre-World War II aircraft flew in their entire lifetime. The Junkers G.38, the "Jumbo" of the thirties, carried 34 passengers; the Boeing 747 can carry 550, and its airframe has to withstand the stresses of takeoff and landing with loads 16 times as great. A modern airframe has to take the strains of flying through turbulence, and of pressurization to some nine pounds per square inch at cruising height, as well as those of normal flight and landing.

An aircraft's strength lies in its monocoque construction: though reinforced by a supporting frame, the skin takes most of the flight loads.

Aircraft are subject to more extreme changes in temperature than any other form of transport. An hour or so in the hot sun of the tropics can heat an airframe to over 120 degrees Fahrenheit, yet within 30 minutes of takeoff it will be cruising at high altitudes where the temperature may be 100 degrees below freezing. Aluminium-copper or aluminium-lithium alloys are the lightest materials able to stand up to this treatment. They account for most of the structure of most modern jetliners. Highly-stressed parts such as the landing-gear are made of forged steel whose extra weight is more than offset by its greater strength. A 747 making a hard landing stresses them to three times its 400-ton weight.

Parallel frames of aluminium alloy, like large hoops, define the shape of the fuselage cross-section. They are held in place by long strips or stringers which run along the length of the fuselage. A skin of light alloy, $\frac{1}{16}$ in to $\frac{1}{8}$ in thick, is stretched around each section and the floor is bolted to the frame. Here, the floor can be seen just below the widest part.

The centre section of the aircraft, where the wing passes through the fuselage, is the strongest part of any airliner. Here the weight of the entire fuselage is transferred to the wing during flight. Long metal spars stretching from one wingtip to the other take the bending loads in flight, and on the ground the weight of the whole plane is channelled down to the landing-gear.

Airframes are as lean as they can safely be. So that aircraft can take off with as big a profit-making load as possible, all excess weight is pared away with computerized precision. Wing skins are chemically milled in acid baths to exactly predetermined thickness, and every rivet and bolt is trimmed to the exact length.

Increasingly, major parts of the structure are made from new composite materials stiffened by amazingly strong fibres of carbon, Kevlar (like spider web) and other advanced materials, all stronger than steel but many times lighter. Many parts, including external skins and control surfaces, are sandwiches of thin skins bonded to a lightweight honeycomb filling inside. Soon whole airliners may be composite structures.

Today's airliners fly up to 15 hours a day for 20 years or more. The stresses produced by continual movement, and even intense noise, cause fatigue, the cracking and breaking that occurs in metals under constant flexure. Fatigue is an aging process that cannot be avoided, but weak points such as holes and joins can be reduced by using adhesives instead of rivets and bolts, and by making wing skins in gigantic panels. Fatigue can start from a scratch, so surfaces are polished and sharp corners rounded off. Safe limits are set to the lives of susceptible components, and they are inspected frequently.

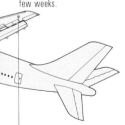

All Airbuses are built in segments by several companies located hundreds of miles apart. Its assembly in Toulouse, shown here, takes just a few weeks.

Each A300B wing has three upper and three lower skin sections. They are machined out of huge slabs of 2 in-thick aluminium-copper alloy. Milling processes remove most of the metal leaving a sheet tapering to about $\frac{1}{16}$ in thick with integral strengthening corrugations as deep as the original slab. These are laid over a framework of ribs and spars which give shape.

Propellers

In the gradual invention of the flying machine one of the most important advances was to separate lift from propulsion. Only when flapping wings had been discarded could the flying machine be made to work. A rigid wing gives lift, and propulsion is effected by accelerating an airflow backward. Until the jet era, this was done with a propeller.

The propeller is simply a rotating wing. It generates lift exactly as a wing does, but the blades direct the air backward so lift becomes propulsive thrust. The faster it turns, the greater the thrust. A propeller would have the effect of rotating the fuselage and the wings in the opposite direction. The aircraft's shape and the use of the control surfaces coun-ter this torque reaction, and some twin-engined aircraft have handed (counter-spinning) propellers.

The propeller's pitch — the angle of its blades to the airflow — decreases from root to tip so that it acts through the air as a screw through wood. The pitch is a measure of the distance it will travel through the air in one revolution. Like the thread of a screw the blade pitch may be set fine for takeoff, matching a fast-running propeller, and can be reset to coarse for high cruising speed, matching a slow-running, economical propeller.

Fixed-pitch propellers are effective at one forward speed, but constant-speed propellers adjust pitch automatically. They keep the engine rpm at a constant-speed setting, permitting it to be used at its most efficient (and economical) speed at all stages of the flight and, twisted into reverse pitch on landing, act as a brake.

Fast-running propellers are noisy, so modern propellers are being made to run more slowly to reduce noise. To maintain thrust they have as many as six blades, made of glass-fibre or carbon fibre for light weight.

The newest development is the propfan. This has 6 to 12 blades, each looking like a sharp-edged scimitar, and it retains efficiency up to jet speeds. General Electric flew a propfan in the 25,000 lb class in 1986, and several kinds are now flying. They can be pusher, tractor or contra-rotating.

Rotating blade

Hub mechanism

Spinner

The blades of a variable-pitch propeller are adjusted — usually hydraulically — to any chosen angle by the hub mechanism, which is covered by a streamlined spinner. If an engine fails, the propeller is feathered (turned edge-on to the air) to minimize drag.

The GE UDF (standing for UnDucted Fan) was the first propfan to fly. The gas turbine engine blasts hot gases through extra turbines downstream. These carry the propfan blades around the outside. Thus, the UDF is a contra-rotating pusher, with no gearbox.

Piston engines and turbojets

Nineteenth-century airships and would-be planes had propellers driven by steam, compressed air or electricity, but every *successful* airliner has had one or more internal-combustion engines. A tiny fraction have had diesel engines, but almost all use the Otto-cycle (four-stroke piston engine) or the gas turbine.

Aviation piston engines are similar to car engines, but larger and more powerful — usually with six or eight cylinders, air-cooled and arranged in horizontally opposed pairs.

Each pair drives one crankpin, via two connecting rods, and the front of the crankshaft is geared down to a slower-running propeller. The rear end of the crankshaft drives accessories and may be geared up to a fast-running supercharger which pumps extra air (to burn more fuel) into the engine as the aircraft climbs into thinner atmosphere; alternatively there may be a turbocharger, a supercharger driven by a small turbine spun at high speed by the white-hot exhaust gas.

Fuel — gasoline (petrol) — is dyed different colours according to type, and the type varies from top-grade motor fuel in light aircraft, up to 115/145 octane in bigger engines. Only small aircraft, and those needing tough low-speed populsion at low altitudes, for example for agricultural work and fire-fighting, still have piston engines.

In 1937 the turbojet brought an entirely new method of propulsion. In this engine, air is converted, by burning fuel, into a blast of hot gas moving at high velocity.

The core of a gas-turbine engine works quite simply: a compressor sucks in air, compresses it and delivers it to a combustion chamber. Kerosene-type fuel is sprayed in and burned to convert the high-pressure airflow into a column of white-hot gas. Fixed, curved blades direct this gas onto the blades of a turbine rotor, spinning it like a windmill. The turbine converts the energy in the gas flow into shaft-power, which drives the compresssor. In a turbojet it extracts just enough power to drive the compressor while the rest of the high-velocity gas roars out of the exhaust nozzle to jet-propel the plane.

Turbojets tend to be noisy and wasteful of fuel. Virtually all modern jetliners have quieter, more efficient turbofans (p. 35).

The axial compressor of a turbojet increases pressure by forcing air through rows of blades like small wings rotating between fixed stators.

Combustion takes place in separate flame tubes or alternatively, in an annular (ring-like) chamber encircling a smaller and lighter engine.

The nozzle is profiled to extract maximum thrust from the flow of hot gas. It often has a complicated shape, in an attempt to reduce noise.

The turbine in this engine has three stages, which can be seen connected to the compressor. Some can generate as much as 100,000 horsepower

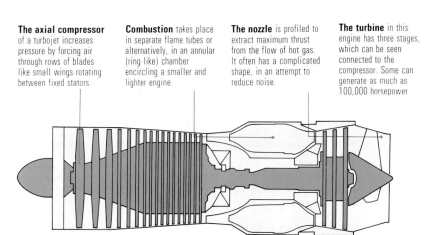

Turboprops

In a turboprop engine, the main thrust comes from the propeller and only a small proportion from the jet exhaust. A turboprop handles a larger airflow than any other aircraft engine and so (at low speeds) generates the largest thrust for any given rate of fuel consumption. But, as forward speed increases, thrust falls away until, at about 450 mph, propeller efficiency is seriously impaired as the blade tips approach the speed of sound.

In the late 1950s jets were all the rage, even for short trips. The 1973 "fuel crisis" served to focus attention on the need for fuel economy, quite apart from the increasingly vexed question of noise. The result was that,

whereas turbojets were superseded and replaced by turbofans (see facing page), turboprops came right back into the picture. Today most small "commuter airliners" have turboprop engines.

Nor is this all. The invention of the propfan (p. 32) promises by the year 2000 to put these advanced propellers on most airliners, even those flying at jet speeds. Indeed, today the turboprop is merging into the propfan, which in turn is merging into the ducted propfan, which is merging into the turbofan!

Many types of helicopter are powered by a turboshaft engine, which is essentially a turboprop minus the propeller. The horizontal output shaft spins at about 6,000 rpm, as in a turboprop. Through a gearbox on the airframe, the shaft turns the main rotor at about 200 to 300 rpm.

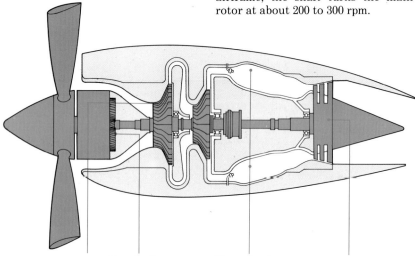

The propeller shown here has four blades (which are cut off to save space). The blue line points out the first of the two centrifugal compressors on this engine. These work like the fan in a vacuum cleaner.

The reduction gear makes the propeller turn much more slowly than the turbine that drives it. Around the gearbox can be seen the curving inlet duct through which the air enters. Some turboprops have an "S-duct" from above or below.

The combustion chamber is where the fuel is burned. Some engines have a single annular chamber, but this engine has a ring of separate tubular chambers. They convert the compressed air into white-hot gas which drives the turbine.

The turbine in this engine has three stages, and it drives both the compressors and the propeller. Most turboprops today use separate turbines, one driving the compressor and a separate one to drive the propeller at a different speed.

Turbofans

Modern airliners use turbofan engines, which incorporate the best features of the turbojet and turboprop. Early turbofans, called by-pass jet engines, were simply turbojets with oversize blades in the first few stages of the compressor. The surplus air compressed by the tips of these blades was ducted round the rest of the engine — "by-passing" it — and discharged through the jet pipe. The resultant slowing-down of the final jet did not reduce power because it was compensated by the increased volume of airflow. But, in comparison with an ordinary turbojet (or "straight jet", as it became known) there were other vital reductions in fuel consumption and, most important, noise. Since noise varies as the fourth power of jet speed (twice the speed of the jet means 16 times the noise), ways had to be found to quieten the jets. Early turbojets experimented with special nozzles — some were shaped like the petals of a flower, others had as many as 21 pipes to mix the jet with the atmosphere quickly. But no method was as effective as the high by-pass ratio turbofan. This engine has revolutionized air transport, dramatically reducing airline fuel bills and noise, with no loss in aircraft operating speeds.

Early turbofans had a BPR (bypass ratio) of less than 1; the amount of air flowing through the bypass duct was less than that through the high-pressure hot core. Today's airliner engines have a BPR between 3 and 8, and soon 15 may be common. They are virtually ducted turboprops.

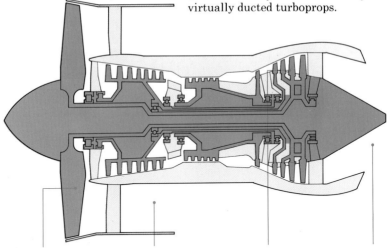

The large-diameter fan, located at the front in a profiled duct, acts like a propeller to supercharge the core engine on the one hand, and to by-pass air around it on the other. The biggest engines have fans of some 90 inches diameter, with giant blades.

The bypass duct is filled with a hurricane flow of air which provides almost all of the engine's thrust. About one-fifth of the air goes through the core, where it is intensely compressed by the axial compressors before reaching the combustion chamber.

The turbine, powered by the small fraction of airflow passing through the core, drives the fan. In some smaller turbofans, the turbine is so tiny and the fan relatively so large that it has to be coupled via a gearbox, just as the turbine is in turboprop engines.

The core jet is hot and fast-moving, but so relatively small that a reverser is seldom fitted (only to the giant flow fron the fan). In the latest engines, the two flows are mixed in a single nozzle, for higher efficiency.

Supersonic aircraft

Most jets cruise at a subsonic speed of 550 mph, about 50 mph slower than the world land speed record, and slower than the speed of sound in the surrounding air. Their passage through the air causes a disturbance which sends out pressure waves in all directions, like ripples in a pond, though the waves are spheres, not rings.

The relatively small pressure differences transmitted ahead of a plane moving at subsonic speed act as warning signals to the air in front, giving the molecules time to move out of the way and flow smoothly round the wings and tail.

Supersonic aircraft cruise at the muzzle velocity of a rifle bullet. As they approach the speed of sound, Mach 1, the warning signals become shorter. The molecules have less time to move out of the way as the plane catches up on the pressure waves ahead, compressing them until at Mach 1 (660 mph at 36,000 ft and above) they form into a vertical wave, a shockwave, more violent than a sound wave. Its pressure rises instantaneously, and near the source it sounds like the crack of a whip.

As the aircraft accelerates beyond Mach 1, the shockwave forms a cone, with the aircraft at the vertex, "towing" it along. Because supersonic transports (SSTs) travel faster than sound only at high altitudes, the shockwave cone has time to expand enormously before it reaches the ground, where it is weak enough to be heard as a dull boom. Even so, many people are concerned that shockwaves may damage human ears or even buildings. There is usually more than one shockwave in the cone, one from the nose and another from the tail 200 feet farther back, giving a double boom, or continuous sound disturbance sounding like thunder or a distant explosion.

The fuselage of an SST is streamlined to a point at the nose, and the

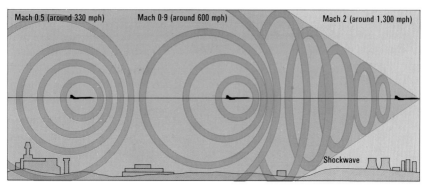

Mach 0.5 (around 330 mph)   Mach 0.9 (around 600 mph)   Mach 2 (around 1,300 mph)

Shockwave

The boom carpet is the strip of ground over which the audible part of the shockwave cone passes. It may be 40 miles wide, so SSTs are allowed to go supersonic only over seas and thinly populated areas; some countries ban SSTs entirely.

SSTs are designed with a thin-sectioned, long, slender fuselage and slim delta wings to fit inside the shock-wave cone, causing least air resistance and avoiding many problems. It is a bad shape for low speeds.

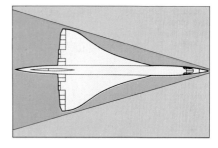

slender delta wings cover roughly half the length of the aircraft. The sharp leading edge is so shaped that at takeoff or landing the air swirls over it to create an extremely powerful vortex (a writhing column of air) which gives increased lift. Passenger windows are smaller than usual to reduce the possibility of fatigue in the highly pressurized cabin.

Passengers are not aware of tran-sonic acceleration, and since super-sonic cruise at Mach 2 (over 1,300 mph) takes place at a height of 50,000 feet, the ground seems to go by at the normal speed. But from a supersonic aircraft the clouds look very, very far below. Identifiable features on the ground look tiny and passengers can see a fantastic distance. The sky is a blackish-violet shade, and the horizon is obviously curved.

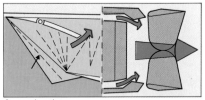

Supersonic cruise

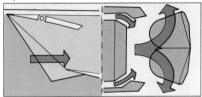

Reverse thrust

SST engines are mounted in easily-accessible nacelles or casings under the wings. To increase the airflow to the engine, and so give extra thrust for takeoff and transonic acceleration, ramps in the roof of the huge air intakes automatically lift up and a spill door opens. The front ramp closes to achieve normal thrust when the plane is cruising at supersonic speeds. The various doors are computer-controlled.

The exhaust assembly alters in area and profile, in time with the engine, to accommodate the aircraft's wide speed range. Two variable geometry ''clamshell buckets'' on the rear of the powerplant are partly closed at takeoff, ''fish-tailing'' or squashing the jet stream to reduce noise. They open fully in normal flight but, shut tight, they act as thrust reversers on landing to slow the aircraft down as rapidly as possible.

Rolls-Royce Olympus turbojet engine

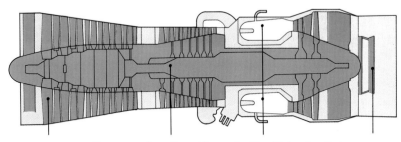

Concorde's Olympus two spool turbojet engine preceded Concorde by more than 20 years. It broke the world altitude record in 1953. Heat-resistant nickel-based alloys and titanium, which will withstand fierce heat, ice and bird strike, are used in the engine's manufacture.

The two spools act like two engines in one. The low- and high-pressure compressors raise the temperature of the intake air so that less fuel is needed to generate up to 40,000 lb of thrust (equal to the horsepower of 10,000 small cars), four times that of the first Olympus.

The annular (ring-like) combustion chamber was an improvement on earlier variants. Together with a new vaporizing fuel injector system, it burns the fuel/air mixture so completely that Concorde is one of the most smoke-free aircraft in present-day service with airlines.

An afterburner or re-heat system is a thrust-booster. Placed between the turbine and the exhaust nozzles, it gives extra thrust for takeoff, and to overcome air resistance on transonic acceleration, by igniting additional fuel in the jet pipe's hot exhaust gases, for brief periods.

Rotorcraft

Helicopters can take off and land vertically on a space little bigger than the diameter of their own rotors. Their value, therefore, is in their ability to operate from conveniently small heliports, saving journeys to and from out-of-town airports.

But helicopters will never replace airliners for long-distance travel because their speed is limited to below 200 mph, at which speed the rotor tips are whirling round at almost 500 mph. Any faster and they approach the speed of sound, overstressing the blades. And helicopters are short-haul vehicles. Most of the energy, and fuel consumed, is used for lift; an airliner with the same engines could travel twice the distance at more than twice the speed for the same fuel consumption.

A rotating-wing aircraft is an old idea only recently developed by complex engineering. Leonardo da Vinci made a sketch of a *helixpteron* (literally "screw-wing") in 1490, but made no allowance for torque reaction, a force familiar to anyone who has felt an electric drill turning in the opposite direction to the spinning motor. This force is neutralized in modern helicopters by the side thrust of a tail rotor (whose variable-pitch blades also permit it to be used as a rudder) or by two counterspinning main rotors.

Igor Sikorsky, a Russian-born American, designed and produced the first practical helicopter in 1939. The versatile Sikorsky S-61 is now produced in various military and civil versions. It flies at an average speed of 138 mph over a range of 450 miles.

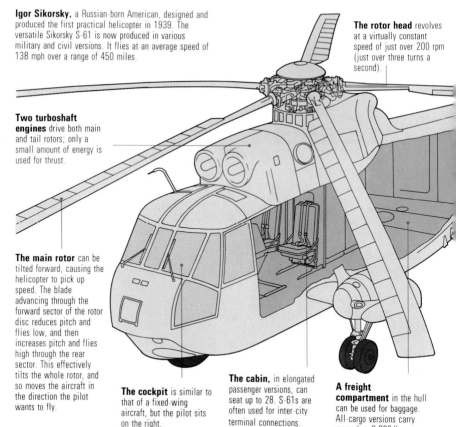

The rotor head revolves at a virtually constant speed of just over 200 rpm (just over three turns a second).

Two turboshaft engines drive both main and tail rotors; only a small amount of energy is used for thrust.

The main rotor can be tilted forward, causing the helicopter to pick up speed. The blade advancing through the forward sector of the rotor disc reduces pitch and flies low, and then increases pitch and flies high through the rear sector. This effectively tilts the whole rotor, and so moves the aircraft in the direction the pilot wants to fly.

The cockpit is similar to that of a fixed-wing aircraft, but the pilot sits on the right.

The cabin, in elongated passenger versions, can seat up to 28. S-61s are often used for inter-city terminal connections.

A freight compartment in the hull can be used for baggage. All-cargo versions carry more than 6,000 lb.

The most complex aerodynamic problems of rotorcraft were solved by a Spanish engineer, Juan de la Cierva, who designed the first autogyro. It looked like a propeller-driven monoplane topped by a large rotor. An autogyro's rotor is set in motion by the engine, but continues to turn in the air by the action of the slipstream though the blades. Similarly, though a helicopter's rotors are power-driven, if the power supply of a helicopter fails completely, it will not stall. When the angles of pitch of the rotor blades are reduced to a minimum, aerodynamic forces maintain their rotation like a falling sycamore seed spinning to the ground.

A helicopter cockpit has two main controls. The floor-mounted collective pitch lever increases the pitch of all the blades simultaneously to provide vertical control. The machine climbs when the angle of pitch of the blades is increased and more engine power is applied to overcome the extra drag created. The cyclic pitch stick, the equivalent of the airliner pilot's control stick, can vary the angles of pitch of the rotor blades alternately as they pass round the rotor disc. The alternating pitch change tilts the rotor plane in whichever direction the stick is pushed to move the helicopter forward, backward or sideways.

A fixed tailplane, mounted on the tail boom, gives stability in forward flight.

A swashplate transfers control lever movements to the rotor head. Its upper part revolves with the head, tilting the rotor.

The pitch change hinge gives control of the rotor in flight by allowing the blades to be twisted, to increase or decrease their angle to the horizontal. Together with the flapping hinge which allows the blades to rise and fall, and the drag hinge on which they can move forward and backward slightly, it forms a kind of universal joint to give the blades free motion about three axes.

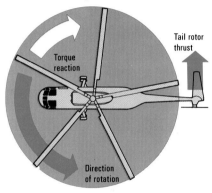

The rotors generate and also control lift. In hovering flight, the speed of the main rotor and the angle of pitch of its blades combine to direct a slipstream downward that exactly balances the aircraft's weight. The tail rotor counteracts torque, the tendency of the fuselage to rotate in the opposite direction to the main rotor.

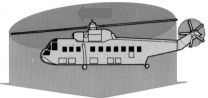

To move forward, the rotor is tilted forward. Most of the airflow is directed downward to give lift, but some is directed backward. Its reaction moves the helicopter forward.

Hovercraft

In 1954 an experiment with coffee cans finally solved a stubborn engineering problem: how to overcome the resistance that water imposes on the speed of ships. Christopher Cockerell, a British electronics engineer, forced air with a vacuum cleaner through a simple compressed-air chamber, made from two cans, to create an annular jet, and tried the idea out on a punt and a motor launch before producing the first successful air-cushion vehicle (ACV).

This had a hoverheight of less than two inches; the flexible skirt, which retains air to make a deeper cushion, was the vital development that made the hovercraft practicable.

Most hovercraft are amphibious, able to ride over waves, ice, sand, mud and marsh. They are not built to negotiate slopes, and steering, effected by moving the fins and pylons to alter the thrust of the propellers mounted on top of them, can be unwieldy, especially in crosswinds. But hovercraft cruise at around 70 knots (80 mph), twice the speed of passenger ships, and need no special harbours.

The illustrations show a typical amphibious ACV, but there is also another kind which can operate over water only. Called the sidewall type, it has thin walls along the sides dipping into the water. The walls contain the cushion of air without expenditure of power (except at the open front and rear ends), but they naturally cause drag and so reduce the vehicle's speed.

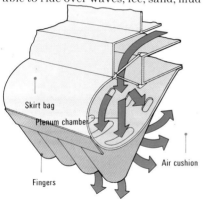

Skirt bag

Plenum chamber

Air cushion

Fingers

Flexible skirts make the hovercraft amphibious, acting as giant shock absorbers enabling the craft to clear obstacles up to 8 ft high. They cushion the impact of waves before it is transmitted to the hull, so high speeds can be maintained in rough seas.

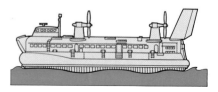

The bag, or upper part of the skirt, is made up of segments. The flexible extensions, or fingers, attached to these extend and contract with the undulations of the surface, providing an air seal.

The SRN4 is powered by four turbine engines (**1**). The airflow from the intakes (**2**) is pumped by lift-fans (**3**) into an expandable air chamber (**4**), and is fed through jets which direct it inward to form the air cushion (**5**) and downward for stability.

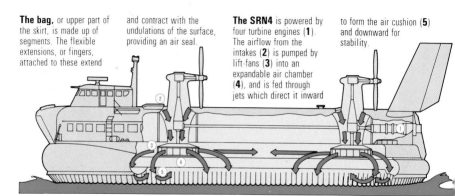

Seaplanes, skiplanes and flying boats

Encouraged by the vast amount of open water available for natural runways, the development of seaplanes began soon after the first successful land flights. Seaplanes have two major advantages over wheeled aircraft: they take off from, and land on, water and need no specially prepared landing site; small seaplanes need only 500 yards or less of unobstructed water. During the 1930s these aircraft were the world's fastest machines.

Seaplanes present unique design problems. Not only must they be able to float on water, but they must also be able to skim along the surface at high speed. They are supported on floats (and are often called floatplanes) which are usually heavier and cause greater drag than wheels because they cannot be neatly retracted.

Skiplanes are designed specifically for landing on snow and need no special landing strip. They have no brakes, but in mountainous areas they usually land on upward slopes. They "weathercock" in wind, making steering a highly skilled technique.

Flying boats, used extensively in the 1930s and still found on some inter-island airline services, have large hulls which create extra drag, but are necessary to keep the wings and propellers clear of the water. The hulls are surmounted by wings with floats at the ends.

The most versatile aircraft are amphibians. These have floats or hulls, and wheels or skis as well.

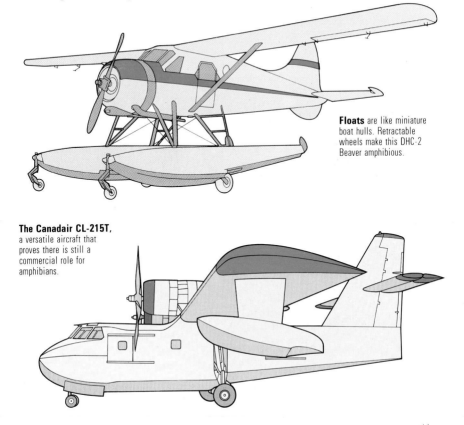

Floats are like miniature boat hulls. Retractable wheels make this DHC-2 Beaver amphibious.

The Canadair CL-215T, a versatile aircraft that proves there is still a commercial role for amphibians.

The flight deck

Inside the flight deck there is calm. The engines can only just be heard and the sensation of movement comes mostly from the sound of air round the nose of the aircraft. Above the cloud layers, the view is far-ranging but dazzling, particularly when flying into the sun. At high altitudes other aircraft are hard to distinguish against the bright light and dark blue of the stratosphere.

Aviation has its traditions. In the early years, influenced by the keep-right rules of the road and at sea, aircraft also kept right on the airways. For ease of visibility captains chose to sit on the left.

All the primary instruments and controls are duplicated and for some there is even a third stand-by instrument. In the unlikely event of one of the pilots collapsing, the other has all the controls needed to fly safely. In flight, each pilot can monitor the other's instruments, and ensure that they are giving the same indications on both panels.

There is also a highly sophisticated centralized warning system on the main instrument panel. Red or yellow illuminated squares accompanied by loud buzzing indicate immediately any failure of any part of the aircraft and its control systems. The strident sound of any of 18 different warning signals could disturb the serenity of a flight deck.

For 50 years after 1920, airliner cockpits merely became more complicated. Then big changes happened, as the result of modern digital electronics. One of the newest airliners in service, the A320, has hardly any "instruments" at all. Instead the

The flight deck of a Virgin Boeing 747 (the co-pilot's seat has been omitted for a clearer view)

1 Overhead switch panel
2 Navigational radio selector
3 Autopilot engage switch
4 Basic T arrangement
5 Inertial navigation warning lights
7 Thrust reverser lights
7 Pitch trim controls
8 Nose gear tiller
9 Landing-gear control handle
10 Water injection control
11 Speed brake handle
12 Thrust levers
13 Inertial navigation controls
14 Brake pressure
15 Computer selection switch
16 Stabilizer trim levers
17 Flap lever
18 Pitch trim wheel
19 Parking brake levers
10 Engine start levers
21 Central console containing: weather radar controls; ADF (automatic direction finder); radio equipment; aileron and rudder trims; intercom switches
22 Observer's seat

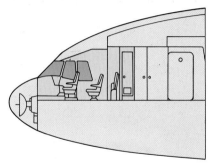

The flight deck is planned for visibility, utility and comfort. Curved windshields and insulation cut down outside noise. Oxygen masks and smoke goggles are near to hand; a built-in ladder leads to an escape hatch. In the nose a weather radar scanner sweeps left and right through 30°.

pilots face large displays like colour TVs. Computers feed these with much more information than could ever be conveyed by electromechanical instruments, but they display only what the pilots need to know at any time. Either of the two pilots can reprogram any display at the touch of a button.

So great and efficient is the symbiosis between the men and the machine, that the crew has changed. In the old days, a flight crew might number two pilots, a flight engineer, a navigator and a radio operator. Today the biggest airliners fly with just two pilots. Trade union pressures resisted this change, claiming safety would be degraded. It remains a controversial subject, but the record shows that safety is actually enhanced.

A minor change in the A320 is that the old control wheels are replaced by small sidesticks.

23 The windshield is 9 in high at the centre. Made of laminated glass and plastic with a hard coating, it is $\frac{5}{8}$ in thick.

26 The flight engineer's panel contains the main circuit breakers and the environmental and engine monitoring systems.

24 Pedals are pushed to control the rudder. Only slight movements are needed to turn the aircraft or keep it level.

25 The control column, pulled and pushed, lowers and raises the elevators hydraulically. The wheel controls the ailerons.

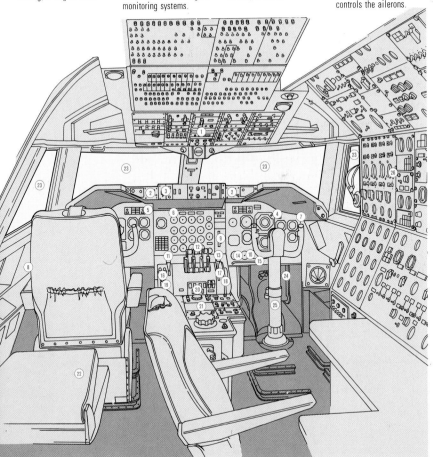

The control panel

A striped pointer indicates maximum permitted airspeed according to altitude

A Mach scale aligned with the pointer indicates Mach 0.35

A pointer indicates an airspeed of 180 knots

The airspeed indicator (ASI) gives the plane's speed in knots and Mach number. A sensor — the pitot probe — leads from the ASI out into the airstream at the nose; the faster the aircraft, the greater the build-up of pressure in the sensor. Airspeed determines the lift generated.

A clear digital read-out is easily scanned

Altitude shown in ft

The large pointer completes one revolution for every 1,000 ft of altitude
The standard setting of 1013.25 millibars is sea level pressure on a normal day
Knob to set surface pressure

The altimeter is an aneroid barometer connected with the atmosphere via a vent on the aircraft's outer skin. The pilot sets the surface pressure before takeoff and subsequent changes, detected by the instrument as the plane climbs or descends, appear as altitude.

Distance to radio beacon
Command track counter in degrees
Fixed lubber indicating magnetic heading
Command track pointer showing new heading
Position relative to radio beam
Systems failure warning flags
Aircraft symbol

The horizontal situation indicator (HSI) displays an aircraft symbol set in the centre of a revolving compass card. It indicates the aircraft's position relative to radio navigation and instrument landing beams, and the bearing and distance in nautical miles to a selected radio beacon.

Artificial horizon
Aircraft symbol and flight director
Angle of pitch
Systems failure warning flag

Pointer indicating angle of bank

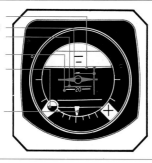

The attitude director shows the attitude (pitch and roll) of the aircraft relative to the Earth's horizon. The aircraft symbol remains fixed and the artificial horizon moves, so that the aircraft symbol seems to climb, dive, bank and turn in view, in step with the aircraft.

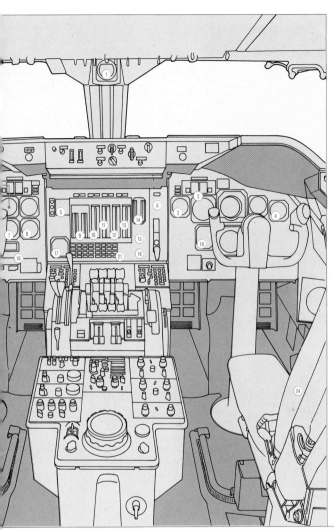

Pilots' controls of a Boeing 747. This is a traditional cockpit, filled with electromechanical instruments of the kinds shown opposite. The latest airliners replace these with giant electronic displays that look like colour TVs. These can display far more information; and when everything is working properly, they are quiescent.

1 **Stand-by compass**
2 **Approach progress indicators**
3 **Clock**
4 **Radio altimeter**
5 **Total air temperature**
6 **Landing gear down/locked indicators**
7 **Vertical speed indicator**
8 **Stand-by altimeter**
9 **Engine pressure ratio indicators**
10 **Low speed engine compressor (rpm)**
11 **Exhaust gas temperature**
12 **High speed engine compressor (rpm)**
13 **Fuel flow indicator**
14 **Flap position indicator**
15 **Static air temperature**
16 **Turn and bank indicator**
17 **Flight control position indicator**
18 **True airspeed indicator**
19 **Radio magnetic indicator**
20 **Map and panel light knobs**
21 **Annunciator light panel**
22 **Weather radar scope**
23 **Pilot's seat**
24 **Co-pilot's seat**

The flight director converts the attitude director into an instrument that tells the pilot how to fly the plane. Its computer processes the attitude and heading information displayed on the other instruments, and by means of two pointers superimposes directives on the artificial horizon. Whenever the aircraft, and consequently the pointers, move out of alignment, the pilot simply has to manoeuvre the plane exactly as the flight director indicates until the pointers cross, and he will find himself flying back onto the required heading. In the diagram, the plane is seen diving and banking to the right. The artificial horizon responds by moving above, and inclining to the left of, the aircraft symbol. The vertical pointer indicates that the pilot must fly still farther to the right; the horizontal pointer below the aircraft symbol indicates that he must descend a little more before intercepting the ILS beam.

The autopilot

In May 1914, a Parisian crowd saw Laurence Sperry, son of the American inventor of the first autopilot, fly a biplane low overhead. He was holding his hands in the air while his companion walked along the wings.

Uncontrolled, an aircraft will not immediately fall out of the sky but, even in calm air, it will gradually bank, turn, climb or dive. Sperry's system overcame those tendencies.

An autopilot is essentially a stabilizing system which takes over the controls during the climb, cruise and descent-to-destination phases of a flight, leaving the pilot free to concentrate on surveillance and communications. In turbulent conditions it relieves him of the fatiguing task of maintaining a smooth ride.

Sophisticated modern autopilots feed essential flight information from electrically-driven gyroscopes, pressure sensors and accelerometers (which measure vibrations and accelerations) into a computer. The data is processed and fed to servomotors (mechanisms which respond to electrical command signals, converting them into hydraulic signals) and these move the aircraft's control surfaces.

Signals to the autopilot computer may be caused by influences within the aircraft. Pitch can be affected as the fuel load lightens, or by people crowding to the back of the cabin to watch a movie. The autopilot compensates by moving the elevators and trimming the aircraft to hold it level.

On the flight deck the pilot merely monitors the trim indicators and keeps an eye on the flight director. Switched to autopilot, this no longer issues commands as in manual flying, but depicts the aircraft movements that the autopilot is bringing about.

Except for a switch lit up on the control panel, the autopilot cannot be seen. But the control column moves as if operated by invisible hands.

The autopilot control panel, mounted at the top of the instrument panel, can be reached by both pilots. From left to right the controls include: a setting knob and course indicator in compass degrees; automatic speed controls; auto approach and landing and flight director buttons; dual autopilot control channels (AP1 and AP2); a press bar (TURB) to reprogram the computer for turbulence; heading selection controls; controls for the altitude at which the autopilot will hold the aircraft; a warning system for a descent below 10,000 ft.

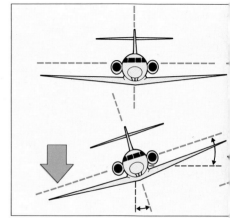

The sensing unit contains pressure sensors, accelerometers and three gyros mounted on different axes

Weather radar scanner

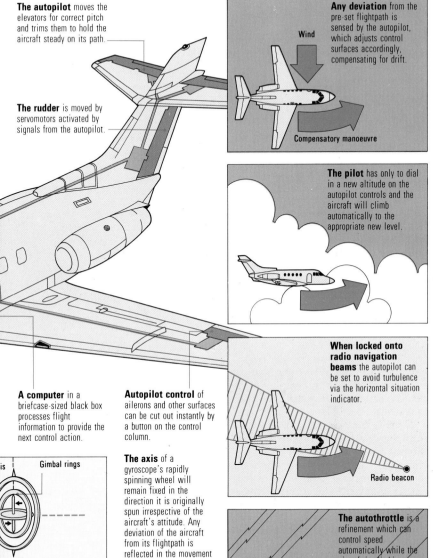

The autopilot moves the elevators for correct pitch and trims them to hold the aircraft steady on its path.

The rudder is moved by servomotors activated by signals from the autopilot.

Any deviation from the pre-set flightpath is sensed by the autopilot, which adjusts control surfaces accordingly, compensating for drift.

Wind

Compensatory manoeuvre

The pilot has only to dial in a new altitude on the autopilot controls and the aircraft will climb automatically to the appropriate new level.

When locked onto radio navigation beams the autopilot can be set to avoid turbulence via the horizontal situation indicator.

A computer in a briefcase-sized black box processes flight information to provide the next control action.

Autopilot control of ailerons and other surfaces can be cut out instantly by a button on the control column.

The axis of a gyroscope's rapidly spinning wheel will remain fixed in the direction it is originally spun irrespective of the aircraft's attitude. Any deviation of the aircraft from its flightpath is reflected in the movement of a gimbal ring in which the wheel is suspended. The amount and rate of deviation is measured and electrical signals sent to servomotors which instantly move the appropriate control surfaces.

Axis

Gimbal rings

Revolving wheels

Radio beacon

The autothrottle is a refinement which can control speed automatically while the aircraft is climbing, cruising and landing.

Aerial navigation/1

To be able to find his way around the skies, a pilot needs to know his position and his direction. Finding direction is easy using the simple magnetic compass, and there is at least one of these on every flight deck. Another kind of aircraft compass uses a gyroscope.

Air travel was always limited as long as pilots had to navigate using only compass bearings, maps and visual recognition of features on the ground. Planes equipped with radio have the aviator's equivalent of the mariner's lighthouse to find position, with one advantage: radio waves do not need to be visible to be effective. They can travel all over the world either in long waves — used in long-range navigation — that curve around the Earth's surface, or in short waves which tend to travel in

Dead-reckoning uses little but the pilot's eyes and suitable maps. The oldest and simplest form of aerial navigation is still used by pilots of light aircraft. It depends on recognizable ground landmarks. The pilot plots his track on the map before takeoff and, using his compass, flies in the right direction. Knowing his speed will enable him to calculate when he should fly over certain landmarks, and so check his progress.

The wind, carrying the aircraft off course, or causing sudden speed-ups or slow-downs, upsets such simple navigation. By relating his last known position to the direction he has flown, and his speed, the pilot will determine an approximate position several times during the flight. This becomes the centre of a circle, called a circle of uncertainty, whose radius is about ten per cent of the distance flown since the last landmark.

Astro-navigation

Above clouds or over featureless country when the Sun or stars are the only familiar sights around, pilots can make use of astro-navigation techniques. Using a sextant (this measures the angular separation of objects by means of adjustable mirrors) the pilot takes azimuth and elevation readings at a given time. To do this he measures the Sun's angle relative to the aircraft's flightpath and to the horizon, and calculates the aircraft's latitude and longitude on the world's surface. An accurate measure of the time of each observation, by chronometer, is essential.

On a clear night astro-navigators use the Pole-star in the northern hemisphere and the Southern Cross in the southern. It is rare for commercial pilots to use astro-navigation techniques today, but military crews are still familiar with them.

Position-fixing

True position will gradually become masked as small measuring errors accumulate and as the aircraft moves. As the illustration shows, a pilot flying an aircraft equipped with radio will take readings from, say, three radio beacon signals, and plot position-lines on a map. Where these intersect a small triangle is formed and the aircraft's position is assumed to be within this so-called cocked-hat.

The best results are obtained when all the measurements are taken within a short period; a one-minute delay in taking a position-reading at jet speed can introduce a ten-mile error. Automatic radio systems, and other modern computerized systems, take almost instantaneous readings and so minimize this problem. Radio beacons register on the pilot's radio magnetic indicator or on the horizontal situation indicator.

straight lines and are used in short-range navigation systems.

On this and following pages are outlined some of the methods used to navigate in the air. They are arranged with the oldest first, and the newest (Navstar) last. With Navstar, anyone on Earth with a receiver knows at all times his exact position, exact height (if above the ground) and exact speed and direction of travel. The possi-bilities are limitless and very exciting.

At present an American military system, Navstar has the great advan-tage of needing only small and fairly inexpensive receivers. Only the big-ger airlines can afford the cost and weight of (for example) Doppler radar or a triple INS — so pilots still have to learn the "ancient" traditional methods.

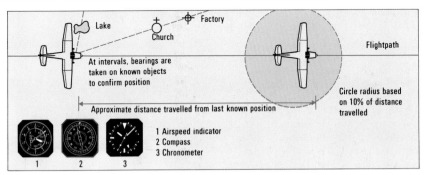

Lake
Factory
Church
At intervals, bearings are taken on known objects to confirm position
Flightpath
Circle radius based on 10% of distance travelled
Approximate distance travelled from last known position
1 Airspeed indicator
2 Compass
3 Chronometer

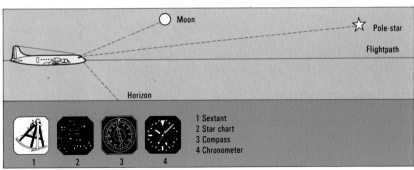

Moon
Pole-star
Flightpath
Horizon
1 Sextant
2 Star chart
3 Compass
4 Chronometer

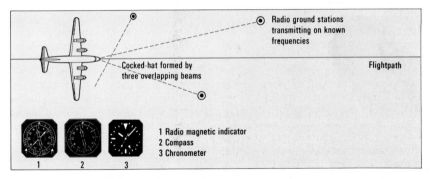

Radio ground stations transmitting on known frequencies
Cocked-hat formed by three overlapping beams
Flightpath
1 Radio magnetic indicator
2 Compass
3 Chronometer

Radio Range and NDB

A Radio Range system consists of a station transmitting two morse letters: A (·—) and N (—·). As the signals merge into a continuous note the pilot knows his aircraft is on the centreline of a designated airway. But this system can give a pilot guidance along up to four routes only, and has been largely superseded.

An alternative is the non-directional beacon (NDB), a station emitting a continuous signal, usually with an identifying message in morse that is repeated at frequent intervals. This can be received by aircraft homing onto the station, just as they would follow the beam of a lighted beacon, from up to 50 miles away. Without a compass a pilot following the signal cannot tell from which direction he is approaching the radio station. The direction to the beacon is displayed on the HSI.

VOR

Very high frequency omnidirectional range is the most commonly used radio system. Each VOR beacon transmits a continuous signal with morse-code identifying letters superimposed. By regulating the frequency of the signal it can be received in different forms by aircraft heading towards it from different directions. A processed signal is displayed on the horizontal situation indicator. Range is determined by distance-measuring equipment transmitting a signal to a VOR station and triggering an automatic reply. The time interval, translated into distance, is read off in nautical miles. At large airports VOR stations guide inbound aircraft to where an NDB, located about five miles from the beginning of the runway on an extended centreline, enables the pilot to home onto the Instrument Landing System.

Long-range radio navigation

Until recently long-wave radio signals were only reliable to a range of about 2,000 miles. Now they extend even farther, and their accuracy is such that a pilot can be sure of his position to within two to five miles. Because it is impractical to build conveniently sized aerials to carry direction-related long-wave information, a number of simple radio stations, one called a master and the others called slaves, are sited about 200 miles apart. Together they transmit synchronized pulses or continuous radio waves whose regular interference with one another sets up a complicated but predictable pattern of interference. This is always stationary relative to the ground even though the aircraft is moving, and so provides a reference against which an aircraft's radio receiver can automatically establish its position.

Weather radar

Nose-mounted weather radar is carried by most airliners. Though very simple — it is a safety device rather than a navigation system — it can be used to make navigation decisions. Its beam, sweeping across the sky up to 200 miles ahead (only 20 minutes away in a jet airliner), reflects off water droplets and detects weather that could be uncomfortably rough or even dangerous to fly through. A pilot usually changes course to avoid severe weather. The display unit in the flight deck gives a phosphorescent map of rainfall ahead, and the strength of the radar returns is approximately equivalent to cloud turbulence levels, but clear air turbulence cannot, unfortunately, be detected by radar. Most weather radars can be tilted downward to give a rough outline map of the terrain immediately beneath the aircraft.

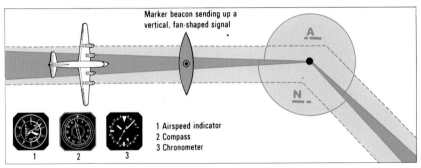

Marker beacon sending up a
vertical, fan-shaped signal

A

N

1 Airspeed indicator
2 Compass
3 Chronometer

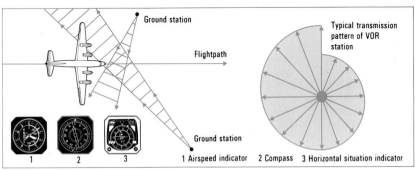

Ground station

Flightpath

Typical transmission
pattern of VOR
station

Ground station

1 Airspeed indicator   2 Compass   3 Horizontal situation indicator

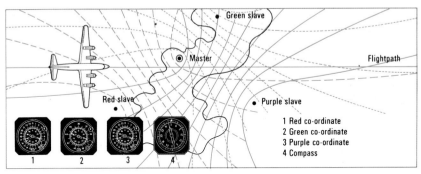

Green slave

Master

Flightpath

Red slave

Purple slave

1 Red co-ordinate
2 Green co-ordinate
3 Purple co-ordinate
4 Compass

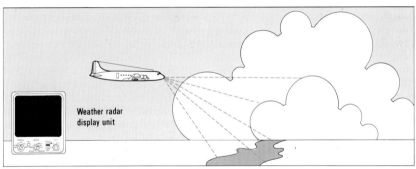

Weather radar
display unit

Aerial navigation/3

Doppler radar

The Doppler system is entirely self-contained. In this navigation system the radar splays up to four beams at a known frequency onto the ground beneath the aircraft. As they are reflected back to the aircraft the frequencies of the forward beams are increased, and the frequencies of the rearward beams are reduced, in proportion to the component of the speed in each direction. By analysing the frequency of radar energy scattered back from the ground the radar's computer can determine data such as the speed of the aircraft across the ground and the angle of drift caused by winds. Recently, such information has also become available from devices such as Omega and inertial navigation systems (INS) that are considerably simpler — so Doppler radar is tending to disappear from commercial aircraft.

INS

The heart of an inertial navigation system is a carefully-balanced platform, held level by gyroscopes, on which three accelerometers are mounted, each pointing in a different direction: fore and aft, up and down, left and right. They measure the aircraft's slightest acceleration, and this is automatically converted to velocity and then to distance covered. On takeoff the system is given the aircraft's exact position, and thereafter a panel display shows position continuously throughout the flight. The INS can also determine how winds are affecting the aircraft. A drift of one mile each hour is typical.

It is usual for large airliners to carry three INS sets so that the crew can check any discrepancies; by comparing the three position indicators they can tell immediately whether one of the systems has failed.

Omega

A recently introduced navigation system whose accuracy surpasses that of the INS, the Omega system is already being used on long-range aircraft. The illustration shows the positions of the Omega transmitters in each hemisphere, each sending out powerful long-wave radio signals that can be picked up by aircraft and also by ships and submarines. Within a ten-second interval, each station transmits three pulses, each on a different radio frequency and lasting for approximately one second. All the signals are synchronized, and super-accurate atomic clocks keep their transmissions in time. On the aircraft a miniature computer, whose many thousand components can fit onto a thumb-nail-sized circuit board, analyses the signals and calculates its position anywhere in the world to within two miles.

Laser navigation

Laser "gyros" can now provide a navigation system with no moving parts; three, mounted in an aircraft, can detect the slightest movement. They consist of triangular tubes with mirrors at each angle. Two laser beams, transmitted in opposite directions, take the same time to travel round the triangle, but when rotated by aircraft movement one beam takes more time and the other less.

Satellite navigation systems

Navstar, several of its satellites already in orbit, is one of various satellite systems under development. It will be fully operational by the 1990s. Its final 24 satellites, orbiting simultaneously 10,000 miles high, will provide continuous high-quality position fixes. When perfected, the system will enable a pilot to know where he is within as little as 20 ft, the width of a Boeing 747 fuselage!

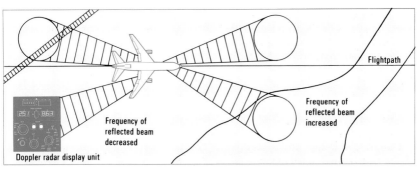

Flightpath

Frequency of reflected beam decreased

Frequency of reflected beam increased

Doppler radar display unit

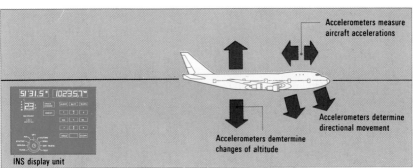

Omega display unit

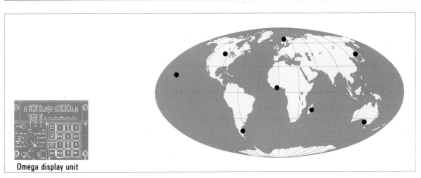

Accelerometers measure aircraft accelerations

Accelerometers determine directional movement

Accelerometers demtermine changes of altitude

INS display unit

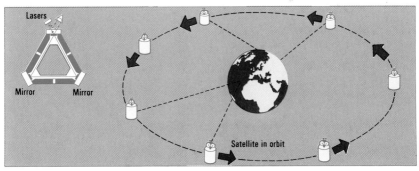

Lasers

Mirror   Mirror

Satellite in orbit

The fuel system

A long-range jet airliner carries 100 tons or more of fuel, enough to drive a small car about 50 times round the world. Of necessity, the earliest of all the complex aircraft systems to evolve was the fuel system.

Light aircraft have piston engines much like those of cars, burning aviation-grade petrol (gasoline). This is pumped into the tanks, flexible neoprene-rubber bags fitted into the wing compartments or fuselage, via a gravity filler.

Jet airliners burn various grades of jet fuel of the kerosene (paraffin) type. There is often no separate tank. Instead, the aircraft structure — the spaces between the wing spars, parts of the body, or tailplane — is coated with layers of rubbery sealant to form a series of fuel-tight compartments. These stay absolutely leakproof even though the structure twists and bends in turbulence or on rough airfields. Baffles in the tanks stop the fuel sloshing about, and one-way valves prevent it from running uncontrolled from tank to tank. The space above the fuel is not filled with combustible air but dry nitrogen, which is inert.

All fuel can serve any engine, the tanks being linked by pipes with one-way or pilot-controlled valves. These allow it to flow no matter what the aircraft's attitude, and they control the flow of fuel or gas through the system to balance out pressure differences at varying altitudes. Vents,

Fuelling sockets may be in the fuselage, as in the BAe One-Eleven **above**, on the landing-gear bays, or under the wing as on the Boeing 747 **below**. They can usually be reached from the ground, but the 747 needs a lifting platform.

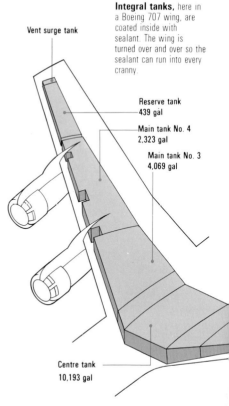

Vent surge tank

Integral tanks, here in a Boeing 707 wing, are coated inside with sealant. The wing is turned over and over so the sealant can run into every cranny.

Reserve tank
439 gal

Main tank No. 4
2,323 gal

Main tank No. 3
4,069 gal

Centre tank
10,193 gal

usually at the wing tips or tail, keep the pressure constant.

The fuel is pumped out of each tank by electric or air-driven booster pumps at the lowest point. Multi-engined aircraft have special proportioners to distribute the fuel accurately between the engines, and high-pressure pumps on the engines.

Extreme care is taken to eliminate water from the fuel, which would freeze at high altitudes and cause blockages, but heated filters melt any ice crystals that do form.

Even though the aircraft's skin may heat to 120 degrees Fahrenheit (49 degrees Celsius) on the ground at hot airports or due to friction at supersonic speeds, the fuel must never be allowed to boil and produce bubbles, despite the fact that it may serve as a "heat sink" to which nearly all unusable heat is rejected, as it does in Concorde. Lightweight foam usually insulates each tank.

In subsonic aircraft, fuel is consumed evenly throughout the system to make the centre of gravity shift by as little as possible. In Concorde it is used to change the centre of gravity, to counteract trim changes between subsonic and supersonic flight.

Refuelling an aircraft, particularly the new-generation, wide-bodied airliners, needs special equipment. Giant mobile tankers and fixed airport fuel hydrants can refuel a wide-bodied aircraft in less than half an hour.

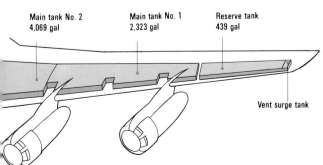

Main tank No. 2
4,069 gal

Main tank No. 1
2,323 gal

Reserve tank
439 gal

Vent surge tank

Pressure-fuelling has replaced gravity fillers. Fuel is pumped aboard at a rate of up to 2,000 gals (2,400 US gals) a minute through high-pressure couplings which seal automatically when the hefty hose is uncoupled. Anti-static fuel additives, and an electrical bonding wire between hose and aircraft, prevent sparks.

The hydraulic system

A pilot of average strength can exert a muscle force of perhaps 100 pounds. This was adequate to operate the wire-controlled ailerons, elevators and rudders of the first airliners, but when flaps and retractable landing-gears were invented, and aircraft began to weigh 50 tons or more, pilots needed mechanical assistance.

Hydraulics provide the muscles that work the moving parts of a large aircraft. The principle is the same as in the brakes of a car: pumps driven by the engines force fluid through pipes and valves.

Most hydraulic fluids used in aircraft are mineral oils, but increasingly, water-based non-inflammable compounds are used. They are virtually incompressible, providing not only an immediate operative force, but a lock, preventing unwanted movement in any part of the system.

Airliners usually have two or more hydraulic systems in case one should fail. Some aircraft have control surfaces divided into separate sections, each controlled by a separately signalled hydraulic power unit. Others couple several systems to single items, with a "majority rule" to overpower any system containing a fault.

Aircraft power steering is so responsive that resistance is built into the column so that pilots can gauge how much pressure to apply.

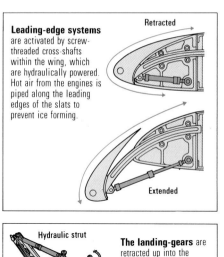

Leading-edge systems are activated by screw-threaded cross-shafts within the wing, which are hydraulically powered. Hot air from the engines is piped along the leading edges of the slats to prevent ice forming.

Retracted

Extended

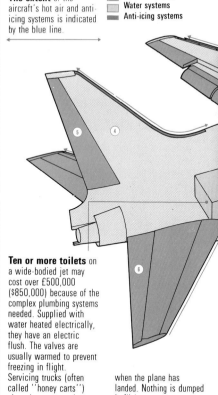

The extent of the aircraft's hot air and anti-icing systems is indicated by the blue line.

▨ Hydraulically operated areas
▢ Water systems
▬ Anti-icing systems

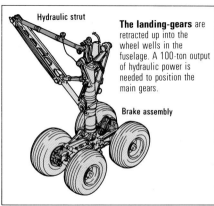

Hydraulic strut

The landing-gears are retracted up into the wheel wells in the fuselage. A 100-ton output of hydraulic power is needed to position the main gears.

Brake assembly

Ten or more toilets on a wide-bodied jet may cost over £500,000 ($850,000) because of the complex plumbing systems needed. Supplied with water heated electrically, they have an electric flush. The valves are usually warmed to prevent freezing in flight. Servicing trucks (often called "honey carts") clear the waste tanks when the plane has landed. Nothing is dumped in flight.

Anti-icing and water

The first airliners were dangerously affected by ice formation during flight. It increased their weight, starved the engines of air and even changed the shape of the wings by forming along the leading edges.

Alcohol sprays and brush-on pastes were the first attempts at anti-icing during the 1930s, but the rubber pulsating boot, still common on slow aircraft, was the first really effective de-icing system. Tubes along the leading edges of the wings and tail alternately inflate and deflate by air pressure, breaking the ice so that the slipstream can carry it away.

On jets, extremely hot air is ducted from the engine compressors along the wing and tail leading edges, and to engine inlets and windshields. Electric elements, embedded in rubber or plastic, heat the windshield and other surfaces until they are too hot to touch. Heated anti-icing fluids protect parked aircraft.

Only since 1950 have clear drinking water, running water for washing, and flushing toilets been installed in all long-range airliners. The popularity of air travel made them indispensable, yet the apparently simple problems of freezing waste pipes at high altitudes, and surge in water tanks during turbulence, needed complex engineering before their efficiency was assured.

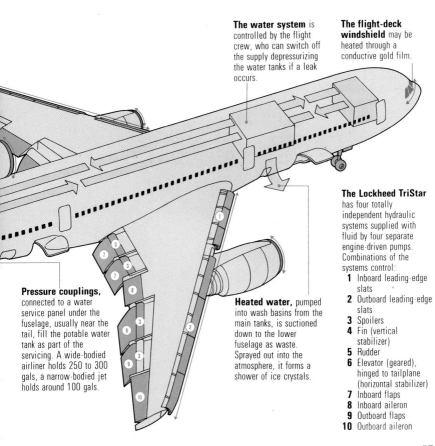

The water system is controlled by the flight crew, who can switch off the supply depressurizing the water tanks if a leak occurs.

The flight-deck windshield may be heated through a conductive gold film.

The Lockheed TriStar has four totally independent hydraulic systems supplied with fluid by four separate engine-driven pumps. Combinations of the systems control:
1 Inboard leading-edge slats
2 Outboard leading-edge slats
3 Spoilers
4 Fin (vertical stabilizer)
5 Rudder
6 Elevator (geared), hinged to tailplane (horizontal stabilizer)
7 Inboard flaps
8 Inboard aileron
9 Outboard flaps
10 Outboard aileron

Pressure couplings, connected to a water service panel under the fuselage, usually near the tail, fill the potable water tank as part of the servicing. A wide-bodied airliner holds 250 to 300 gals, a narrow-bodied jet holds around 100 gals.

Heated water, pumped into wash basins from the main tanks, is suctioned down to the lower fuselage as waste. Sprayed out into the atmosphere, it forms a shower of ice crystals.

Pressurization and air-conditioning

The higher a plane flies, the colder the temperature of the air around it. At 35,000 feet and above, the outside air is around minus 70 degrees Fahrenheit (minus 57 degrees Celsius) far, far colder than an icebox.

As an aircraft climbs, atmospheric pressure falls too, from about 15 pounds per square inch at sea level to around four pounds per square inch at airliner cruising height, which may be 10,000 feet above the highest altitude that will sustain human life. Cabin pressure is usually allowed to fall gently to the equivalent of 8,000 feet, and maintained at that level by pressurizing the fuselage.

Piston-engined aircraft and turbo-props have air compressors to maintain cabin pressure. Jet engines handle so much air that pressurization supplies can be bled from them under great pressure, and already very hot. These are cooled in a heat-exchanger, from where some is fed to the cabin and the excess expelled. Full pressurization can add a ton of weight to a Boeing 747.

Oxygen masks are installed above passenger seats for emergency use in the event of pressurization failure.

Fresh air for the environmental control system (ECS) is heated in the same heat-exchanger, humidified and fed into the cabin to air-condition it to a constant level of comfort.

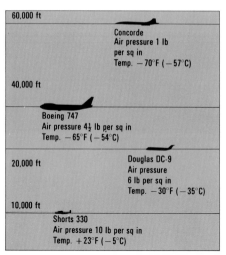

60,000 ft

Concorde
Air pressure 1 lb
per sq in
Temp. −70°F (−57°C)

40,000 ft

Boeing 747
Air pressure 4½ lb per sq in
Temp. −65°F (−54°C)

Douglas DC-9
Air pressure
6 lb per sq in
Temp. −30°F (−35°C)

20,000 ft

10,000 ft

Shorts 330
Air pressure 10 lb per sq in
Temp. +23°F (−5°C)

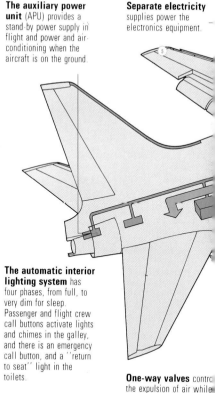

The auxiliary power unit (APU) provides a stand-by power supply in flight and power and air-conditioning when the aircraft is on the ground.

Separate electricity supplies power the electronics equipment.

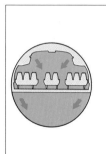

The Lockheed TriStar has five automatically controlled temperature zones: one in the flight deck, three in the cabin and one in the galley. Engine bleed air is ducted to each zone, vented through the cabin floor, through the cargo holds and electrical service centres.

The automatic interior lighting system has four phases, from full, to very dim for sleep. Passenger and flight crew call buttons activate lights and chimes in the galley, and there is an emergency call button, and a "return to seat" light in the toilets.

One-way valves control the expulsion of air while keeping fuselage pressure constant.

Electrics and electronics

Simple one- or two-seater planes have a direct current (DC) system to run the radio and navigation lights; large airliners usually have other kinds of current on board, suited for specific purposes. They have over 15,000 electric and electronic devices, served by systems as complicated as those of a complete city. They generate most of their electric power as AC (alternating current), the same as a house supply, by alternators on each engine. For emergency use there are other generators: a ram air turbine (a windmill spun by the slipstream), and an auxiliary power unit (APU) which can either be used in an emergency or on the ground when the engines are not running. AC is used for all the heavy loads: for anti-icing the airframe (needing the largest AC supplies) for powering hydraulic systems, for heating ovens in the galley, for powering radio masts, toilet and galley drains, and accounts for about half the total power.

The avionics (aviation electronics) use about one-twentieth of the power, but need a precisely controlled frequency of AC current generated by alternators which turn at the right speed no matter how fast the engines may be turning. Absolute integrity of these supplies must be guaranteed; they have total priority over non-essential loads.

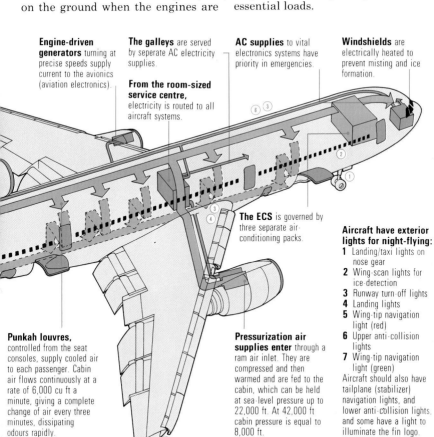

Engine-driven generators turning at precise speeds supply current to the avionics (aviation electronics).

The galleys are served by seperate AC electricity supplies.

From the room-sized service centre, electricity is routed to all aircraft systems.

AC supplies to vital electronics systems have priority in emergencies.

Windshields are electrically heated to prevent misting and ice formation.

The ECS is governed by three separate air-conditioning packs.

Punkah louvres, controlled from the seat consoles, supply cooled air to each passenger. Cabin air flows continuously at a rate of 6,000 cu ft a minute, giving a complete change of air every three minutes, dissipating odours rapidly.

Pressurization air supplies enter through a ram air inlet. They are compressed and then warmed and are fed to the cabin, which can be held at sea-level pressure up to 22,000 ft. At 42,000 ft cabin pressure is equal to 8,000 ft.

Aircraft have exterior lights for night-flying:
1 Landing/taxi lights on nose gear
2 Wing-scan lights for ice-detection
3 Runway turn-off lights
4 Landing lights
5 Wing-tip navigation light (red)
6 Upper anti-collision lights
7 Wing-tip navigation light (green)
Aircraft should also have tailplane (stabilizer) navigation lights, and lower anti-collision lights, and some have a light to illuminate the fin logo.

59

Cabin layout

An airline's profit depends upon each of its aircraft carrying as many passengers as possible. The less cabin space devoted to passenger seating, the more expensive the air ticket will be. The designers of aircraft are therefore required to accommodate the largest number of seats, while retaining reasonable comfort.

In the early days of airline operation, during the 1920s and 1930s, aircraft could carry few passengers. The wooden-winged Fokker F.XII which flew KLM's Amsterdam to Batavia (now Djakarta) service, the longest air route in 1931, carried only four. As the technology of air travel advanced, seats were positioned one behind another, usually with a side aisle.

When long-established air travel became established, after 1930, aircraft were fitted with sleeping compartments. As late as the 1950s, the Douglas DC-7, which operated the first regular non-stop transatlantic services in 1956, taking about ten hours, was fitted with "slumberette" reclining seats and bunks. These were not needed in later, faster jets.

The economic significance of high-density seating was soon exploited, and a line of seats on each side of a central aisle became the classic configuration; the second-generation jet airliners had rows of five (three plus two) or six (three plus three) seats.

Not all airliners have alternative economy (coach) and first-class accommodation. Some commuter and shuttle aircraft, charter operations and small island-hoppers have a single class. The distinction is most evident in the different seat layouts.

In narrow-bodied airliners, the economy-section rows of triple-seat units usually give way to two plus two rows of double-seat units in the first-class cabin. In the wide-bodied airliners the standard seating pattern

The inside wall of the passenger cabin, which appears solid to the passengers, is completely removable **above**. Walls, ceiling and floor are made up of lightweight panels which can be removed individually or *en bloc*, enabling maintenance engineers to service the system behind and beneath, replace damaged fittings and examine the windows. Storage units, galley and toilet walls and doors, partitions and bulkheads are also removable. Wall panels are one-piece vacuum mouldings made from lightweight synthetic materials, and floor panels are constructed from plastic honeycomb panels bonded between glass-fibre or carbon-fibre skins.

Airbus A300   **McDonnell Douglas MD-80**

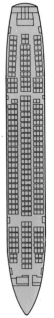

The Airbus A300
single-class layout has nine seats abreast. The mixed-class layout has eight abreast in economy and six abreast in first class.

The MD-80 seats 12 first-class passengers in rows of two plus two, and 125 tourist-class travellers in rows of three plus two.

consists of rows of up to nine or ten abreast with two aisles: two plus five plus two in the Douglas DC-10, or three plus four plus three in the Boeing 747. The first-class seating pattern is usually two plus two, with extra luxury provided in the additional lounge areas.

Although an airliner is a parallel tube for most of its length, the cabin tapers at each end, most noticeably in wide-bodied jets, so in the front and back of most aircraft the number of seat rows is reduced.

Ultimately the number of seats is determined by the number of seat rows. Seats are usually spaced about 34 inches apart in first class, 32 inches apart in the economy section. This distance, measured from the front of a seat to the same point on the one behind, is known as the seat pitch. To keep fares low, in charter flights, seats may have a pitch of only 29 inches, much closer than for the (more expensive) scheduled services on which an airline's reputation is built.

Most major airlines will permit passengers to select the seats they prefer on mixed-class scheduled flights, as long as they book early enough. A seat at the front is likely to be in a no-smoking area, and in small airliners especially, may give a view into the flight deck. Smokers are located at the back, because the smoke drifts backwards, although air-conditioning changes the cabin air once every three minutes. Window seats on the side away from the Sun give the best view, and seats with most leg-room are by the doors or emergency exits where seat-pitching is most generous. A few airlines mark off a "business end" of the cabin for executives, and most aircraft have special cot-holders, where babies should be stowed whenever the "Fasten seat belts" sign flashes up.

Business jets like the British Aerospace 125 **above** can be fitted out more or less to a customer's requirements, with customized interior colour schemes, materials and furnishings. Five-, eight- or ten-seat configurations are available, but most business jet interiors are designed as lounges, the seats arranged to make the most of the available interior space. Optional luxuries can include stereo tape and radio units, bars and even beds. An air-to-ground telephone/telex link, desks, tables, computers and displays can turn a small jet into a flying boardroom or office.

Concorde

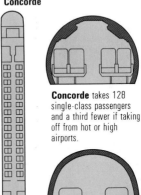

Concorde takes 128 single-class passengers and a third fewer if taking off from hot or high airports.

Beechcraft B99

The Beechcraft B99 commuter aircraft carries up to 15 passengers in single seats flanking an aisle.

Cabin comfort

Wicker garden seats were fashionable in the smoking lounges of Imperial flying boats of the 1930s. Modern seats may be less elegant but they are safer; and the handful of manufacturers who supply all the world's airlines ensure that the core of comfort provided by adjustable backrests and cushioned upholstery is surrounded by all possible conveniences: plug-in or fold-away meal trays, ashtrays, magazine racks, footrests and luggage restraint devices.

The world's civil aviation authorities set the safety standards. To be able to take the strain of severe air turbulence, or of an emergency stop, passenger seats must be able to withstand several times the normal takeoff acceleration and landing deceleration rates. The UK and US authorities demand that an occupied seat be able to withstand an acceleration of nine times that of gravity (a mass of one pound accelerated by 32 feet per second per second) forward, and one and a half to four and a half times gravity rearward, sideways, upward and downward. Extensive testing ensures the strength and resistance of all welds, bolts and safety-belt anchorages. Adjustable backrests break forward on a sudden stop so that passengers in the seat behind

Passenger seats are designed in sets of two, three, four or five seats. The main frame assembly is made of tubular steel. The legs are braced for extra rigidity and the ''feet'' lock into seat railtracks on the floor so that no forward, backward or sideways movement is possible. Seat units can be removed to give maintenance engineers access to underfloor systems.

The centre seat of a triple unit may have a table built into the contoured backrest. This folds down and locks onto the armrests, converting the centre seat into a centre table.

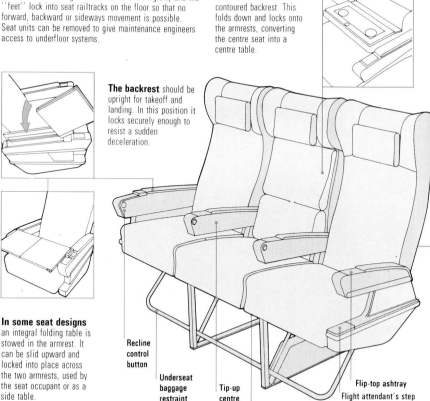

The backrest should be upright for takeoff and landing. In this position it locks securely enough to resist a sudden deceleration.

In some seat designs an integral folding table is stowed in the armrest. It can be slid upward and locked into place across the two armrests, used by the seat occupant or as a side table.

Recline control button

Underseat baggage restraint unit

Tip-up centre armrest

Life-jacket

Flip-top ashtray

Flight attendant's step

will not hit them if thrown forward on a sudden deceleration.

Most passenger seats face forward, toward the aircraft nose. Backward-facing seats would be safer: passengers would be supported by the backrest during sudden deceleration instead of forward against the seat in front, unrestrained except for the seatbelt fastened across the abdomen. Because passengers would rather see where they are going than where they have been, airlines have refused to alter this practice but, significantly, whenever military use is made of civil aircraft, seats are turned around into the safer position.

Lifejackets are usually stored beneath each seat where they are readily accessible. Above the passengers' heads, or sometimes released from the seat in front, oxygen masks drop down automatically if the cabin pressure should fall below the optimum level. Seats are upholstered in flame-resistant materials. On some airliners the cushions can be removed and used as floating life-preservers.

In structure and standard of upholstery there is little difference between first and tourist (coach) class seating. But there is an obvious difference in size. First-class seats are larger and are farther apart, and contoured backrests, often fitted with "slumber" headrests, provide a little extra comfort.

Noise levels vary little between different points on an aircraft, although passengers near a galley or toilet may be disturbed frequently. The engine noise is more noticeable at the back of a rear-engined airliner; the first-class cabin is located away from the engines. From a seat positioned near the landing-gears, the sound of the doors locking into the up and down positions can be disturbing, but noise from the wheels on the runway tends to be transmitted throughout the fuselage. Aircraft could be made quieter, but a level of mechanical noise diffuses the sound of 400 passengers talking at once.

To protect themselves in an emergency, forward-facing passengers **left** must brace themselves in a forward-leaning position, head protected by the arms and cushioned on the knees. Rear-facing passengers **right** are more protected and need only brace hard against the seat back.

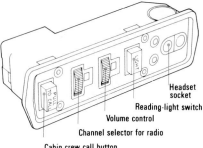

Headset socket
Reading-light switch
Volume control
Channel selector for radio
Cabin crew call button

Individual control units, set into the armrest or high above each seat, enable passengers to call the cabin crew, operate individual light and fresh-air units, and listen through headsets to the variety of music usually offered by major airlines. One of the channels gives the film soundtrack, which may be available in alternative languages. The film projector, generally located below the ceiling storage units, aims the picture at a mirror which produces an almost horizontal beam, preventing distortion. Screens are located on the cabin bulkheads, or arranged so that they hinge down from the ceiling.

Released by a latch, a meal table slides or folds down from the seat in front.

Cabin service

Before the first airlines had found their own identity, they mimicked the stately luxury of the great sea-liners. During the 1930s, graceful airships and elegant flying boats were staffed with a full complement of chefs and stewards who served leisurely meals in grand dining rooms.

But mass travel, and the pursuit of speed rather than comfort, brought the need for mass catering: a large airline such as TWA serves over 16 million meals in flight every year, and Singapore Airlines invests about 5.9 per cent of its budget in cabin services.

Airline food is prepared in vast catering centres, often leased at airports at both ends of the routes. Catering may be contracted out to large hotels or restaurants, or specialized companies contracted to load flights 20 to 40 minutes before departure with pre-cooked meals ready for reheating, and trays of cold food. Only pre-browned steaks are cooked on board, in ovens powered by the aircraft electrics. Frozen meals take 30 seconds to defrost in microwave ovens. Frozen meal packs are essential on flights to airports with inadequate catering facilities. Fresh food would not survive delays, but the use of frozen food and powdered instead of fresh milk (which sours quickly in a pressurized cabin, and is not readily available in some parts of the world) limits the standards of airline catering. Yet airlines go to great lengths to plan varied menus, and to transport delicacies such as coffee beans, tropical fruit, fresh fish and even caviar for first-class passen-

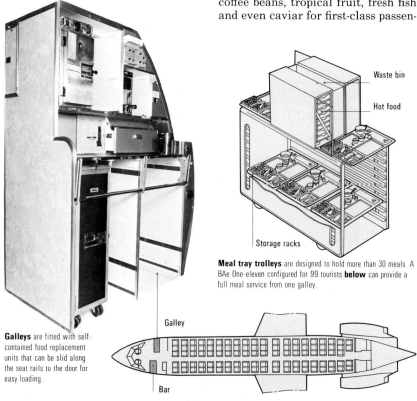

Waste bin

Hot food

Storage racks

Meal tray trolleys are designed to hold more than 30 meals. A BAe One-eleven configured for 99 tourists **below** can provide a full meal service from one galley.

Galleys are fitted with self-contained food replacement units that can be slid along the seat rails to the door for easy loading.

Galley

Bar

gers, from distant parts of the world.

Most airlines serve a choice of two main meals but Virgin Atlantic offer a choice of three main meals, including a vegetarian choice as standard.

National dishes vary the "international" sautéed chicken and steak, and some transatlantic airlines serve turkey and cranberry sauce on Thanksgiving Day. Some airlines offer special ethnic dishes.

On average, economy meals cost about £5 ($10) a head; first-class meals cost about twice as much, and as a rule, only first-class passengers are offered free drinks. Some airlines present free gifts to first- and business-class passengers. The crew may be served a more varied menu. For fear of food poisoning the captain and co-pilot usually eat different meals and shellfish may be banned to them.

Passengers on special religious or medical diets can ask for vegetarian, Moslem, kosher, Hindu, salt-free, dietetic ulcer, diabetic or slimming meals when they book their tickets. Children may be served special meals and infants' bottles will be made up by the cabin crew.

Mealtimes depend on departure times, and follow an international clock. They may be changed to avoid service during turbulence. Heating and serving are timed so that no passenger is served lukewarm food.

The catering trucks are usually the first servicing vehicles to arrive at the aircraft parking bays. Catering staff remove soiled utensils and waste, and reload the aircraft. British Airways handles over 500,000 items of cutlery, 168,000 glasses, 50,000 tray dishes and 40,000 cups and saucers, and launders around 100 tons of linen and blankets a week.

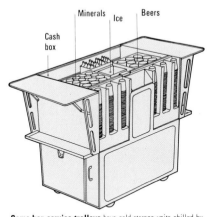

Cash box

Minerals Ice Beers

Some bar-service trolleys have cold storage units chilled by gas-activated dry ice. Aircraft bars are installed and sealed by Customs. A mixed-class Boeing 747 configured for 385 passengers **below** need six galleys to provide a full meal service.

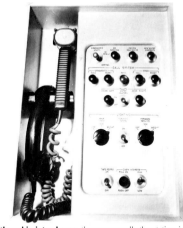

On the cabin interphones, the crew can call other stations in different parts of the aircraft, and override an existing conversation to contact the flight crew in an emergency.

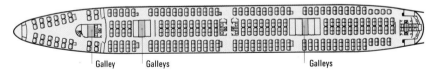

Galley Galleys Galleys

Emergencies

Accidents do happen, and when they do, crew training, aircraft equipment and the good sense of the passengers may be fundamental to survival. To be alert to (but not obsessed with) the possibility of an emergency increases the chances of surviving it.

Aircraft seat belts, like the seats, are designed to withstand sudden deceleration. Work out how to fasten and unfasten them quickly. Cabin crews check that they are fastened at takeoff and landing, and that babies are installed in special cot-holders.

Do not, unless you are well versed in them, ignore the safety demonstrations at the beginning of a flight. Learn how to put on a lifejacket, and how to use the emergency oxygen masks stored above the seat or in the back of the seat in front: should depressurization occur suddenly at high altitudes, there would be very little time to find out how to put them on. In each magazine pocket is a card of safety instructions in pictures. It gives the positions of the emergency exits. Each of these has a sign giving the operating instructions in one or more languages, so they can be opened by passengers.

Fire extinguishers and sometimes axes are stowed at the cabin crew stations. Life raft stowages are usually near each main exit; in wide-bodied jets they are extensions of the escape slides, and in many well-known types of aircraft they are stored in the ceiling above the aisle. The survival, first-aid and polar kits

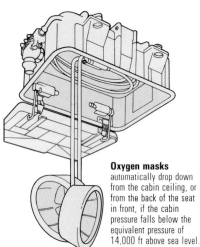

Oxygen masks
automatically drop down from the cabin ceiling, or from the back of the seat in front, if the cabin pressure falls below the equivalent pressure of 14,000 ft above sea level.

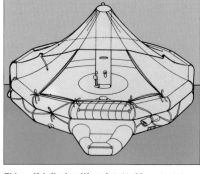

This self-inflating life raft holds 26 people. It is stocked with lifejackets, floating cots, supplies, a floating non-puncture knife, a lifeline, paddles and a drogue (sea anchor), and may have a radio transmitter. The canopy acts as a rain-catcher.

Emergency and evacuation equipment
carried on the McDonnell Douglas DC-10 includes:
1 Asbestos gloves
2 Axe
3 General-purpose fire extinguishers
4 Door barrier straps
5 Carbon-dioxide fire-extinguisher
6 Survival packs
7 Escape ropes
8 Flashlights
9 First-aid kits
10 Floating baby-survival cots
11 Spare lifejackets
12 Oxygen masks for portable bottles
13 Megaphones
14 Oxygen bottles
15 Oxygen bottles with face masks
16 Extension seat belts
17 Smoke goggles
18 Paddles

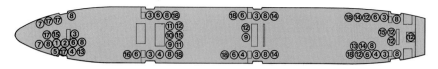

are usually found near, perhaps attached to, the life rafts or exits.

If the "fasten seat belts" signs flash on in flight, obey them quickly; the aircraft may be about to enter turbulence and passengers walking about, especially at the back, could be thrown around.

Extinguish cigarettes immediately the "no smoking" signs go on (in the ashtray, never on the floor). *Never smoke in the toilets* where inflammable materials are often still used in the furnishings. Many accidents are caused by in-flight fires or smoke; many began in the toilets.

In an emergency, obey the cabin crew without question. They will order passengers to fasten seat belts, extinguish cigarettes and brace themselves (bracing positions are illustrated on the "safety instructions" card) for sudden deceleration. They control the exits when the aircraft stops, instruct passengers on the procedure, and collect emergency equipment and supplies. If doors are inoperative, they activate the emergency exits, ordering passengers to unfasten seat belts, leave everything behind (including all hand baggage), and make for the designated escape chutes indicated by the cabin staff.

At the doorway, jump or slide down the chute to the ground (or into the life raft). Then get away from the aircraft. Move fast, and *forget your belongings*. In a fire, stragglers may be overcome by toxic fumes released by burning cabin furnishings.

Polar suits are replacing the fur coats carried on Arctic flights. Big enough to fit anyone, they are made of fire-resistant, water repellent material and are insulated on both sides with aluminium coating. They weigh half a pound.

On the Lockheed TriStar (below) emergency exits are located clear of the wing for the safest evacuation of passengers directly onto the ground, or into life rafts. Four exits on either side enabled 345 passengers plus a crew of ten to be evacuated in 82 seconds during demonstrations conducted for US Federal Aviation Administration certification.

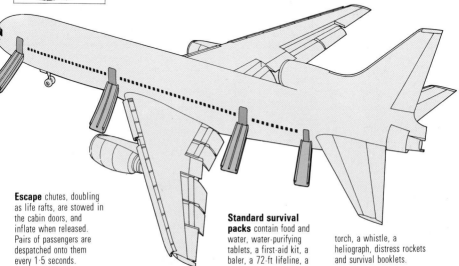

Escape chutes, doubling as life rafts, are stowed in the cabin doors, and inflate when released. Pairs of passengers are despatched onto them every 1·5 seconds.

Standard survival packs contain food and water, water-purifying tablets, a first-aid kit, a baler, a 72-ft lifeline, a torch, a whistle, a heliograph, distress rockets and survival booklets.

Skyscape

As an airliner climbs through city smog or wintry murk into the clear sunshine of the upper air, the world and its weather spread out below like a map. In bright sunshine the shadow of the aircraft can sometimes be seen on the clouds below, with a rainbow halo all around it. The Earth may be ringed by a sharp horizon, or, in warmer climates, obscured by the dazzling peaks and purple ravines of 30,000-foot-high thunderstorms. The aircraft may travel through wispy ice-cloud cirrus that patterns the sky like translucent lace, or grey banks of cloud that give only brief glimpses of the ground beneath.

The clouds have information to give. Light puffy cumulus is made in rising warm air and grows more quickly over land than on sea; on a featureless ocean crossing a cluster of distant cumulus can indicate islands still hidden by the curving Earth — a navigational aid used by Viking and Polynesian sailors.

Clouds come in every shape, and are not difficult to identify. Cumulus

The earth may be dappled with puffs of fine-weather cumulus **above** which make shadows on the fields beneath; ground features can be easily identified as the plane comes in to land.

A peak of the English Cumbrian hills breaks out from a mass of hill fog **right above**. Thunder-clouds **right** are easily recognized by the anvil-shaped clouds on their tops.

clouds usually lie far below a jet; they rarely grow above 12,000 feet even in warm sub-tropical skies. Light aircraft fly in the smooth air just above their tops, and seldom below them in the turbulent thermals, the currents of rising warm air that produce them.

Pilots of small aircraft also avoid flying through the dark hearts of thunderstorms, though the crew of a jetliner may not always clear their pinnacles. These cumulo-nimbus sometimes grow so fast they can be seen "boiling" upward and wearing small eyebrow-shaped clouds called pileus on their heads. Because they grow so tall, thunder-clouds remain bathed in golden sunlight after it has become dark on the ground.

The long-distance jet flies above most of the clouds, giving passengers a grandstand view of the world's weather in all its moods. On windy days strange lens-shaped lenticular clouds may be spotted hanging in the sky above mountains or even solid cloud. They grow to the lee of mountains like gigantic versions of the ripples that form downstream of rocks in a river. These waves of cloud may go as high as Concorde, to 50,000 feet. Pilots flying smaller aircraft are wary of such massive streams of up and down air.

In high latitudes at night, the spectacular aurora borealis, northern lights from outer space, may be visible from the cabin window. Often in the form of an arc, sometimes with rays shooting skywards, this eerie display of greenish light is caused by electrical discharge more than two

miles high, in outer space.

The degree of latitude affects the length of twilight. The northern Sun's low path gives a long half light, but towards the tropics, where the Sun is high and plummets steeply at the end of the day, dark — and dawn — come rapidly. Travelling westwards across either hemisphere in summer, passengers at jet speed have the impression that night has disappeared.

Few passengers realize how easy it is to identify the fascinating geography over which they fly, but from six

miles up on a clear day so much can be seen that an airline route map or a pocket atlas can make a long flight more interesting. High over the incredible blue of the Mediterranean the Greek islands, Cyprus or Malta are unmistakable, and it is easy to visualize the ships of the ancient civilizations voyaging between them. Quite different are the Pacific islands, or the American Florida Keys linked into a great curve by the roads and bridges of a new concrete world.

In the dark, cities below look like islands; 25,000 feet from the ground they show up so clearly that it is sometimes possible to see streets lighted as brightly as runways, and even large buildings. Mercury vapour lights are bluey pinpoints with coloured halos, and sodium lights make a yellowy-orange glow. The aircraft lights, reflected off a million water droplets, may dazzle passengers as the plane flies through a cloud.

Watching the aircraft in flight can be absorbing. Seats at the front may give glimpses into the flight deck. The propellers of short-range aircraft may be seen to change pitch when speed is altered. There is a wispy vortex from propeller tips at takeoff if the atmosphere is moist. Wingtip vortices may be visible in a turn, but Concorde's are quite spectacular. After takeoff, when the jet is at a steep angle, a huge cloud forms at the front of the wing and rolls back along the leading edge in the form of a thin tube. In flight, it seems to trail after the wing tip in a stream.

Aircraft wings are designed to flex up and down in flight, helping to give a smoother ride. The flaps, slats and spoilers can be seen working as the plane climbs, turns and descends. Back seats give the best view of the flaps and spoilers working together when landing. Passengers near the wing may be able to see right through it when they are full out.

Holding patterns

A pilot on a long-distance route starts his descent more than 100 miles out, but long before he reaches the last stage of the flight, preparations for guiding him in are already being made.

As the incoming flight shows up, a bright "blip" on his radar screen, the area controller contacts the destination airport's approach controller by direct communication link to give a "release". He identifies the flight by its flight plan details and confirms the altitude that the pilot will descend to and the radio beacon that he will be told to head for.

By the time the inbound crew contacts approach control, the controller has already decided where the aircraft will be positioned in the sequence of other inbounds, outbounds and overflights. This he does by using his minimum separation of 1,000 feet vertically and three miles horizontally on radar. Using speed control he regulates the constant flow of fast jet and slower turboprop and piston-engined aircraft.

At the beginning of the descent, he tells the pilot of the inbound flight the type of approach to make to the designated runway, and gives a resumé of local weather conditions.

At most major airports, aircraft make a radar controlled approach to the Instrument Landing System for a particular runway. For the approach the pilot is guided by the radar controller, who will put him into a "hold" if the airport is busy. The hold is an area of airspace in the airport's control zone where aircraft are kept flying safely around a radio beacon until they can be cleared to start the approach to landing. In no-wind conditions a properly-flown holding pattern should take the form of a racetrack, and take four minutes from beginning to end, but if the wind is strong, one side of the racetrack will elongate and the other shorten as the

aircraft fly before or into it.

Guided into the uppermost level, each flight descends in turn, layer by layer, 1,000 feet at a time, until it reaches the lowest level. The busiest airports may have four or five stacks, smaller airports have two. Aircraft may be held for up to an hour.

Traffic inbound from the hold is separated according to the runway configuration at the destination airport. If there is only one runway, used for both landing and takeoff, landing aircraft must be spaced six miles apart. In good weather conditions, aircraft landing at airports with a separate runway for landings only will be brought out of the stack in a steady stream, three miles apart. But they may be spaced six miles apart in gusty, turbulent conditions. The controller ensures that the first aircraft is clear of the runway before the next one touches down.

At a range of nine miles and a height of 3,000 feet, the aircraft intercepts the ILS glidepath. Under the instructions of the air controller in the tower, the captain starts his final descent to the runway.

The progress of each flight, from takeoff to roll-out, appears in alpha-numeric display on the approach controller's radar screens, and is automatically video-recorded. In the event of an accident, the stored tapes can be played back and studied by investigators.

8 "Roger, seven-three-two. You are cleared to land two-eight-right"

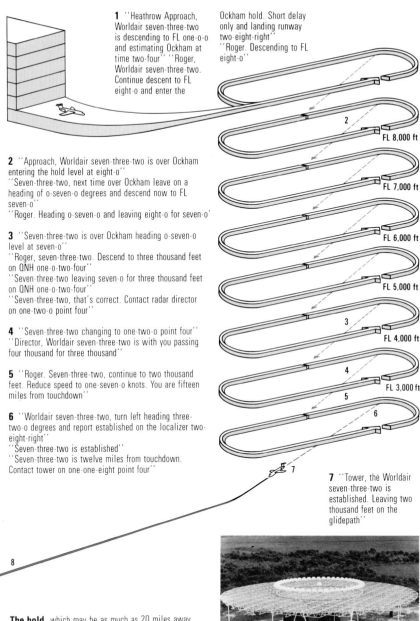

1 "Heathrow Approach, Worldair seven-three-two is descending to FL one-o-o and estimating Ockham at time two-four" "Roger, Worldair seven-three-two. Continue descent to FL eight-o and enter the Ockham hold. Short delay only and landing runway two-eight-right" "Roger. Descending to FL eight-o"

FL 8,000 ft

2 "Approach, Worldair seven-three-two is over Ockham entering the hold level at eight-o"
"Seven-three-two, next time over Ockham leave on a heading of o-seven-o degrees and descend now to FL seven-o"
"Roger. Heading o-seven-o and leaving eight-o for seven-o"

FL 7,000 ft

3 "Seven-three-two is over Ockham heading o-seven-o level at seven-o"
"Roger, seven-three-two. Descend to three thousand feet on QNH one-o-two-four"
"Seven-three-two leaving seven-o for three thousand feet on QNH one-o-two-four"
"Seven-three-two, that's correct. Contact radar director on one-two-o point four"

FL 6,000 ft

FL 5,000 ft

4 "Seven-three-two changing to one-two-o point four"
"Director, Worldair seven-three-two is with you passing four thousand for three thousand"

FL 4,000 ft

5 "Roger. Seven-three-two, continue to two thousand feet. Reduce speed to one-seven-o knots. You are fifteen miles from touchdown"

FL 3,000 ft

6 "Worldair seven-three-two, turn left heading three-two-o degrees and report established on the localizer two-eight-right"
"Seven-three-two is established"
"Seven-three-two is twelve miles from touchdown. Contact tower on one-one-eight point four"

7 "Tower, the Worldair seven-three-two is established. Leaving two thousand feet on the glidepath"

The hold, which may be as much as 20 miles away from the airport it serves, passes over a VOR beacon. A pilot locates it by following the radial leading to it. This shows up on the VOR receiver on his control panel. Looking like a broad-brimmed white top hat, the VOR station **right** broadcasts its signals from frequencies 108 to 118 on the FM dial.

Landing

As the descent begins, the calm relaxation of the flight crew changes to intense concentration. Between staccato bursts of radio talk and crackle, the captain makes critical decisions with precision.

His choice of approach speed is defined in exhaustive specifications made by the aircraft's manufacturers. They determine a minimum speed for final approach under ideal conditions, "V_{ref}", for which they guarantee landing performance data. Actual approach speeds are higher, 120 to 180 mph for most jets.

The heavier the aircraft, the higher the V_{ref} and the longer the distance needed to stop. For various gross weights and an approach speed of V_{ref} the manufacturers calculate the required runway length by measuring the distance from the point at which the plane is 50 feet high to its stopping position, and multiplying this by one and two thirds.

But more than this distance may be necessary on wet and slippery surfaces and the captain has to limit landing weight correspondingly.

Airliners approaching touchdown follow a shallow glideslope, miles long. The more steeply they descend, the less noise disturbance they cause to nearby residents. Just before the final descent the pilot lowers the landing-gears and extends the flaps fully, to slow the aircraft while maintaining lift. Unnecessarily early extension of the gears and flaps causes high drag and thus higher fuel consumption and noise levels.

Crossing the runway threshold, he "flares out", lifts the nose slightly to reduce the rate of decent, and gently throttles back. He aims for the VASIs, the Visual Approach Slope Indicators; but a 747 pilot, his eyes some four storeys above the wheels, aims at the 1,500-foot point to ensure adequate wheel clearance. Runways with no visual aids are difficult, especially at night or if the runway slopes, and heavy rain can cause insidious optical illusions from its prismatic effect on the windshield.

As the aircraft sinks down onto the main wheels, the captain raises the spoilers, "dumping" lift. Because of their drag, they also act as air brakes. He engages reverse thrust and ap-

Reverse thrust buckets, basically similar to these clamshell buckets used on Concorde, are used to slow aircraft down after touchdown. In normal flight they are open; when they are shut, exhaust gases are deflected forward and outward, providing a backward thrust that helps the wheel brakes to kill the landing speed. The wheel brakes alone are able to slow an aircraft in an emergency, but they may become dangerously overheated. To reduce the danger of explosion, nitrogen is used to fill aircraft tyres.

All high-lift surfaces are extended on this Airbus A300B as it lands. Slats have been extended from the leading edge along the full wingspan, and Fowler flaps have been run out along the tracks visible at the trailing edges. This configuration, needed to lower a plane weighing around 120 tons gently onto the runway, creates high drag, but each of the turbofan engines has up to 58,000 lb of thrust to accelerate the aircraft in case the landing has to be aborted.

plies the wheel brakes by gently pressing the tops of the rudder pedals. Maximum wheel-braking capacity is applied only in an emergency. With multiple fixed and moving discs between the wheels, modern brakes can absorb well over 60 million foot-pounds of energy.

On the slippery runway the brake pedals can be fully depressed. The sophisticated anti-skid system senses when each tyre begins to slide, releases the brakes momentarily to allow the wheel to grip again, then reapplies them. This occurs several times a second, maintaining an optimum slip ratio for stopping.

The worst hazard of wet runways is aquaplaning (hydroplaning) when wheels may "ski" on the film of surface water, losing adhesion. Runways can be grooved, like highways, with transverse slits a quarter of an inch deep give stopping characteristics almost equivalent to dry conditions on a wet runway.

Slowing a heavy-laden 747 to a safe taxiing speed is equivalent to bringing 6,000 family cars to a halt from over 40 mph.

Slats on the leading edge and flaps on the trailing edge are extended in low-speed flight to increase lift and drag. Air channelled through the slots holds the main airflow to the wing and flaps, maintaining lift.

Raising a spoiler disturbs the airflow over the upper wing surfaces. The resulting increase in drag slows the aircraft and is useful in controlling a steep descent. One spoiler can also be raised to bank the plane.

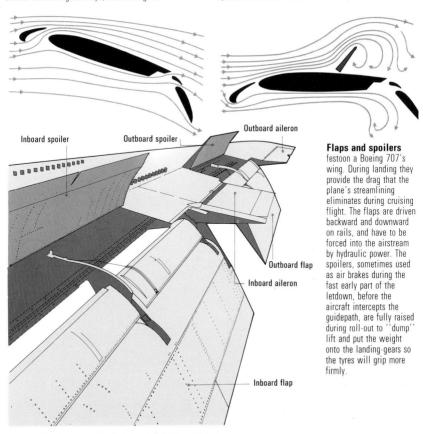

Inboard spoiler
Outboard spoiler
Outboard aileron
Outboard flap
Inboard aileron
Inboard flap

Flaps and spoilers festoon a Boeing 707's wing. During landing they provide the drag that the plane's streamlining eliminates during cruising flight. The flaps are driven backward and downward on rails, and have to be forced into the airstream by hydraulic power. The spoilers, sometimes used as air brakes during the fast early part of the letdown, before the aircraft intercepts the guidepath, are fully raised during roll-out to "dump" lift and put the weight onto the landing-gears so the tyres will grip more firmly.

Runway lighting

The distinctive pattern of lights marking the runway approach says "home" to the pilot who may have flown his aircraft through long hours of darkness. Two lines of lights along the runway sides give the perspective for judging the angle of approach and round-out for touchdown, such essential guidance that airports still keep at hand portable lighting units for emergencies.

Sophisticated, expensive lighting systems are also essential for a rapid alignment check during daytime approaches if visibility is poor. For a pilot breaking out of low cloud, high-intensity approach lights are the only visual clue that the ground is near. In fog, even approach lights may hardly be visible, but the bright runway lights will guide the roll-out after touchdown.

Fog-plagued airports may have individual lights that peak at an intensity of 30,000 candelas (twice the illumination of a set of car headlamps). To prevent dazzle they can be dimmed — from 100 per cent for sunlight or fog, to one per cent for a clear night.

On the taxiways the pilot follows blue edge lights and sometimes green centre lights marking the route. Red stop bars may appear when another plane crosses the path.

Failure of the electricity supply could be catastrophic to a landing jet, so most civil airports have emergency systems that switch in automatically within 15 seconds of a failure, and those with all-weather facilities have a stand-by system that switches in within one second.

National differences have made the standardization of airport lighting systems difficult. London's Heathrow Airport is among the most complex, with 28,000 individual lamps, but the American system illustrated here, is widely used.

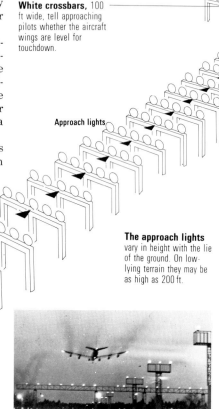

White crossbars, 100 ft wide, tell approaching pilots whether the aircraft wings are level for touchdown.

Approach lights

Sequence flashers, lines of white strobe lights, illuminate in sequence to guide the pilot's eyes towards the runway centreline.

Sequence flashers

The approach lights vary in height with the lie of the ground. On low-lying terrain they may be as high as 200 ft.

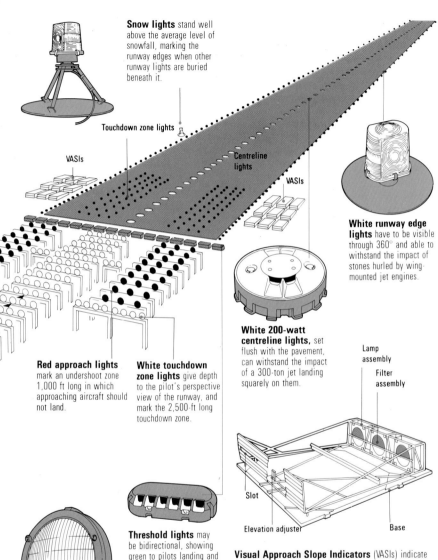

Snow lights stand well above the average level of snowfall, marking the runway edges when other runway lights are buried beneath it.

Touchdown zone lights

VASIs

Centreline lights

VASIs

White runway edge lights have to be visible through 360° and able to withstand the impact of stones hurled by wing-mounted jet engines.

White 200-watt centreline lights, set flush with the pavement, can withstand the impact of a 300-ton jet landing squarely on them.

Lamp assembly

Filter assembly

Slot

Elevation adjuster

Base

Red approach lights mark an undershoot zone 1,000 ft long in which approaching aircraft should not land.

White touchdown zone lights give depth to the pilot's perspective view of the runway, and mark the 2,500-ft long touchdown zone.

Threshold lights may be bidirectional, showing green to pilots landing and red on the reverse side, marking the runway end for pilots taking off.

Visual Approach Slope Indicators (VASIs) indicate the pilot's angle of approach and help to prevent overshoot or undershoot in all but the poorest visibility. They consist of two parallel rows of lights angled to project a white beam above the ideal approach path, and a red beam beneath it. If the pilot is approaching at the correct angle he sees red lights above white. If all the lights are white he is too high and if they are red he is too low. Runways used by Boeing 747s need a three-row configuration because of the height of the flight deck about the wheels. The individual unit illustrated in this cutaway diagram is mounted on a frangible stem, and is strong enough to withstand jet blast.

Approach lights have frangible stems that snap off if accidentally hit.

Landing aids

Breaking out of cloud at a height of 200 feet, a jet pilot has 20 seconds or less before touchdown. Finding himself immediately at decision height (the point where he has to decide whether it is safe to land, or whether he should put the aircraft into a go-around climb) he has a last few critical moments in which to assess instrument readings and take corrective action. But he loses vital time refocusing his eyes on the runway to identify his position in relation to the centreline and glidepath.

The prevalence of fog, mist and low cloud at British and European airports (where, for instance, British Airways makes over 200,000 landings a year) led to the development of an automatic landing system.

An autoland system is a super-autopilot which detects and responds to Instrument Landing System (ILS) radio beams. In fog or poor visibility, it guides aircraft onto the runway accurately and safely, and in good visibility it gives a more consistent and therefore safer approach and landing than might always be possible under manual control. By guiding flare-out accurately, it can lower the decision height for a safe go-around to less than 20 feet.

The ILS consists of a localizer beacon whose beam, radiating along the straight line of approach to the runway, guides the aircraft onto the centreline, and a glidepath transmitter, set about 450 feet to one side of the runway, with a beam, angled at about three degrees to the horizontal, that guides aircraft down at an even rate of descent.

The position of an aircraft in relation to these beams is shown on the flight director. Once the autopilot has locked onto the ILS beams, the pilot has no need to touch the controls until the aircraft is on the runway.

Glidepath signals are usually "captured" by aircraft at a height of about 1,000 feet. Pilots fly either manually

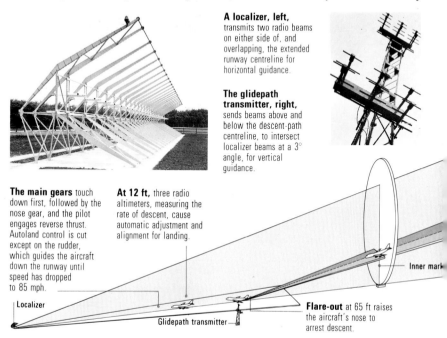

A localizer, left, transmits two radio beams on either side of, and overlapping, the extended runway centreline for horizontal guidance.

The glidepath transmitter, right, sends beams above and below the descent-path centreline, to intersect localizer beams at a 3° angle, for vertical guidance.

The main gears touch down first, followed by the nose gear, and the pilot engages reverse thrust. Autoland control is cut except on the rudder, which guides the aircraft down the runway until speed has dropped to 85 mph.

At 12 ft, three radio altimeters, measuring the rate of descent, cause automatic adjustment and alignment for landing.

Localizer

Glidepath transmitter

Inner mark

Flare-out at 65 ft raises the aircraft's nose to arrest descent.

or on autopilot toward the airport's navigation beacon until they intercept the ILS radio beams and follow them down to the runway. At 65 feet, radio altimeters trigger flare-out, raising the nose so the aircraft sinks gently onto the runway.

The first passenger-carrying autoland was made in 1965. Subsequent refinements improved the system, but ILS beams bend if they pass over buildings, stretches of water, or even highway traffic, making the system unsuitable for some airports.

The new Microwave Landing System (MLS) is gradually being adopted at major airports. This system transmits a radio beam from left to right and right to left across the sky. By automatically timing the intervals between successive interceptions of the sweeping beam, the landing system can accurately calculate an aircraft's position relative to the runway. It is cheaper than the ILS to install at airports (although the aircraft equip-

ment is more costly) and, because the beams spread more widely, it offers a number of alternative approach paths.

To date, only about 1,000 out of 4,000 major world airports are equipped with ILS suitable for autoland, and only about 30 runways have the most accurate versions enabling aircraft to land safely in zero visibility with a less than one in 10,000,000 probability of failure.

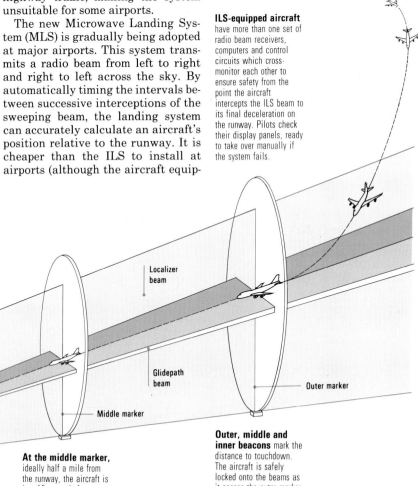

ILS-equipped aircraft have more than one set of radio beam receivers, computers and control circuits which cross-monitor each other to ensure safety from the point the aircraft intercepts the ILS beam to its final deceleration on the runway. Pilots check their display panels, ready to take over manually if the system fails.

Localizer beam

Glidepath beam

Outer marker

Middle marker

At the middle marker, ideally half a mile from the runway, the aircraft is just 15 seconds from touchdown.

Outer, middle and inner beacons mark the distance to touchdown. The aircraft is safely locked onto the beams as it passes the outer marker.

After touchdown

An airliner landing at a large airport may have to negotiate a mile of taxiways to reach a stand or parking place. Pilots usually have maps of the airport layout, and taxiways are marked with lights and other signals. But if a pilot loses his way despite the radioed directions of controllers in the tower giving him the route to be taken, an airport truck with a large "Follow me" sign may be sent to lead him in.

Lines painted on the concrete apron adjoining the taxiways lead the pilot to his final positioning; he will aim to keep his nosewheel on the appropriate line, and the aircraft's stopping point must be precise if the airbridges (the telescopic walkways joining aircraft to terminal) are to reach the doors. Various optical or electrical signs assist the manoeuvre: some of these are illustrated.

Moving walkways are often installed to speed passengers disembarking; each stand can be as much as

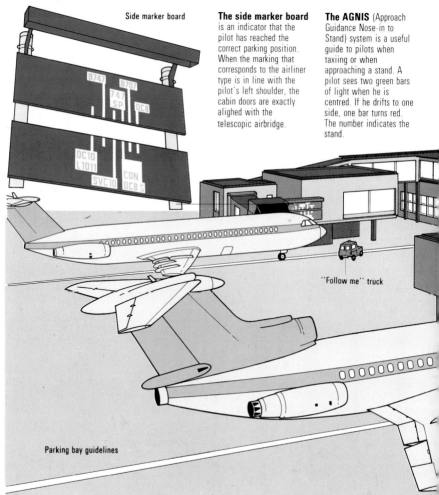

Side marker board

The side marker board is an indicator that the pilot has reached the correct parking position. When the marking that corresponds to the airliner type is in line with the pilot's left shoulder, the cabin doors are exactly alighed with the telescopic airbridge.

The AGNIS (Approach Guidance Nose-in to Stand) system is a useful guide to pilots when taxiing or when approaching a stand. A pilot sees two green bars of light when he is centred. If he drifts to one side, one bar turns red. The number indicates the stand.

"Follow me" truck

Parking bay guidelines

200 feet wide, and a pier that can accommodate half a dozen planes will be hundreds of yards long.

If the airliner has to park at a stand remote from the piers, mobile passenger steps are driven out to the aircraft and passengers will be collected by bus, or by a mobile passenger lounge, perhaps capable of holding 150 people. Such lounges are mounted on hydraulic "stilts" whose height can be changed so that the exit

aligns with the doors of any type of plane and with the terminal doors. An airline may choose to save the expense of a ramp disembarkation and bus passengers to the terminal.

Immediately all passengers have disembarked the airliner can be refuelled and reloaded with cargo, galleys replenished, toilets emptied and the systems checked. Turnaround may take only 20 minutes for an airliner plying a short-haul route.

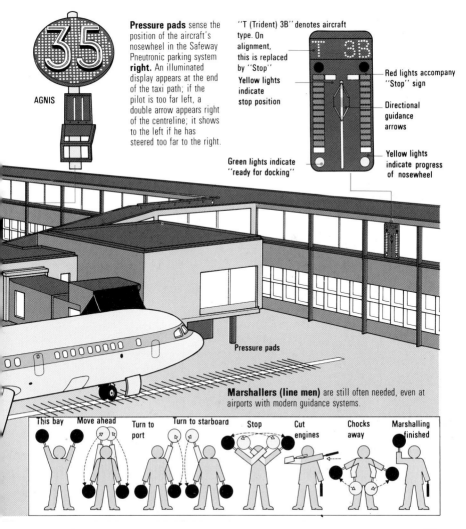

Pressure pads sense the position of the aircraft's nosewheel in the Safeway Pneutronic parking system **right.** An illuminated display appears at the end of the taxi path; if the pilot is too far left, a double arrow appears right of the centreline; it shows to the left if he has steered too far to the right.

AGNIS

"T (Trident) 3B" denotes aircraft type. On alignment, this is replaced by "Stop"

Yellow lights indicate stop position

Green lights indicate "ready for docking"

Red lights accompany "Stop" sign

Directional guidance arrows

Yellow lights indicate progress of nosewheel

Pressure pads

Marshallers (line men) are still often needed, even at airports with modern guidance systems.

| This bay | Move ahead | Turn to port | Turn to starboard | Stop | Cut engines | Chocks away | Marshalling finished |

Airliner spotter's guide

To the untrained eye, the array of modern airliners all look much alike. But to the keen spotter, each aircraft has its own individual characteristics and is immediately recognizable. The purpose of this section of the book is to provide a recognition guide for the uninitiated air traveller.

Airliners can be divided into seven main categories, depending on the number and type of engines (jet or propeller) and where the engines are located on the aircraft.

Two underwing jets
Characteristic of some of the smallest and very largest jet airliners, such as the Boeing 737 and the Airbus 300.

Two tail jets
Favourite configuration of many medium-sized airliners such as the BAe 1-11 and the Douglas DC-9.

Two propellers, low wing
There are many small turboprop aircraft with this arrangement, pioneered by the classic DC-3.

Three jets
Engines may be located at the tail (BAe Trident, Boeing 727, Tu-154) or wings and tail (TriStar, DC-10).

Four jets
Configuration found in some of the largest airliners (Airbus A340, Boeing 747, Il-86) and fastest (Concorde).

Two propellers, high wing
Another popular formula for small turboprops, adopted by de Havilland (DHC-6 -8) and Fokker (F27 and F50).

Four propellers
Four-engined turboprops include the DHC-7, DC-6B, Il-18, L-100 and the aging Vickers Viscount.

Airbus A300

Built by:
Airbus Industrie

Entered service:
1974

Maximum range:
5,000 miles

First flown in 1972 and in service since 1974, the A300 was the world's first twin-engined "wide body" or twin-aisle aircraft, bringing Boeing-747 technology of spaciousness, quietness and economy to shorter routes.

The only builder of big jetliners to compete with the United States, Airbus Industrie is a consortium formed by Aérospatiale (France), British Aerospace (UK), CASA (Spain) and MBB (West Germany). Fokker (Netherlands) shares in some programmes, and the engines and many other parts come from the United States.

The first A300s carried up to 267 passengers on routes up to about 1,000 miles. Airbus kept improving the design, so that today's A300-600R can fly a larger load over ranges exceeding 5,000 miles. Yet the aircraft looks virtually unchanged (the 600 has small triangular fences on the wingtips).

The A300s are close relatives of the A310, but are larger (overall lengths: 300, 177 ft 5 in; 310, 153 ft 1 in). Also the 310 has smaller wings, and if it has wingtip fences they are more prominent. The Boeing 767 is similar to both, but its fuselage slopes down at the tail whereas the 300 and 310 both have a straight top line. A minor point to look for is that the 767's nose gear is

The sophisticated Airbus design means that for a similar passenger capacity, a wide-bodied trijet (superimposed) has an extra engine, 7° more wing sweepback, 27 per cent extra wing area, 60 per cent more tailplane (stabilizer) and 20 tons of additional structure.

The A300 carries 20 containers in the hold and, in the A300C4 (convertible), 13 cargo pallets 88 in wide and 125 in long, loaded on to the passenger deck through a large side cargo door.

Easily adapted to mixed payloads, the A300 can carry a maximum of 343 tourist-class passengers, or 90,250 lb of cargo. With six pallets on the main deck, it can still accommodate 145 passengers.

Cargo configuration

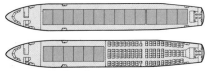

Mixed payload configuration

81

Airbus A300

farther forward, well ahead of the front entrance door.

The wings of the A300 are made in Chester, England; the nose, lower centre fuselage and engine pylons are constructed at St Nazaire, Nantes and Toulouse in France; the fuselage and vertical tail are manufactured at plants in West Germany (and Italy); the moveable parts of the wings and wingtips are made in the Netherlands; and the horizontal tail and doors are fabricated in Spain. To make it even more international, the giant slabs of alloy that form the wing skins come from Iowa, USA, before going to Chester, then to Bremen (West Germany) where all the Dutch parts are added, and then finally to the assembly line in Toulouse.

Well over 300 A300s are flying throughout the world. Even in the highly competitive North American market they fly with Eastern, PanAm, American and Continental. From 1993 production will switch to the bigger A330 (see A340, p. 105).

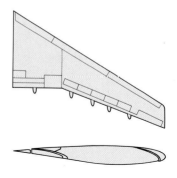

The supercritical Airbus wing has a more convex underside, a flatter top and a down-curved trailing edge so that lift is spread more evenly from the front to the rear section. This advanced design delays formation of sonic shock waves at high speeds, permitting the wing to be thicker yet producing no more drag at high speeds than a wing with a conventional section. It is also 2,500 lb lighter and has less sweepback.

The European Airbus was backed by the governments of France, the Netherlands, Spain and West Germany. The wing was designed and developed by British Aerospace, and the engines are manufactured in the United States.

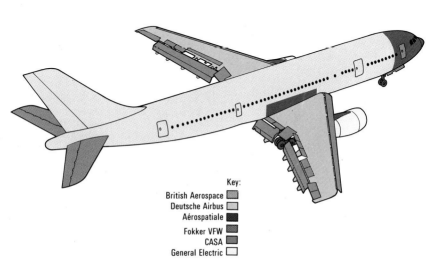

Key:

British Aerospace ▢
Deutsche Airbus ▢
Aérospatiale ▮
Fokker VFW ▨
CASA ▦
General Electric ▢

Airbus A310

Built by:
Airbus Industrie

Entered service:
1982

Maximum range
5,700 miles

The first A310 flew in 1982 and about 150 were in service in the late 1980s. It has a shorter body than the A300, with three instead of four doors on each side. It also has a smaller and very efficient wing, whose outer flap sections ride out on three projecting fairings instead of four. These fairings, together with the giant fin and many other parts, are made of new-technology carbon fibre.

Airbus Industrie saw a need for a smaller version of the A300. One possible solution was merely to put fewer seats in an A300; another was to put a smaller body on an A300 wing; a third was to spend vast sums on developing a smaller aircraft which, in consequence, was likely to be more expensive than the existing A300.

Eventually in 1978 Airbus Industrie made the decision to build a completely new aircraft with about 200 seats. The body cross-section is the same as on the A300, as are some other parts, but Airbus did not compromise the A310 in any way and they believe the new aircraft to be the most efficient jetliner flying today.

In 1985 the A310-300 entered service with sweptback fences on the wingtips to give even better efficiency. It is also fitted with extra fuel tanks located within the horizontal tail, to increase fuel capacity and avoid the need for aerodynamic download on the tail (which causes drag). As a result, the latest Dash-300 version can fly a full passenger or cargo load up to 5,700 miles.

The Airbus A310-300 has a long range because of extra fuel tanks in the horizontal tail. The sweptback wingtip fences are a distinguishing feature of the Dash-300 version of the aircraft.

Airbus 320

Built by:
Airbus Industrie

Entered service:
1988

Maximum range:
3,600 miles

Unlike previous Airbuses, the A320 is a "narrow body" single-aisle aircraft (although still wider than any other single-aisle aircraft). Basically a 150-seater, it can carry up to 179 passengers and still set a superb standard of comfort.

In every respect the A320 is the newest airliner in the sky. In the cockpit traditional handwheels are replaced by small sidesticks, and the instruments take the form of coloured electronic displays with incredible versatility. The "fly-by-wire" digital computerized controls command the aircraft to do everything perfectly, never to do anything hazardous, and automatically respond to windshear or gusts that could endanger older airliners. An unprecedented proportion of the structure is carbon fibre instead of metal, including the complete tail. The engines, in the 25,000-lb thrust class, may be CFM56s or V.2500s.

At first sight, the A320 could be confused with the Boeing 737-300 or 737-400, the Boeing 757 or the Tupolev Tu-204. Points to look for are that the 737 has no wingtip fences, a kinked fin leading edge and is less streamlined (see p. 85). The 757 and Tu-204 are bigger and have bogie main gears. The Tu-204 has different wingtip fences, and the 757 gives an appearance, particularly when it is on the ground, that is often described as being "down at the nose".

Distinguishing features between the A320 and the Boeing 737 can be seen by comparing this photograph with the one at the top of the next page, particularly the longer projection of the A320's rear fuselage behind the tail.

Boeing 737

Built by:
**Boeing Commercial
Airplane Co**

Entered service:
1967

Maximum range:
2,900 miles

In 1965, Boeing must have been un-easy at the gamble they were taking. Nobody seemed to want their smallest jet, the 737, except Lufthansa of West Germany. Nevertheless, on the strength of this one foreign order, Boeing went ahead with their 100-seater. Costs were kept down by using the same cockpit and cabin section as the earlier 707 and 727, and two of the 727's engines (JT8Ds) were suspended close under the wings.

Boeing need not have worried: their baby has become the best-selling jet airliner of all time. In June 1987 it passed the 727's previous record (1,832 aircraft sold), and by 1989 nearly 2,000 had been built.

The original 737-100 looked stumpy. No other airliner sits so close to the ground, or has engines that project both ahead of and behind the wings. Soon Boeing replaced the -100 with the -200, with a longer body seating about 115 passengers, and offered cargo, convertible and business versions. Some airlines opted for a special "gravel kit", which prevents gravel from getting into the engines and enables the 737 to operate from rough

The 737 can be fitted with a "gravel kit" consisting of protective features which enable it to operate from unpaved or gravel airstrips.

A gravel-deflecting "ski" is fitted to the nose-gear, and there are other deflectors on the main gears.

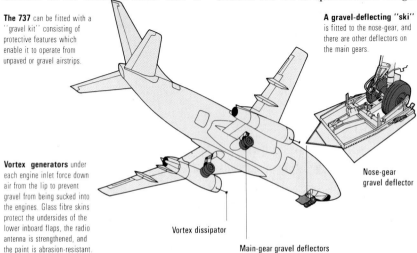

Vortex generators under each engine inlet force down air from the lip to prevent gravel from being sucked into the engines. Glass fibre skins protect the undersides of the lower inboard flaps, the radio antenna is strengthened, and the paint is abrasion-resistant.

Vortex dissipator

Main-gear gravel deflectors

Nose-gear
gravel deflector

Boeing 737

or sand-affected runways.

By the 1980s the Pratt & Whitney JT8D — the world's most common airliner engine, with 12,000 in use at 14,000 to 16,000 lb thrust — was becoming obsolescent on such grounds as fuel efficiency and unacceptably high noise levels. In 1984 Boeing flew the first 737-300 with new CMF56 turbofans in the 20,000-lb class, which eliminated both defici-

encies. They are hung on pylons entirely ahead of the wing.

The Dash-300 was stretched by 9 ft 5 in, to seat up to 149 passengers, which required the addition of a small dorsal fin giving a characteristic kinked leading edge to the vertical tail. Further stretching by 10 ft gave the -400 (168 passengers), and shortening to 100 ft produced the smaller -500 (130 passengers).

The 737-300 is easily distinguished from the earlier -100 and -200 by the position of the engines well ahead of the wings.

The engine necelles on the -300 and -400 are slightly flattened on their undersides to give better ground clearance.

Boeing 757

Built by:
Boeing Commercial Airplane Co

Entered service:
1983

Maximum range:
4,600 miles

Boeing spent many years considering how to replace the 727. It tried 727s with new engines hung under a new wing, and went ahead with the 757 in 1978 with an aircraft that retained the 727's cockpit and tail. Finally it made the 757 into an all-new aircraft, with a low tailplane and the same cockpit as the 767.

Longest of the single-aisle narrow-bodied jets, the 757 retains the same cabin section as the old 707, with an internal width of 11 ft 7 in and seating 178 to 239 passengers in triple seats each side of the aisle. What the cabin lacks in width it makes up in length —

the cabin occupies a total of 118 ft 5 in out of the aircraft's overall length of 155 ft.

The 757's wing is totally new, with little sweepback. The first batches had British Rolls-Royce 535 engines, of 37,000 to 40,000 lb thrust. These have set a marvellous record of reliability and quietness, but five of the 25 customers for the 757 chose the rival Pratt & Whitney PW2037. One such customer is United Parcel Service, which bought a cargo version with a wide door and no cabin windows. All 757s have bogie main gears and three flap tracks behind each wing.

A plan view of the 757 reveals the shape of the wing, with comparatively little sweepback, which has an area of nearly 2,000 sq ft and can lift an all-up weight in excess of 100 tons.

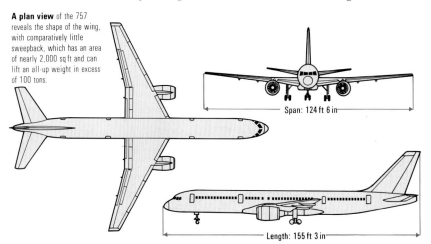

Span: 124 ft 6 in

Length: 155 ft 3 in

Boeing 767

Built by:
Boeing Commercial Airplane Co

Entered service:
1982

Maximum range:
7,000 miles

At first sight a copy of the rival Airbus A300, the Boeing 767 differs in having a bigger wing and a narrower body (with an interior cabin width of 15 ft 6 in, compared with 17 ft 4 in for the European airliner). The overall length of the basic 767–200 is 159 ft 2 in, compared with 153 ft 1 in for the A310 and 177 ft 5 in for the A300. The later 767-300 was lengthened to 180 ft 3 in. Other recognition features – see the lower illustration on this page – include a nose gear mounted farther forward (well ahead of the forward door), three unobtrusive flap tracks on each wing, and a rear fuselage that tapers both above and below (in the A300 and A310 the top line is straight).

The first 767 flew in September 1981, and large orders were placed by Amer-ican trunk operators such as Amer-ican, Delta, TWA and United. In 1984 Boeing flew the first 767-200ER (Ex-tended Range), suitable for such routes as the North Atlantic. In 1986 came the first stretched 767-300, with typical seating increased from 216 to 269. The latest version is the 767-300ER, which combines the greater passenger capacity with the longer operating range.

All these versions have various General Electric or Pratt & Whitney engines, although British Airways, one of the very few customers outside the United States and Japan to buy a large fleet of the aircraft, specified Rolls-Royce RB.211 engines uprated to 60,600 lb thrust. All three makes of engine look very similar.

Twin-jet Boeings

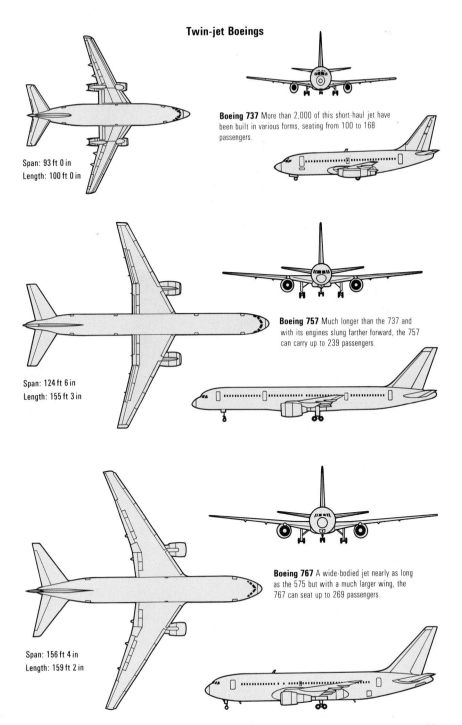

Boeing 737 More than 2,000 of this short-haul jet have been built in various forms, seating from 100 to 168 passengers.

Span: 93 ft 0 in
Length: 100 ft 0 in

Boeing 757 Much longer than the 737 and with its engines slung farther forward, the 757 can carry up to 239 passengers.

Span: 124 ft 6 in
Length: 155 ft 3 in

Boeing 767 A wide-bodied jet nearly as long as the 575 but with a much larger wing, the 767 can seat up to 269 passengers.

Span: 156 ft 4 in
Length: 159 ft 2 in

Tupolev Tu-204

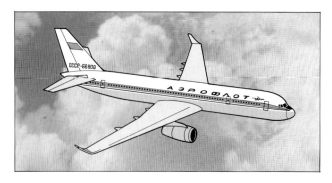

Built by:
Soviet industry

Entered service:
Planned for 1992

Maximum range:
2,855 miles

Just as the Tu-154 (see p. 103) appeared rather like a Soviet copy of the Boeing 727, so does its replacement Tu-204 closely resemble the 727's replacement, the Boeing 757. Compared with the American aircraft, the Tu-204 will have a bigger and more sweptback wing (like the wing of the 767, in fact), a slightly shorter fuselage, about the same engine power, rather less payload, lower maximum weight and considerably shorter range.

The Soloviev D-90A turbofan engines are rated at 35,275-lb thrust, and they are installed in curved, full-length nacelles rather like those of the 757's 534E4 engines (but not other 757 engines). The graceful wing has a span of nearly 138 ft, compared with 124 ft 10 in for the 757, and it has prominent winglets (wingtip fences).

Other obvious external features of the Tu-204 include four passenger doors on each side, three flap-track fairings on each wing and bogie main landing gears. Seating will normally be for 170 to 214 passengers.

The first Tu-204 was to fly in 1988. It is unlikely to appear in service with Aeroflot, the giant Soviet airline, until about 1992.

137 ft 9½ in

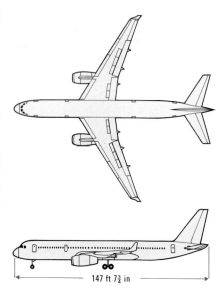

147 ft 7¾ in

Aérospatiale Caravelle

Built by:
Aérospatiale, France

Entered service:
1959

Maximum range:
2,200 miles

As the first short-haul jetliner to enter service, the Sud-Est (now Aérospatiale) Caravelle created a stir, despite predictions that it would not sell. The high-flying, long-range Comet was the only jet airliner in service, and it was thought that the Caravelle would be too costly in fuel at low cruising altitudes.

Its design became a classic: to reduce cabin noise the designers mounted two turbojet engines in nacelles on the rear fuselage. There were many variants, including later marks with turbofan engines, and in all a total of 270 Caravelles were bought by various European operators and United in the United States.

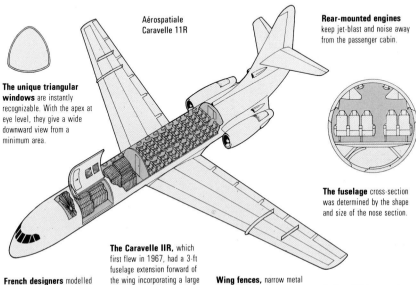

Aérospatiale
Caravelle 11R

Rear-mounted engines keep jet-blast and noise away from the passenger cabin.

The unique triangular windows are instantly recognizable. With the apex at eye level, they give a wide downward view from a minimum area.

The fuselage cross-section was determined by the shape and size of the nose section.

French designers modelled the Caravelle around the complete nose section of the British Comet.

The Caravelle IIR, which first flew in 1967, had a 3-ft fuselage extension forward of the wing incorporating a large freight door to admit bulky cargo. The Super Caravelle was even longer.

Wing fences, narrow metal strips, keep the airflow straight, reducing drag and improving lateral control.

Spoilers, 20 ft long, can be raised from the upper surfaces to increase drag.

91

British Aerospace BAe 1-11

Built by:
**British Aerospace and
IAv Bucaresti, Romania**

Entered service:
1965

Maximum range:
2,300 miles

Designed mainly by the team at Weybridge, Surrey, which created the best-selling Viscount, the trim One-Eleven (as it was first designated) used two of the Rolls-Royce Spey engines in the 10,000-lb class already developed for the three-engined Trident. The first 1-11s seated 65 to 89 passengers, but most were stretched to seat about 109.

Recognition features include a straight-edged T-tail with a bullet fairing at the top, a rear access stairway below the auxiliary power unit in the tailcone, wings with a fence around the leading edge at mid-span and three flap tracks along the trailing edge of each wing, and a fairly pointed nose.

BAe built 230 1-11s, including the Series 475 modified for rough dirt airstrips and quick-change passenger/cargo versions. In 1979, under an international agreement, production was transferred to Romania, where the first "Rombac 1-11" was completed in 1982. Today Romania builds the refined Series 495 for rough strips and the heavier Series 560, with engine nacelles lengthened by special "hush-kits". Similar modifications were also fitted retrospectively on some British-built aircraft.

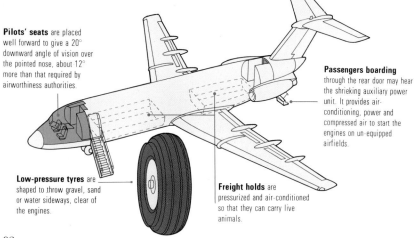

Pilots' seats are placed well forward to give a 20° downward angle of vision over the pointed nose, about 12° more than that required by airworthiness authorities.

Passengers boarding through the rear door may hear the shrieking auxiliary power unit. It provides air-conditioning, power and compressed air to start the engines on un-equipped airfields.

Low-pressure tyres are shaped to throw gravel, sand or water sideways, clear of the engines.

Freight holds are pressurized and air-conditioned so that they can carry live animals.

Douglas DC-9

Built by:
Douglas Aircraft Co

Entered service:
1965

Maximum range:
3,060 miles

The DC-9 was the first American twin-jet. Compared with the rival BAe 1-11 (opposite page) it is very low to the ground and has a more rounded, down-sloping nose, a slightly curved tail with the horizontal tail not quite at the top of the fin (and no bullet fairing), a pointed rear tailcone (whereas the BAe 1-11 has an auxiliary power unit exhaust), squarish instead of elliptical cabin windows, no rear access under the tail, and a nose gear near the tip of the nose.

More than with any other aircraft, Douglas kept stretching the DC-9 (as shown below). This helped to sell 976 of all versions, including USAF, Navy and Marines versions with wide cargo doors and equipment for carrying medical patients. But that was only the beginning — see the McDonnell Douglas MD-80 on page 96.

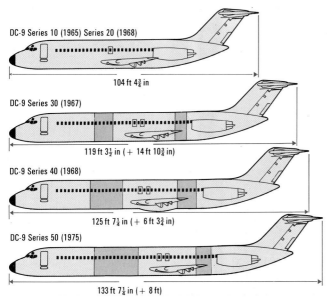

DC-9 Series 10 (1965) Series 20 (1968)

104 ft 4¾ in

DC-9 Series 30 (1967)

119 ft 3½ in (+ 14 ft 10¾ in)

DC-9 Series 40 (1968)

125 ft 7¼ in (+ 6 ft 3¾ in)

DC-9 Series 50 (1975)

133 ft 7¼ in (+ 8 ft)

The 90-seat Series 10
began service only 10 months after its first flight; 137 were built. SAS ordered 10 STOL-20s, identical in size but with the -30 wing and the -40 engines.

The 115-seat Series 30
with long, high-lift wings was a popular mixed-traffic version; 503 were sold.

The 125-seat Series 40
had more powerful 15,500-lb thrust engines and increased fuel capacity; 24 were produced for SAS.

The 139-seat Series 50,
with 16,000-lb thrust engines, increased total sales of the DC-9 to nearly 1,000 aircraft.

Fokker F28

Built by:
**Fokker Aircraft,
Netherlands**

Entered service:
1969

Maximum range:
2,000 miles

The Fokker F28 Fellowship is powered by a lighter version of the Rolls-Royce Spey engine, the 9,900-lb thrust RB.183. The aircraft is smaller and lighter than rival twinjets, seating 65 passengers (or up to 85 in stretched models). Designed for short, rough airstrips, the F28 has a wing with hardly any sweepback, engines very close behind the wing, a tail like that of a DC-9 (see p. 93) but with a dorsal fin that gives a kinked leading edge, and a blunt rear fuselage which

opens to provide powerful airbrakes. The cabin windows are elliptical (like those on the BAe 1-11), but there are only two flap-track fairings on each wing.

Purchasers had a choice of two wingspans (with or without leading-edge slats) and two fuselage lengths (with or without a cargo door). This agile aircraft outsold the BAe 1-11, with 241 sales to 57 customers in 37 countries. In 1987 production was switched to the Fokker 100.

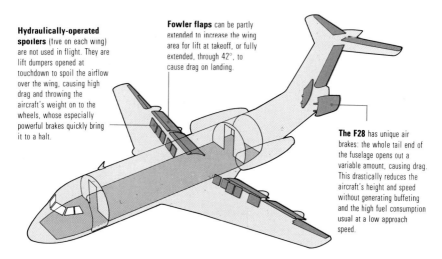

Hydraulically-operated spoilers (five on each wing) are not used in flight. They are lift dumpers opened at touchdown to spoil the airflow over the wing, causing high drag and throwing the aircraft's weight on to the wheels, whose especially powerful brakes quickly bring it to a halt.

Fowler flaps can be partly extended to increase the wing area for lift at takeoff, or fully extended, through 42°, to cause drag on landing.

The F28 has unique air brakes: the whole tail end of the fuselage opens out a variable amount, causing drag. This drastically reduces the aircraft's height and speed without generating buffeting and the high fuel consumption usual at a low approach speed.

Fokker F100

Built by:
**Fokker Aircraft,
Netherlands**

Entered service:
1987

Maximum range:
1,840 miles

Compared with most of its rivals, Fokker has much less finance and a microscopic home market. It cannot afford to be wrong, and it took years of study before, in late 1983, the company announced the successor to the F28.

The designation of the new aircraft, the Fokker 100, is approximately its seating capacity (actually 97 to 119 passengers). The twinjet airliner is obviously a stretched version of the F28, but it is much more than this. Features include a new "electronic" cockpit, redesigned wings, revised systems, and improved cabin and totally new Rolls-Royce Tay engines rated at 13,850 to 15,100 lb thrust yet much quieter than the F28's Speys.

To share the financial burden and the risk, the wings are made by Shorts in Northern Ireland, most of the fuselage and tail by MBB in West Germany, and the nacelles and reversers (not fitted to the F28) by Grumman in the United States. At the time of writing, Fokker had sold about 90 of the aircraft, with a similar number on option.

92 ft 1½ in

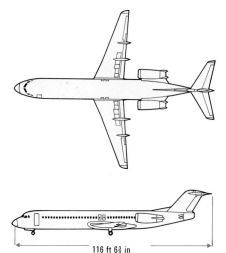

116 ft 6¾ in

The Fokker F100 is a much longer ''stretched'' version of the F28 (see previous page).

McDonnell Douglas MD-80

Built by:
Douglas Aircraft Co

Entered service:
1980

Maximum range:
3,060 miles

Like Boeing, Douglas watched the gradual obsolescence of the Pratt & Whitney JT8D engine and were relieved when P & W developed this into the JT8D-200 series, with a much bigger fan increasing thrust to 18,500 to 21,000 lb (depending on the version), with far better fuel economy, and a fraction of the noise. These engines enabled Douglas to make a further giant stretch of the DC-9 to produce what was called the DC-9 Super 80 but later renamed MD-80.

It is an unmistakable aircraft: low to the ground and very long indeed.

Seating capacity is 172 passengers. The later MD-81, -82, -83 and -88 differ in engine power, fuel capacity and range; the MD-88 also has a more modern cockpit with electronic displays. The MD-87 is a shorter version (109 to 130 passengers) but with a longer range. Like its precursor the DC-9, the MD-80 has proved to be a smash hit, with sales exceeding 900 aircraft by 1988.

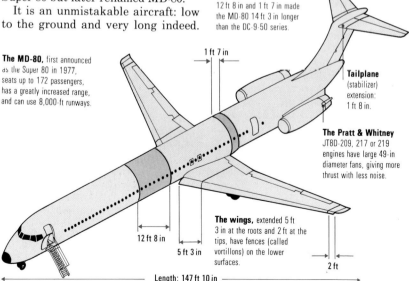

Fuselage extensions of 12 ft 8 in and 1 ft 7 in made the MD-80 14 ft 3 in longer than the DC-9-50 series.

The MD-80, first announced as the Super 80 in 1977, seats up to 172 passengers, has a greatly increased range, and can use 8,000-ft runways.

1 ft 7 in

Tailplane (stabilizer) extension: 1 ft 8 in.

The Pratt & Whitney JT8D-209, 217 or 219 engines have large 49-in diameter fans, giving more thrust with less noise.

The wings, extended 5 ft 3 in at the roots and 2 ft at the tips, have fences (called vortillons) on the lower surfaces.

12 ft 8 in

5 ft 3 in

2 ft

Length: 147 ft 10 in

Tupolev Tu-134

Built by:
Soviet industry

Entered service:
1964

Maximum range:
1,175 miles

The giant Soviet design bureau headed by A. N. Tupolev produced one of the world's first short-haul jetliners, the Tu-104 of 1956. This was uneconomic, but the smaller turbofan-engined Tu-124 was developed into the Tu-134 (first flown in 1962). A highly streamlined aircraft, it has been built in large numbers and widely exported to China and other countries in the Communist bloc.

Features of the Tu-134 include a glazed "bomber-type" nose, bogie main gears set very far apart on the swept wings and retracting backwards into distinctive pods behind the wings, engines mounted fairly high near the pointed tailcone, and a T-tail with a pointed bullet fairing at the junction as well as a dorsal fin which gives a kinked leading edge. The original 134 seated 64 to 72 passengers, but gave way to the slightly longer 134A, with a "solid" radar nose and up to 80 seats. Each wing has two fences, and the passenger windows are circular. In all about 600 of the type were built.

Underside view of a Tu-134A emphasises the long nose, sweptback wings, and underwing pods into which the main bogie landing gears retract backwards.

British Aerospace Trident

Built by:
British Aerospace

Entered service:
1964

Maximum range:
2,500 miles

The Trident began life in 1958 as the de Havilland 121, first of the new rear-engined T-tailed trijets. Designed to cruise at more than 600 mph, faster than contemporary civil jets, it had a squat tail, triplex powered controls (three separate power units driving each control surface), four small wheels side-by-side on each main landing gear, and an offset, sideways-retracting nose gear.

The Trident pioneered truly blind autolanding, and in 1965 became the first airliner to be certificated for automatic landing in passenger service. The advanced flight control system, together with the autopilot, enabled the aircraft to lock onto ground radio beams and, using auto-throttle to control airspeed, descend along the glidepath to touchdown. Altogether 117 Tridents, including over 30 of the stretched long-range 3Bs, were constructed.

A few Trident 1s and 1Es are still flying, as well as some of the longer-range 2s and stretched 3s. On the Series 3, the three 11,930-lb thrust Rolls-Royce Spey engines were aug-

mented with a small booster jet for use at takeoff. This version can seat up to 180 passengers, and a few of the ex-British Airways machines of this type found second-time buyers. Many more are in full service in China, together with two Super 3Bs with extra fuel capacity and range.

Küchemann wingtips extend the wing area of the Trident 2E and 3B, giving the extra lift necessary to carry much heavier loads.

A Rolls-Royce RB.162 booster engine (blue), based on a military vertical lift engine, proved a cheaper and better way of increasing performance from hot Mediterranean airfields than uprating the main Spey turbofans. The extra 5,250-lb thrust could also be utilized in flight if necessary.

Trident 3B

Boeing 727

Built by:
Boeing Commercial Airplane Co

Entered service:
1963

Maximum range:
2,800 miles

From 1956 until 1960, Boeing worked on the design of a short-haul jet smaller than the 707, and then launched the 727. It has the same overall configuration as the earlier British Trident (see p. 98), but is in detail quite different. Because of the 14,000-lb thrust of the Pratt & Whitney JT8D engine it is bigger, seating up to 125 passengers. Because of high-lift leading-edge slats and triple-slotted flaps it can use short runways, and because of 32° of sweepback, it can cruise at 600 mph. Later, in the 727-200, the fuselage was stretched to seat up to 189 passengers—and then sales really boomed. Eventually Boeing sold 1,832 727s, at the time a record for

any civil airliner in the Western world (ignoring wartime military versions of the DC-3).

Features include the same cockpit and cabin cross-section as the 707, with a bank of triple seats on each side of the aisle and small retangular windows, main gears with two wheels side-by-side and three rear engines. The central engine inlet is faired into the huge sharply-swept tail and its outlet nozzle is in the end of the fuselage (above a rear stairway, which some operators do not use).

The 727-200 (QC) is a quick-change version with seats, galleys and toilets fixed to pallets which can be quickly removed and replaced with roller floors for all-cargo operations.

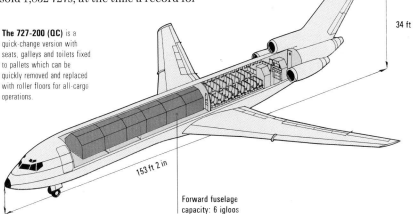

34 ft

153 ft 2 in

Forward fuselage capacity: 6 igloos

Lockheed L-1011 TriStar

Built by:
Lockheed Corporation

Entered service:
1972

Maximum range:
7,300 miles

This wide-bodied trijet was initially launched in 1968 with large orders, a strong part of its appeal being the new Rolls-Royce RB.211 engine. But the first RB.211 was a disaster, bankrupting Rolls-Royce in 1971 and throwing the L-1011 programme into jeopardy. Eventually it went ahead, with excellent 42,000-lb thrust RB.211-22B engines, but the delay was serious. Even more crippling was the fact that struggling Rolls-Royce was in no position to compete with North American firms in offering engines in the over-50,000-

lb class, and this put the rival DC-10 airliner in a commanding position. Lockheed were able to sell only 249 of all versions.

Later a more powerful RB.211 did appear, and Lockheed built longer-ranged L-1011s, culminating in the Series 500 with extended wings, a shorter body and a range of up to 7,300 miles.

The L-1011 can be distinguished from the DC-10 because its centre engine is inside the rear fuselage (not completely above it).

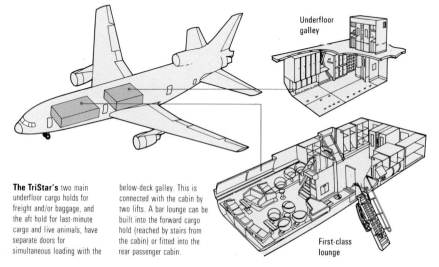

Underfloor galley

The TriStar's two main underfloor cargo holds for freight and/or baggage, and the aft hold for last-minute cargo and live animals, have separate doors for simultaneous loading with the below-deck galley. This is connected with the cabin by two lifts. A bar lounge can be built into the forward cargo hold (reached by stairs from the cabin) or fitted into the rear passenger cabin.

First-class lounge

McDonnell Douglas DC-10

Built by:
Douglas Aircraft Co

Entered service:
1970

Maximum range:
6,600 miles

Like the rival L-1011 (see p. 100), the DC-10 was planned to meet a 1966 specification by American Airlines, which placed the launch order in early 1968. The first DC-10-10 was designed for coast-to-coast range (across the United States), carrying up to 380 passengers and powered by three 40,000-lb thrust General Electric CF6-6 engines in a novel arrangement — two under the sharply sweptback wings and one completely above the rear fuselage with the vertical tail above it. In 1972 it was joined by the DC-10-30, with an increased wingspan (from 155 ft to 165 ft), much greater fuel capacity, an extra twin-wheel main gear on the centreline and CF6-50 engines in the 50,000-lb class.

The first DC-10s weighed 386,500 lb loaded, whereas later DC-10-30s weigh up to 572,000 lb and can carry a maximum payload for 4,600 miles. The last DC-10s of all are the DC-10-30ER (Extended Range) version, with 54,000-lb thrust engines and extra fuel for ranges up to 6,600 miles. There are

also the DC-10-45 (an extended range -10); the DC-10-40, similar to the -30 but with Pratt & Whitney JT9D engines; and the -30F freighter and -30CF convertible models. The US Air Force uses a tanker/transport version, the KC-10 Extender.

Having had to survive harsh treatment from the media after a spate of crashes, the DC-10 has always been a basically excellent aircraft. A total of 380 were built.

The centre (No. 2) engine is mounted in the base of the tail. Changing it involves dismantling the rear fuselage panels.

Large windshields and side-panel windows give good flightdeck visibility. Each pilot can see 62° up and 22.5° down, and rearward vision through 135° gives a sideways view as far as the wingtips.

McDonnell Douglas MD-11

Built by:
Douglas Aircraft Co

Entered service:
Planned for 1990

Maximum range:
7,920 miles

In December 1986 British Caledonian, then an independent airline, placed the launch order for the MD-11. Derived from the DC-10 (see p. 101), the MD-11 capitalizes on the 60,000-lb thrust available from the General Electric CF6-80C2 and Pratt & Whitney PW4000 turbofans, which make possible take-off weights in the order of 650,000 lb. As a result the MD-11 is 198 ft 7 in long (18 ft 7 in more than the DC-10). The giant trijet will look like a lengthened DC-10 with winglets.

Other changes include modern digital electronics and a two-crew cockpit, winglets above and below the wingtips, an improved cambered horizontal tail (smaller than that of the DC-10 and, like the later Airbuses, filled with fuel for trimming purposes) and a restyled cabin.

Scheduled to fly in March 1989 and enter service a year later, the MD-11 is designed to carry 250 to 405 passengers, and carry a medium load of 321 passengers 7,920 miles.

Maximum flexibility is designed into the MD-11, which can carry all passengers, a mixture of passengers and cargo or all cargo in its cabin space, as well as cargo and/or baggage in its lower cargo hold. The mixed payload, or Combi, configuration

(above) provides accommodation for 147 passengers in three classes (16 first, 41 business and 90 economy) and space for ten palletted cargo containers (total about 10,000 cu ft) on the main deck alone.

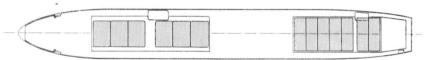

The lower deck arrangement is also variable but can accommodate up to a further 10,000 cu ft of cargo after making allowance for baggage (calculated at 4·5 cu ft per passenger). The configuration illustrated has 6 pallets (86 or 96 in by 125 in) in

the forward hold, 14 of the smaller LD-3 pallets (totalling 2,212 cu ft) in the central hold and bulk cargo space of 510 cu ft in the after hold. There are plans for Power-deck passenger cabins

Tupolev Tu-154

Built by:
Soviet industry

Entered service:
1968

Maximum range:
1,710 miles

The Tu-154 was probably influenced by the Boeing 727, which it closely resembles (see p. 99). It has almost the same cabin cross-section and general layout, although the Soviet aircraft is bigger and much more powerful.

Early Tu-154s were powered by three Kuznetsov NK-8-2U turbofans of 23,150-lb thrust each, but since 1982 the standard version of the aircraft has been the Tu-154M with Soloviev D-30-KU engines. These generate the same thrust but are more modern and burn less fuel, and have clamshell-type reversers. Overall length exceeds 157 ft, gross weight is 220,460 lb and seating capacity is up to 180 passengers. The 154C cargo version has a wide side-loading door.

All Tu-154s have unique six-wheel bogie main gears, retracting backward into faired boxes behind the wings, which have two fences on each side. Another obvious feature is the long pointed bullet at the junction of the fin and horizontal tail. More than 600 154As and 154Bs were built, and probably 150 154Ms have so far been delivered to Aeroflot, Balkan Bulgarian, LOT and other airlines.

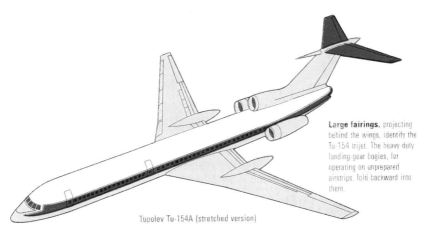

Large fairings, projecting behind the wings, identify the Tu-154 trijet. The heavy-duty landing-gear bogies, for operating on unprepared airstrips, fold backward into them.

Tupolev Tu-154A (stretched version)

Yakovlev Yak-42

Built by:
Soviet industry

Entered service:
1975

Maximum range:
560 miles

A major local airliner within the Soviet Union is the Yak-40. It is a unique example of a jet designed for short rough airstrips and ignoring the need for speed. Powered by three 3,300-lb thrust AI-25 turbofans at the tail, it has a long-span unswept wing and seats up to 32 passengers.

A development from the Yak-40 is the Yak-42, which is bigger and faster. Many hundreds are expected to be built to replace Tu-134s in Aeroflot. Seven were also ordered by Aviogenex of Yugoslavia, but development has been troubled. After trying a sweep angle of 11° the designers decided on an angle of 23°, and to replace the twin-wheel main gears by four-wheel bogies. But seven years after the first flight the Yak-42 was withdrawn after a crash, and today's aircraft have additional changes.

The Yak-42 seats up to 120 in triple seats, and is designed to be tough and self-contained for services to airports where there is just ice and snow and no maintenance facilities. The main airstair hinges down under the tail (location of the 14,330-lb thrust Lotarev D-36 turbofans), and there is a second airstair that hinges down near the nose. The inlet to the centre engine slopes backwards, and the passenger windows are circular.

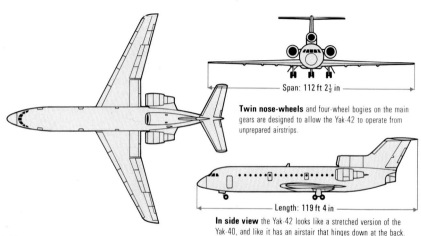

Span: 112 ft 2½ in

Twin nose-wheels and four-wheel bogies on the main gears are designed to allow the Yak-42 to operate from unprepared airstrips.

Length: 119 ft 4 in

In side view the Yak-42 looks like a stretched version of the Yak-40, and like it has an airstair that hinges down at the back.

Airbus A340

Built by:
Airbus Industrie

Entered service:
Planned for 1992

Maximum range:
8,870 miles

When in 1987 Airbus Industrie launched the A330 and A340 it completed the range of airliners it will offer. The two new giants will be the biggest in the family. They will share the same wing, and this will be the most efficient in the sky, designed and mostly made in England. This super wing has a span of 192 ft 5 in, and has tall winglets (wingtip fences) at the tips. On it rides a body with the same cross-section as the A300 and A310 but it is longer.

The A330 is a giant twin, with engines in the 64,000-lb-thrust class, and a length of just over 205 ft. It will carry 328 passengers 5,760 miles. The A340-200 will have four CFM56 engines of 31,200 lb thrust each, and with a length of 194 ft 10 in will carry 262 passengers up to 8,870 miles. The even bigger A340-300 has the same engines, but with a length of almost 209 ft will carry 295 passengers, although over a slightly shorter range of 7,890 miles.

In each case these passenger numbers are based on comfortable multi-class seating; maximum capacity (with high-density seating) is much greater. There will also be an A340-300 Combi carrying (for example) 77,160 lb of cargo and 201 passengers. All versions will have a very large underfloor cargo capacity, with room for up to 32 standard containers.

A view from above shows the slim proportions of the A340s giant wing, which has a span of more than 192 ft.

105

Boeing 707

Built by:
Boeing Commercial Airplane Co

Entered service:
1958

Maximum range:
6,450 miles

In 1952 Boeing gambled far more than the net worth of the company in building the prototype of what became the 707. They need not have worried. They built 820 military versions and 992 bigger 707s in various forms, and still make the distinctive E-3 Sentry "AWACS" radar aircraft (including some for the British RAF), which use the same airframe.

The 707 introduced airlines to swept wings, with four jet engines hung across the leading edge. Most have Pratt & Whitney JT3D turbofans of 18,000-lb thrust. Among many others the commonest (and last) variant is the 707-320C, with a length of 153 ft, gross weight of 333,600 lb and typically carrying up to 219 passengers at over 550 mph for up to 4,300 miles. Features include clean sharply-swept wings, bogie main gears with a fairly narrow track folding inwards, a tall fin (often including a small under-fin) with a distinctive radio antenna projecting forwards at the top, and an unbroken row of small rectangular windows. In its day the 707 was thought to be huge — now it is only a minnow among the monsters.

Spare 707 engines can be transported in streamlined underwing "pod-paks" which do not impair the handling. With this capability, an airline needs fewer spare engines.

The 707 families are identified by "dash" numbers. The original -120, -220 and -720 families (seating up to 180 passengers) were domestic models. The stretched -320s and -420s (seating up to 219) were intercontinental versions.

Boeing 707-120B

Boeing 707-320C

Boeing 747

Built by:
**Boeing Commercial
Airplane Co**

Entered service:
1970

Maximum range:
7,090 miles

When it was introduced, the Boeing 747 — soon to be known everywhere as the Jumbo — had twice the capacity, power and weight of any existing airliner. A completely new factory — arguably the largest building in the world — had to be built near Seattle in the United States to assemble $2\frac{1}{2}$ million components around a fuselage big enough to have contained the Wright Brothers' first flight. There was no prototype; Number 1 was first off the production line. At a Paris Air Show, the power of the engines was forcibly demonstrated when the 150-mph jet blast 100 ft behind the aircraft blew the runway sidelights out of their holders.

On 21 January 1970, less than a year after the first flight, Pan Am began scheduled services. Up to 500 passengers disembarking at once (a Qantas 747 evacuated a record 674 people after a hurricane in Darwin) caused chaos at air terminals. But fears about the runway length needed for take-off with two-and-a-half times the capacity of a 707 proved unfounded, thanks largely to the wing's high-lift devices. Big, trailing-edge flaps fan out to increase the wing area; slots permit the air to flow smoothly through. And the variable camber slats on the leading edge curve to the most efficient high-lift profile as they extend.

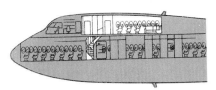

The weight of the 747 demands four sets of four-wheel bogies, like giant roller-skates, to land safely. The tubeless tyres are designed like modern car tyres to eject runway water through channels on each side.

The height of the 747 flight deck means that the pilot has to take extra care in judging clearance on a final approach to land. But it leaves space behind for a 16-seat ''penthouse'' suite, or in later versions for up to 91 seats.

Boeing 747

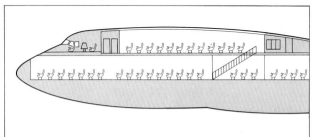

The extra space on the upper deck of the 747-300 **above** and -400 can provide seating for 91 more passengers or house 26 sleeper seats. The familiar spiral staircase is replaced by a straight flight of stairs near the foward entry door.

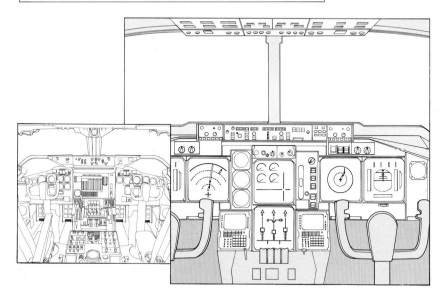

The flight deck of the 747-400 has completely new avionics **(above)** and is much less cluttered than the older 747 layout (see p. 43). The most noticeable difference is the presence of coloured television-type screens, duplicated to present information to the pilot and co-pilot.

Plans to stretch the 747 by inserting ''plugs'' in the fuselage in front of and behind the wings **(right)** would increase the passenger capacity even more to about 700 seats. Boeing have also considered extending the upper deck along the length of the aircraft, to give a 1,000-passenger Super Jumbo.

Boeing 747

The huge 747 has room for six galleys, 16 toilets, 6,190 cu ft of cargo and baggage space, and 146 survival suits carried as part of the emergency equipment on polar flights.

There are various versions of the original 747. The 747SP (Special Performance version) flies higher and farther than any other subsonic commercial aircraft. The all-cargo 747-200F first flew in 1971. It is easy to recognize because it has no windows along the sides of the fuselage (except the short upper deck), and a nose that hinges up like a crocodile's mouth for loading anything from a 40-foot container to a Cadillac.

During the 1970s, Pratt & Whitney improved the JT9D engine, producing versions that give up to 54,750 lb thrust, and in the 1980s introduced the PW4000 engine in the 60,000-lb class. Other 747s are powered by the General Electric CF6 or Rolls-Royce RB.211, and the diagram shows how the engine pods differ in shape. With the more powerful engines, the maximum loaded weight of the 747 has risen from 710,000 lb to 850,000 lb, enabling it to carry greater payloads longer distances.

From the outset, the 747 has never had any serious competition. Most of the 800 Jumbos in service are of the 747-200 type, only about 44 being the short-bodied 747 SPs. In 1982, however, Boeing began flying the 747-300, with an upper deck extended by 23 ft. Fitted with seats, this extra space increased the upper deck's passenger capacity from 32 to 91. Because of the contours of the fuselage, the walls slope and Boeing have arranged panniers for hand baggage outboard of the outer seats. Alternatively, the upper deck can be equipped to sleep 26 first-class passengers. New doors are added on each side.

The first 747-400 was flown in May for 1988. It has the same extended upper deck and, in addition, long-span wings with winglets at the tips, digital avionics, and many other new features.

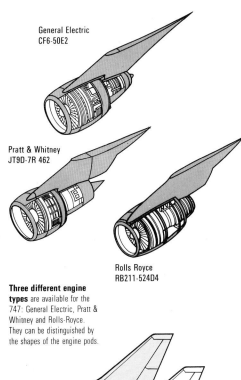

General Electric CF6-50E2

Pratt & Whitney JT9D-7R 462

Rolls Royce RB211-524D4

Three different engine types are available for the 747: General Electric, Pratt & Whitney and Rolls-Royce. They can be distinguished by the shapes of the engine pods.

British Aerospace 146

Built by:
British Aerospace

Entered service:
1983

Maximum range:
1,924 miles

Utterly distinctive, the 146 is by far the quietest jetliner even built, but its real purpose was to bring jet speed and comfort to small aircraft flying comparatively few passengers to small airports. Because of its clever design, the fairly small and simple wing can lift it after a takeoff run of only 700 yards, and it can make an amazingly steep climb away without any noise obtruding above the general background level. On landing, a steep approach can be followed by giant airbrakes flicking open at the tail and powerful brakes on the twin-wheel landing gears, which fold into the streamlined fuselage. Much of the credit for this performance is due the Lycoming ALF502 turbofan engines, each of 6,970 lb thrust.

One of the widest single-aisle aircraft, the 146 has a comfortable interior with no wing to spoil the view. It is available in three lengths: the 146-100, seating 82–93 passengers; the -200, seating up to 111; and the -300, seating 100 in sumptuous 3+2 instead of 3+3 seats. There are also cargo, executive and military versions.

Two of the short (86-ft) -100 versions are in Britain the flagships of The Queen's Flight, but by far the biggest market has proved to be the United States, where passenger appeal, fuel economy and minimal noise are important. Parts are made at many factories in Britain, the fixed parts of the wings and the engines come from the United States, and the movable surfaces and high tailplanes are manufactured in Sweden.

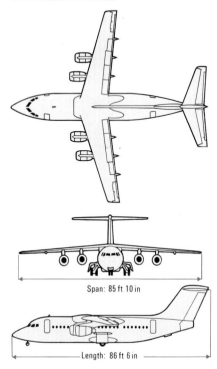

Span: 85 ft 10 in

Length: 86 ft 6 in

Concorde

Built by:
Aérospatiale/BAC

Entered service:
1976

Maximum range:
4,490 miles

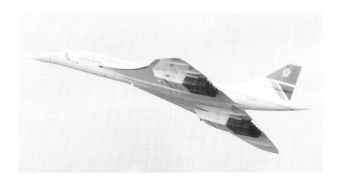

Only 29 years after the first aircraft broke the sound barrier, two Concordes took off from London and Paris to establish the first supersonic passenger service. This was in January 1976, and the westbound flight beat the Sun — arriving (by the clock) before it had started.

After the Anglo-French Supersonic Treaty was signed in 1962, years of intensive research and more than 5,000 hours of wind-tunnel tests proved that the long, streamlined fuselage and slender ogival delta wings finally reconciled good control at speeds as low as 230 mph with a low drag up to 1,300 mph (Mach 2.2).

The wings (produced by Aérospatiale) have elevons which work together as elevators and differentially as ailerons. There are no flaps; control is built into the wings through camber, taper, droop and twist.

Rolls-Royce designed the power plant — so called because the four Olympus turbojet engines constitute just one part of a complex four-part system made up of air intakes adjustable for high and low speeds, engines with two independent compressors for low fuel consumption at sub- and supersonic speeds, a reheat system to give extra thrust for takeoff and transonic acceleration, and variable geometry exhaust nozzles that also serve to provide reverse thrust on landing.

There could be no margin of error in the power-plant design. Concorde's payload is less than a third of that of a subsonic airliner, so the slightest reduction in engine efficiency could

The Concorde programme was a truly 50–50 Anglo–French undertaking, with about 50,000 people in ten locations around France and Britain directly involved and several times that number indirectly. The cost, in each country, was nearly £1.5 million ($3 million) a week.

■ French manufacture
□ British manufacture

Concorde

turn an operating profit into a loss.

The cruising speed is Mach 2.2, just below the "heat barrier", and the airframe (designed for a life of 60,000 hours) is constructed of an aluminium alloy that is resistant to variations in temperature from −35°C to over 120°C (−31°F to 248°F). Above this speed rises in temperature would demand the use of more costly steel and titanium.

Concorde flies high — at 55,000 ft or more — where air density is around one-tenth that at sea level, temperatures are low and supersonic engines efficient. Pilots report that it handles easily, and the transonic acceleration is not noticeable.

Supersonic aircraft have to be slender, and the cabin of Concorde is only 8 ft 8 in wide, although the overall length is 204 ft. Again, although the wingspan is less than 84 ft, the fuel capacity is 26,350 gal (31,650 US gal), takeoff weight 408,000 lb and the thrust of each engine more than 38,000 lb.

Normal seating, in wide double seats each side of the long aisle, is for 100 passengers, although more could be accommodated. They remain almost unaware of the thunder of a Concorde takeoff, when the Captain calls "Rotate" at about 246 mph. Often vivid white vortices appear writhing above the slim wings (see diagram). As the Concorde climbs, passengers can watch these gradually fade, move outboard and become thin white trails from the wingtips. By the time the Concorde reaches the stratosphere, they have disappeared.

The transparent visor, in high-strength glass, is raised in supersonic flight to protect the windshield from heat.

The droop nose gives a streamlined nose-up attitude in flight, and lowers by 15° to give a good view for landing.

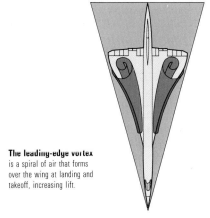

The leading-edge vortex is a spiral of air that forms over the wing at landing and takeoff, increasing lift.

Concorde's fuel is pumped between tanks to trim the aircraft. In supersonic flight, fuel is pumped rearward to cancel out the rearward movement of the lift of the wing.

Concorde's centre of gravity is shifted rearward when the aircraft is landing, but to a lesser extent than when it is going supersonic.

McDonnell Douglas DC-8

Built by:
Douglas Aircraft Co

Entered service:
1959

Maximum range:
6,185 miles

In 1955, the Douglas Aircraft Company took a risk and gambled the company's net worth on the DC-8, which followed the Boeing 707 as the second jet airliner from the United States. Originally powered by the same Pratt & Whitney JT3 turbojets as used on the 707, it had a fractionally more slender body, less wing sweep, and fully powered flight controls. To reduce drag and avoid stress between the wing and fuselage, the aerofoil changes shape towards the root, becoming flatter on top and more curved beneath.

Unlike Boeing, Douglas made the first five versions the same size, differing only in power and fuel capacity. A DC-8-40 became the first jet airliner to exceed the speed of sound when, in 1961, it reached Mach 1.012 (667 mph) in a shallow dive.

In 1965 Douglas injected new life into the popular "Diesel 8" (as pilots called it) with the first of the Super 60 series. These were made longer (see diagram) and had many other improvements, and extended production to 556 aircraft, completed in 1972. Since then these popular aircraft have mostly continued in service, and 110 Series 61, 62 and 63 were rebuilt in 1982–86 to Super 71, 72 and 73 standard with new-technology CFM56-2C

engines. Rated at 22,000 lb, these engines look much bigger, but cut fuel consumption and noise dramatically.

Unlike the 707 the DC-8 looks slender, has no antenna projecting ahead of the fin tip, has bigger squarish windows, and the cabin conditioning inlets are on each side under the nose instead of above the engines. Today many 8s are freighters, with wide side doors and no passenger windows, and Aeronavali Venezia in Italy is still doing conversions.

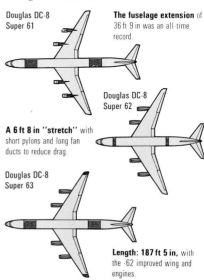

Douglas DC-8 Super 61

The fuselage extension of 36 ft 9 in was an all-time record.

Douglas DC-8 Super 62

A 6 ft 8 in "stretch" with short pylons and long fan ducts to reduce drag.

Douglas DC-8 Super 63

Length: 187 ft 5 in, with the -62 improved wing and engines.

Ilyushin Il-62

Built by:
Soviet industry

Entered service:
1967

Maximum range:
6,216 miles

When it entered service in 1967 this long-range jet appeared to be a British VC10 in Aeroflot markings, but actually it was a wholly Soviet design. The first versions were powered by Kuznetsov NK-8-4 engines of 23,150-lb thrust, but in 1974 Aeroflot introduced the Il-62M with Soloviev D-30KU engines of 24,250 lb and with many other improvements. All versions have a sharply swept wing of 141 ft 9 in span with a slightly kinked leading edge, a length of 174 ft 4 in and a cabin the same width as a 707 seating up to (in the latest 62MK version) 195 passengers. Maximum weight of the MK is 368,170 lb, and a full load can be carried about 5,000 miles.

With VC10s no longer likely to be seen, these big Soviet-built jets are the only ones with four engines at the tail. An odd feature is that, when parked at an airport, the Il-62 extends a small twin-wheel strut vertically downward under the tail, presumably in case incorrect loading should inadvertently tip it up.

The IL-62 is similar in design to the obsolete VC 10 (right), but can be distinguished from it by its taller tail, small doors and short landing gears, and an 8-ft bullet fairing on the fin.

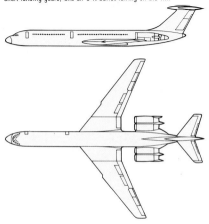

Ilyushin Il-86

Built by:
Soviet industry

Entered service:
1980

Maximum range:
2,860 miles

At first (entering service in 1976) this Soviet wide-body looked like a Boeing 707 that had been over-pressurized! In fact it is a very useful machine, ideal for carrying 350 people between icy airports lacking all amenities, and has been described as the Soviet equivalent of the Airbus. It is bigger than a 707, with a length of 194 ft 4 in and Kuznetsov NK-86 engines of 28,660-lb thrust each. This whale of an aircraft has distinctive main landing gears: three four-wheel bogies side-by-side, two folding inward and the middle one forward. On boarding, passengers carry their baggage and climb one of three airstairs hinged down from low on the left side. On board, they stow their baggage and coats and then climb further stairways to the vast main deck.

In the 1990s the totally new Il-96 will replace the 86 in production. This has a very efficient wing of much greater span, Soloviev D-90A engines of 35,275 lb thrust with much reduced noise and fuel consumption, and a shorter fuselage for up to 300 passengers. With much greater range of some 6,000 miles, the Il-96 is intended for use between big airports, and passengers will go aboard the normal way through doors located at the main-deck level.

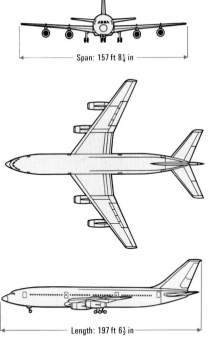

Span: 157 ft 8¼ in

Length: 197 ft 6½ in

To support its weight (up to 454,150 lb) on rough fields, the Ilyushin-86 has three four-wheel main bogies.

Beechcraft 99 and 1900

Built by:
**Beech Aircraft
Corporation**

Entered service:
99: 1968; 1900: 1984

Maximum range:
**99: 910 miles; 1900;
1,583 miles**

Beech Aircraft are the most "up market" of the giants of the lightplane world, and the 99 and 1900 are their biggest products. Both are trim, low-wing machines powered by two Pratt & Whitney Canada PT6 turboprops. The current C99 Airliner (a registered name) has 715-hp PT6A-36 engines, and normally seats 15 passengers in single seats each side of the aisle. It has a row of closely spaced square windows, giving a marvellous view but showing that the cabin is unpressurized.

The Beech 1900C Airliner is a quite different aircraft, with PT6A-65B engines of 1,100 hp. Overall length is 57 ft 10 in, compared with the C99's 44 ft 7 in, and standard seating is for 19. Because it is pressurized the windows are small ellipses, eight on each side. The most distinctive feature is the T-tail, which has small fins sticking down under the tailplane and a second, smaller, horizontal tail lower down on the fuselage. Like the C99, the 1900 can cruise at about 285 mph, mainly on commuter services.

Beechcraft B99 was one of the first turboprop aircraft for commuter use, seating up to 15 passengers.

Beechcraft B1900 A bigger aircraft with more powerful engines, the B1900 carries up to 19 passengers.

Span: 45 ft 10½ in

Span: 54 ft 6 in

Length: 44 ft 6¾ in

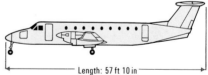

Length: 57 ft 10 in

British Aerospace 748

Built by:
British Aerospace

Entered service:
1962

Maximum range:
1,635 miles

First flown in 1960, the 748 is a tough and simple transport powered (most versions) by two 2,280-hp Rolls-Royce Dart turboprops. Altogether 381 were built of many civil and military versions, most seating up to 58 passengers and some having wide cargo doors. Many are operated from short dirt airstrips in harsh conditions. Features include black de-icer boots along the leading edges, large elliptical windows and twin-wheel landing gears, the main units retracting forwards under the engines.

Now the same BAe factory in Manchester, England, is making the ATP (Advanced TurboProp), first flown in 1986. It uses some of the 748 parts but is almost wholly new, bigger and an outstanding aircraft which probably costs less per seat-mile than any other airliner. The 2,653-hp Pratt & Whitney Canada engines drive six-bladed propellers, giving a cruising speed of 308 mph. Seating up to 72, the ATP has a long row of small rounded rectangular windows, a pointed nose and slightly swept fin.

The tabbed Fowler flaps, powered by an electric motor through a clutch and gearbox, have stand-by manual control. They give lift at slow speeds.

The engine nacelles are big enough to accommodate the Rolls-Royce Dart engines and the landing gears. The "petal" doors give access for servicing.

De-icing is by pulsating boots, two sets of rubber tubes which are alternately inflated and deflated to crack ice on the leading edges.

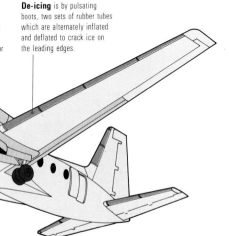

British Aerospace Jetstream

Built by:
British Aerospace

Entered service:
1982

Maximum range:
783 miles

Derived from an earlier design by the defunct company of Handley Page, the Jetstream 31 first flew in 1982. Since then it has become a smash hit, largely because unlike many of its rivals it has a comfortable "stand-up" cabin. Normal seating is for up to 19 passengers, with full pressurization despite the size of the elliptical (almost circular) picture windows. The main door aft of the wing has an integral airstairs.

Some Jetstreams are fitted with a baggage pod on the underside of the fuselage under the wing.

Engines are American Garrett TPE331s, of 940 or 1,020 hp, driving four-bladed propellers. The tailplane is mounted halfway up the slightly swept fin, the steerable twin-wheel nose gear folds forward into the long nose, and the wide-track single-wheel main legs retract inward into the wings. Span is 52 ft, length 47 ft, maximum weight 16,200 lb and cruising speed up to 300 mph. The BAe factory in Scotland is turning out 48 of these popular commuter airliners each year, most of them for the North American market.

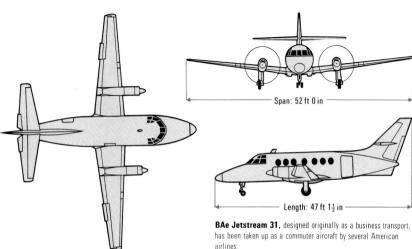

Span: 52 ft 0 in

Length: 47 ft 1½ in

BAe Jetstream 31, designed originally as a business transport, has been taken up as a commuter aircraft by several American airlines.

Convair CV-580

Built by:
Convair (General Dynamics)

Entered service:
1960

Maximum range:
1,950 miles

In July 1946 Convair, of San Diego, flew the first CV-240, a pressurized 40-seater intended to succeed the DC-3 as a standard short-haul transport. It was the forerunner of 1,000 related aircraft, military as well as civil, all powered by two Pratt & Whitney R-2800 Double Wasp piston engines of 2,100 or 2,500 hp, and distinguished by their twin-wheel tricycle landing gear, long slender wings, curvaceous fin and big square windows. The CV-240 was slightly stretched into the 44-seat CV-340, with span increased from 91 ft 9 in to 105 ft 4 in, followed by the CV-440 with up to 52 seats and various refinements.

Over the years many Convairs were fitted with nose radar, and in 1960 the first CV-580 appeared, with piston engines replaced by 3,750 hp Allison 501-D13 turboprops driving propellers with four huge rectangular blades. Another 129 conversions followed, while Convair itself produced the CV-600 (rebuilt 240) and CV-640 (rebuilt 340 or 440) powered by 3,025-hp Rolls-Royce Dart engines. These conversions were naturally faster and smoother, and many are still in use along with a handful with piston engines.

In 1988 Convair introduced the Super 580ST — a new 78-seat stretched version — and the engine builder is developing the Allison Turbo Flagship, again seating up to 78, with 5,000-hp engines and many other changes.

Span: 105 ft 4 in

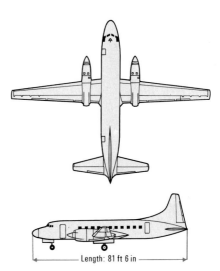
Length: 81 ft 6 in

Convair 580 was originally a turboprop version of the piston-engined Convair-Liner. In its final form (the stretched Super 580ST) it can, with maximum fuel, carry up to 78 passengers nearly 2,000 miles.

Douglas DC-3

Built by:
Douglas Aircraft Co

Entered service:
1936

Maximum range:
1,510 miles

By far the most important airliner in civil aviation history, the Douglas DC-3 (sometimes known by its military name, the Dakota) evolved from a proposition made by TWA, in 1932, that Douglas should build a more modern successor to the Fokker and Ford trimotors. With only two engines on a low cantilever wing, the resulting DC-1 (Douglas Commercial 1) flew in 1933. Its advanced design included retractable main wheels, flaps, fully-cowled engines, variable-pitch propellers and all-metal stressed-skin construction. The 196-mph DC-2, an improved version, provided the first non-stop flights over the Newark–Chicago route.

American Airlines commissioned an enlarged DC-2 for its transcontinental sleeper services. In September 1936 it made the eastbound journey in 16 hours. The daytime version, the 21-seat DC-3, was already flying the New York–Chicago route.

A total of 448 examples of this fast, reliable and economical aircraft had been delivered by 1939. During World War II military versions took the total to 10,691 (discounting thousands made under licence in the Soviet Union). Its multi-spar wing construction enabled it to fly for up to 90,000 hours without dangerous fatigue, and

hundreds of examples of this classic of aviation are still in service.

Thousands of modified DC-3s were built in the Soviet Union as the Li-2, and some of these are still flying in "outback" regions of Asian countries. Meanwhile, several American companies have replaced the 1,200 hp Pratt & Whitney piston engines by much lighter PT6 turboprops of the same make. One such conversion has three engines, the extra one being located in the nose.

Commodious in its day, the DC-3 carried up to 36 passengers in its 30-foot-long cabin. Its successor, the DC 10, carries 10 times as many passengers.

DC-3

DC-10. 181 ft 4¾ in

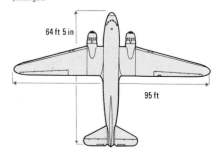

64 ft 5 in

95 ft

Embraer EMB-110 and -120

Built by:
Embraer SA, Brazil

Entered service:
EMB-110: 1973;
EMB-120: 1983

Maximum range:
EMB-110: 1,180 miles;
EMB-120: 1,800 miles

EMB-110, a popular business transport aircraft, was originally built for the Brazilian air force.

EMB-120 was developed from the EMB-110 for short-range business and commuter use.

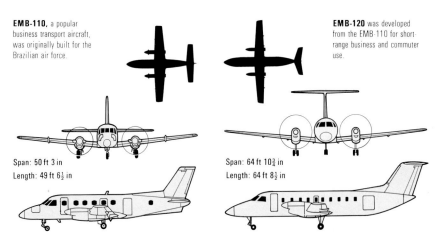

Span: 50 ft 3 in
Length: 49 ft 6½ in

Span: 64 ft 10¾ in
Length: 64 ft 8½ in

Although it has been at work only since 1970, Embraer has catapulted Brazil into the forefront of the world's aerospace exporters. One of its most successful products is the EMB-110 Bandeirante (Pioneer), 500 of which are flying in 34 countries. Powered by 750-hp Pratt & Whitney Canada PT6A turboprops, the Bandeirante has been built in many civil and military versions, but the standard airline model seats up to 21 passengers who enter via an airstairs door just behind the cockpit. The landing gear units each have a single wheel, the wings and tailplane have sharp dihedral (upward slope), the fin is swept and has a long dorsal extension giving a kinked leading edge, and the panoramic windows have straight sides but are curved top and bottom.

The newer (first flight 1983) EMB-120 Brasilia is bigger, and with a cruising speed of 343 mph is one of the fastest of the small turboprops. Powered by 1,800-hp P&W Canada PW118 engines, it has a pressurized cabin and so has a circular-section fuselage and rather smaller rectangular windows. Normal seating is for 30 passengers. Features include twin-wheel landing gears, a very high T-tail and distinctive strakes on each side under the rear fuselage.

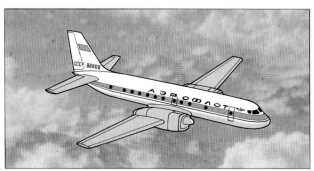

Fairchild Metro
Ilyushin Il-114

Fairchild Metro

Built by:
Fairchild Swearingen

Entered service:
1971

Maximum range:
715 miles

Ilyushin Il-114

Built by:
Soviet industry

Entered service:
Planned for 1990

Maximum range:
1,500 miles approx.

Fairchild Metro

Built for speed rather than spacious-ness, the Metro has a pressurized cabin that is nowhere higher than 4 ft 9 in (along the central aisle). Today most are Metro IIIs, powered by 1,000-hp Garrett TPE331 turboprops and seating up to 20. Maximum cruising speed is 320 mph. Features include a narrow airstairs door at the front and a big upward-hinged baggage/cargo door at the back, air inlets above the propeller spinners, twin-wheel land-ing gears and a sharply sweptback tailplane mounted a little way up the distinctive vertical tail. The Metro VI will have a more efficient wing, 1,250-hp engines and a high T-tail. Cruising speed is expected to be 400 mph.

Ilyushin Il-114

With an appearance and specification like a carbon copy of Britain's BAe ATP, the Il-114 is likely to become a familiar sight throughout the Soviet Union and Eastern bloc countries in the 1990s. Powered by 2,500-hp en-gines driving propellers with six, or possibly even eight, blades, it will seat 60 passengers who will enter via an airstairs door at the front. Fea-tures include a bluff nose, elliptical windows, low tailplane (although not as low as the ATP) and tall fin with slight sweepback. Another difference from the ATP is the absence of a dorsal fin. Various East European nations, including Yugoslavia, will share in making the 114s.

Saab 340

Built by:
Saab-Scania, Sweden

Entered service:
1985

Maximum range:
1,080 miles

Originally this attractive 35-seater was a Swedish–American product, but the American partner, Fairchild, progressively withdrew from the project between 1985 and 1987. Today Saab have delivered well over 100 aircraft, more than half to American customers. Powered by 1,735-hp General Electric CT7 engines driving advanced propellers made by Dowty Rotol in Britain, the 340 is quite a big machine, with a span of 70 ft 4 in and maximum weight of 27,275 lb.

The pressurized cabin is 7 ft 1 in wide and 6 ft high at the aisle, seats being arranged 2 plus 1 alongside the "rounded rectangular" windows. The airstairs door is at the front of the fuselage, and there is a wide baggage/cargo door at the rear. All landing gears have twin wheels. The tail is distinctive, with a large dorsal fillet leading into a slightly swept fin, low-set tailplane with very acute dihedral (upward slope) and long shallow strakes along the bottom of the rear fuselage. Maximum cruising speed is 313 mph.

Span: 70 ft 4 in

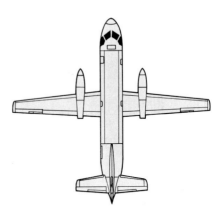

Length: 64 ft 6 in

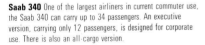
Saab 340 One of the largest airliners in current commuter use, the Saab 340 can carry up to 34 passengers. An executive version, carrying only 12 passengers, is designed for corporate use. There is also an all-cargo version.

123

Airtech CN-235

Built by:
Airtech (CASA-IPTN)

Entered service:
1986

Maximum range:
(reduced payload) 2,933 miles

Airtech is a partnership between CASA of Spain and IPTN of Indonesia, who previously shared manufacture of more than 400 of the smaller CASA C-212 Aviocar. Like the C-212, the CN-235 is visibly intended to fly bulky cargo as well as passengers, and serve air forces as well as airlines. First flown in 1983, it has a very efficient wing located very high on the fuelage, with pointed tips, on which are the 1,750-hp General Electric CT7 engines driving four-bladed glass-fibre propellers. Span is 84 ft 8 in.

The pressurized fuselage has an internal width of 8 ft 11 in and height of 6 ft 2 in, and in the passenger role seats up to 45, who enter via an airstairs door at the rear. The crew enter via a service door at the front on the right. There is a single nose-wheel and tandem main wheels on each side, retracting into large fuselage blisters. Vehicles can drive up the rear ramp door, the tail being sharply swept upward on the broad flat rear fuselage. Deliveries began in 1986. Half the sales have been for civil aircraft, half for military ones.

The CN-235 is an obvious development of its older brother, the C-212, and both are used by commuter airlines in Europe and the Third World.

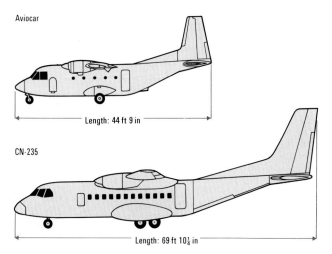

Aviocar

Length: 44 ft 9 in

CN-235

Length: 69 ft 10¼ in

ATR 42

Built by:
Avions de Transport Régional

Entered service:
1985

Maximum range:
**(maximum payload)
1,427 miles**

In November 1981 Aérospatiale of France and Aeritalia of Italy formed Avions de Transport Régional to build a superior regional transport. They might have thought the market already saturated, but the ATR 42 (the number is the seating capacity) was first flown in 1984 and has since proved to be a global best-seller. Before the end of 1987 ATR had sold 240 of these versatile aircraft to 57 operators worldwide.

Features include a small but efficient wing (with ailerons projecting slightly beyond the tips) carrying the 1,800-hp PW120 engines driving four-bladed propellers, a circular-section pressurized fuselage with 17 small windows on each side (cabin width 8 ft 5 in, height 6 ft 3 in), an airstairs door at the back and wide cargo/baggage door at the front, and twin-wheel landing gears with the main units folding into a giant blister extending round the underside of the fuselage. The aircraft has a distinctive kinked-outline fin carrying the tailplane not quite at the top. Maximum weight is 36,817 lb and cruising speed up to 307 mph.

The ATR 71 is a bigger and more powerful version planned to enter service in 1989, with 24 windows each side and seating for 72 passengers.

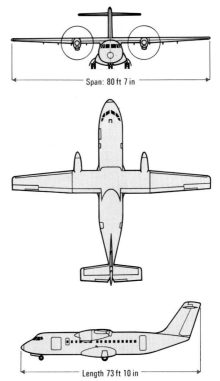

Span: 80 ft 7 in

Length 73 ft 10 in

ATR 42 A new regional transport in a highly competitive market, the joint French-Italian ATR 42 was an immediate success with airlines throughout the world. The basic 42-seat version has been stretched to carry up to 74 passengers in the form of the ATR 72.

Short legs to the main landing gear (easier to accommodate in the fuselage side-pods) put the ATR 42 close to the ground.

Antonov An-24
DH Canada DHC-6 Twin Otter

Antonov An-24

Built by:
Soviet industry

Entered service:
1963

Maximum range:
(reduced payload) 1,500 miles

DH Canada DHC-6 Twin Otter

Built by:
de Havilland Canada

Entered service:
1966

Maximum range:
800 miles

Antonov An-24

Oleg K. Antonov's design bureau at Kiev flew the first An-24 in 1960, and subsequently more than 1,000 of the type were constructed. A model called Y-7 is still built in China. There are many versions, all powered by 2,500-hp AI-24 engines driving four-bladed propellers on a wing with a slight anhedral (downward slope), whereas the tailplane has sharp dihedral. Passenger aircraft seat up to 44 people, the door being at the back and the windows circular. The twin-wheel main gears retract forward into the long nacelles, and some models have a small turbojet in the rear of the right nacelle. The An-24 has a large rear ramp door for loading vehicles.

DH Canada DHC-6 Twin Otter

The once proud de Havilland Aircraft of Canada is now owned by mighty Boeing. It specializes in STOL (short takeoff and landing) transports, and one of its best-sellers (more than 840 aircraft) is the trim DHC-6 Twin Otter.

Powered by 620-hp PT6 engines driving three-bladed propellers, on an untapered wing braced by a single strut each side, it seats up to 20 passengers in an unpressurized cabin with square windows and doors at the rear. The landing gears are fixed (non-retractable), and the tailplane is located a little way up the big, straight-edged vertical tail. Maximum cruising speed is 210 mph.

DH Canada DHC-8
Dornier Do 228

DH Canada DHC-8

Built by:
de Havilland Canada

Entered service:
1984

Maximum range:
1,020 miles

Dornier Do 228

Built by:
**Dornier GmbH,
West Germany**

Entered service:
1982

Maximum range:
(Dash-100) 834 miles

DH Canada DHC-8
First flown in 1983, the Dash-8 was designed for proper airports, so STOL capability was sacrificed for speed (309 mph). Powered by 1,800-hp PW120 engines driving four-bladed propellers, it has a pressurized fuselage seating up to 40 passengers in a cabin 8 ft 2 in wide with an airstairs door at the front, wide cargo/baggage door at the back, and small "rounded rectangular" windows. The vast fin, with a dorsal fillet extending as far as the wing, carries the tailplane right at the top. The downsloping nose is distinctive, and the twin-wheel main gears retract backward into the long nacelles. In 1988 deliveries began of the Series 300 version, seating 56.

Dornier Do 228
The famous German company of Dornier has built a succession of STOL transports. The Do 228 of 1981 introduced an advanced-technology wing whose diagonal pointed tips are distinctive. Powered by 714-hp or 776-hp Garrett TPE331 engines driving four-bladed propellers, the 228 comes in two lengths: the Do 228-100 seats 15 passengers, and the Do 228-200 seats 19. The fuselage is unpressurized and so can have a square section, with big square windows. The wide double-door is at the back. There are twin nosewheels and single mainwheels folding inward into a giant blister under the fuselage. The nose is long and the tailplane behind the fin.

127

Fokker F27 and 50

Fokker F27

Built by:
**Fokker Aircraft,
Netherlands**

Entered service:
1958

Maximum range:
1,375 miles

Fokker F50

Built by:
**Fokker Aircraft,
Netherlands**

Entered service:
1987

Maximum range:
2,100 miles

The Netherlands has a tiny home market, yet by being first succeeded in selling more F27s (786) than any other European builder of airliners. Part of the credit went to the reliable 2,200-hp Rolls-Royce Dart engines, in long nacelles which also house the twin-wheel main landing gears. The circular-section pressurized fuselage (8 ft 2 in wide) has ten giant elliptical windows each side.

Ideally there are double seats opposite each window, but some airline operators squeeze in 50 or more passengers, who board at the rear. The single nosewheel is right at the front of the upturned nose, there is a long dorsal fin extending all along the fuselage to the wing, and the tailplane is attached to the top of the fuselage.

In 1987 production switched to the Fokker 50. Though an obviously improved F27, only 20 per cent of the parts are the same. Seating up to 58, the new Fokker has a row of 21 or 22 small rectangular windows each side, 2,250-hp PW125B engines driving six-bladed propellers, twin nosewheels and a slightly more pointed tailcone.

The main landing gears, extending on long struts from the engine nacelles, come from Britain. They have low-pressure tyres for rough fields previously usable only by DC-3s.

hotel provided, some tour operators have been able to cut the prices of some package holidays still further, by-passing international fare regulations by offering air trips as "tour" packages which include poor or merely nominal accommodation.

The wide range of discount fares is worth investigating. Spouse fares give a reduction to one partner if the other pays full fare; group flights can be booked with a group as small as two; there are still youth fares, although these are gradually being phased out under the rash of other budget fares on offer, and student fares, which require an International Student's Union card. Those who do not qualify for a card can join an affiliation group. Groups of people with professional affinity (all lawyers, for instance) or with similar vocational interests, can charter aircraft to fly their members together. A minimum period of membership is usually necessary before such parties qualify for the low fares.

Despite the fierce competition between airlines flying the same route, scheduled fares do not vary greatly. This is largely because IATA keeps a firm control on price cutting to protect airlines and their passengers.

It is, however, well worth shopping around for cheaper fares, which can often be found through travel agents. They may have places on charter flights, but can also sometimes provide seats on scheduled services at considerably reduced rates.

Some airlines have circumvented the IATA regulations by allowing ticket agencies (known as GSAs and PSAs) a generous profit margin (as much as 400 per cent). The agent can then afford to sell at whatever price he chooses. The ticket bears the official price and the agent's stamp. If any questions are asked, the airline can deny any knowledge of the discounted price, pointing to the agent.

Fare regulation exists to protect passengers, provide insurance and so on, and the airline would invariably pay on a claim. This is because it would not want to antagonize IATA, which could remove a route from an airline.

Internal flights

Internal commuter or shuttle flights, as casual as bus services, are operated on an increasing number of busy routes. Passengers may board the plane with seconds to spare, and pay in the air. Places are guaranteed: provided that a passenger turns up by check-in time, which is typically only ten minutes before departure, he will fly, even if a back-up plane has to be brought out for him alone. On well-used routes such as New York/Washington fares may be lower at weekends or during off-season periods.

The Book of Bargains
The ABC World Airways Guide* gives a world-wide survey of flight information: dates, times, fares, special rates and alternative services. Its data allows the flier to calculate his own journey costs:—

Example
A London businessman wants to visit Denpasar and Jakarta in Indonesia. The round fare to Denpasar is £1,766. If he can arrange his itinerary to fit the time restrictions on excursion fares, he can take an APEX fare (to be booked a month in advance) to Singapore and back, costing £619, allowing him to return from 14 days to three months later. From Singapore he can either buy a local ticket (where the sale is limited to the country of departure) at a concessionary excursion price of £204 (Singapore $734), which restricts him to ten days to one month of travel, taking a similar ticket in London at £260 (Singapore $935) with a saving of nearly £900. Where tickets can only be bought in the country they apply to, they can be booked from any large travel agency.

* Published by Reed Telepublishing, London

145

Ticket check

Air tickets, transferable between all IATA airlines, are standard in form. The first page is torn out at check-in, at which point passengers are given their boarding passes and, usually, a seat assignment, although at some airports seat assignments may be made in advance by telephone.

1 Endorsements: here are recorded any non-transferable APEX and other flights restricted to a certain time on a certain day.

2 Name: should correspond to name on passport. Tickets are transferable to another flight or airline, *not* to another name. Check the spelling.

3 Coupons not valid: an unused ticket can be refunded or renewed up to 30 days after the expiry of the (365-day) period of validity, and thereafter at the airline's discretion.

4 Good for passage: check departure and destination points are correctly entered.

5 Conjunction tickets: if your trip involves more than four stopover points reference numbers for additional tickets are entered here.

6 Issued in exchange: could be a PTA (pre-paid ticket advice) if the ticket is paid for in foreign currency. Details entered below.

7 Ticket designator: single-class Concorde (''R'' code) or staff discount flight (''sub law'') entered here.

8 Tour code: check tour number for your package-deal holiday is entered here.

9 Departure date: must be correct date for the flight number.

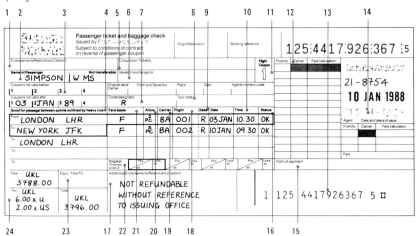

21 Fare basis: check. ''F'' = first class; ''J'' = business class ''Y'' = economy (coach).

22 Baggage checked: weight and number of items checked in. Compensation is not payable on items not entered. **Unck'd:** hand baggage is not checked.

23 Equivalent fare: local equivalent of the fare if paid in foreign currency.

24 Airport tax: not always charged. **Total:** fare plus tax.

17 Additional endorsements/restrictions: comments such as the example filled in should not show on page 2 if not applicable to return trip.

18 Flight number: is always the same for the same route. Check against date and time.

19 Carrier = airline.

20 Allow: baggage allowance, different for different classes. US airlines calculate by piece, not weight.

13 Ticket number: the carrier's code number is followed by the ticket number. The single digit is the coupon number.

14 Agent, date and place of issue: the office stamp of the agent or carrier gives the date of issue of the ticket.

15 Payment can be by cash, cheque, credit card or account.

16 Status: query if not marked ''OK''.

10 Departure time: given in local time. Check in one hour earlier for international flights; half an hour earlier for internal flights.

11 Flight coupon: marked ''1'' on page 1 for the outward trip (torn off at check-in) and ''2'' on page 2 for the return journey.

12 From/to; Carrier; Fare calculation: for official use only; intended for revenue accountancy.

146

Booking and paying

Reservations may be made by telephone and confirmed at the same time, but tickets are not issued until paid for in cash, by cheque or by credit card; payment does not have to be in the local currency, but payments in foreign currency will be at the current rate of exchange.

Tickets can be bought by a friend or company in the country of destination and sent by the airline PTA (Prepaid Ticket Advice) to the user. The cost will be the same, but it may be more convenient to pay abroad.

An account with a reputable travel agent is worthwhile for regular air travellers, not only for the credit facilities made available but also for the preferential services. It is standard practice for agents to book their clients on more than one flight to ensure that a seat is available within a given period. The bookings, made at intervals, are computerized under different numbers and will not be cross-checked; if all bookings are made simultaneously to a single airline they will be computerized under a single number. As soon as the first option comes up, the airline will ask the client to confirm one of the bookings. Agents sometimes book several seats on a flight offering stand-by bargains between London and New York to increase the possibility that there will be a seat for a client to use on a stand-by ticket.

If fares increase between payment and departure, the extra may have to be paid, particularly if the airline has endorsed the ticket to this effect to cover itself at times when fare rises are imminent. The carrier has to refund if fares suddenly decrease.

Children usually travel half-fare and babies under two years at ten per cent of the adult fare, or free.

If a scheduled flight has to be cancelled, the ticket is valid for a year, or payment can be refunded by cash, cheque, or a Miscellaneous Charges Order giving credit to the value of the original ticket.

Cancellation of a discount or budget flight, or a package holiday, may mean forfeiting part or all of the money paid. Breaking the conditions of a return discount flight by returning earlier or later than specified may mean paying the different between the discount and full standard fare. On European routes, cancellation of an APEX booking more than one month from departure date means forfeiting half the price of the fare; less than a month, the whole fare must be forfeited. On routes to the US, cancellation at any time means forfeiting about ten per cent and, on other routes, usually 25 per cent. The only acceptable reason for breaking the conditions of a discount fare is a death in the family, and a full refund is made only on production of the death certificate.

Since airline computers record details of all ticket sales, to fill in an indemnity form and provide proof of identity is all that is required for a replacement ticket to be issued if the original is lost. The purchaser pays twice if the lost ticket is used.

Compensation for cancelled or delayed flights varies from country to country. In the US, airlines must provide meals, transport to hotels, overnight accommodation if needed and telephone and telegraph communication costs. Airlines elsewhere may be less generous. No airline is obliged to compensate for lost time; but it must reroute its passengers if a flight is cancelled or a connection missed through delays. Holiday packages should always be checked out for cancellation procedures; there may be a 24-hour money back guarantee.

Airport taxes are not levied by all airports, but may have to be paid at check-in. The carrier, or your travel agent, should be able to inform you of charges on your journey.

Check list

Passport

Check that your passport has not expired — a new one may take several weeks to arrive. Make sure that any additional children have been incorporated and note the number. Report loss or theft to the police and to the passport office. If abroad, your consulate will issue a travelling document. If you forget your passport, you *may* be allowed out for short trips on proof of identity. You will be required to sign an indemnity form protecting the airline from legal responsibility for you. Passports are usually needed to cash travellers' cheques.

Visas

Consult travel agents, airlines or the embassy concerned about whether or not you need a visa for the country you are visiting (visas are required for the US, but an American does not need one to enter Britain). Submit your passport and, if necessary, vaccination certificates to the appropriate embassy or consulate well in advance. Airlines and package tour organizers often take care of visas for their customers, but it is the traveller's responsibility ultimately. Carry extra photographs for any additional visas needed en route.

Medical

It is wise to have polio, typhoid and tetanus vaccinations regardless of where you are going. Check with the relevant embassies which certificates you will need to enter their countries. You must be vaccinated even if your stopover in a potentially infectious area is brief. Have the injections well before the trip, in case of side effects.

Take with you any medicines you regularly use. Even aspirin mixtures vary greatly from country to country. There is no vaccination against malaria, so take anti-malaria tablets if going through a malarial country.

Money

Buy travellers' cheques in the most advantageous currency for exchange (local economic crises can make a difference) and list the serial numbers in case of loss or theft. Familiarize yourself with rates of exchange. Make sure that local currency can be taken in — and out — and carry only small amounts.

Insurance

The Warsaw Convention automatically insures all travellers while in the air. Otherwise, you should be covered for money and goods, medical expenses, flight cancellation and personal accident and liability. Residents of countries with socialized medicine can find treatment without it being dismayingly expensive; they should buy health insurance. Airlines insure baggage, but do set limits; so take out additional insurance on valuables.

Comprehensive holiday insurance schemes can be had which promise cover for all these things, based on the areas to be visited and the duration of the stay. Selective policies enable the traveller to choose the cover he or she requires.

Baggage

Baggage allowances vary for first, business and economy (coach) class. In the US it is calculated by number and size of pieces. All airlines allow additional carry-on items, usually a bag, coat, umbrella, baby food and baby carrier. Half-fare children have a full luggage allowance. Remove old baggage destination tags, to reduce the chance of lost luggage. Put your name and home address inside your bags, and display your destination address only on the outside, so as not to advertize your departure to professional housebreakers; keep a list of the contents. Excess baggage may be cheaper sent as air freight.

Check-in

Getting there

Your airline, or another one acting for it, will almost certainly have a terminal in town, often associated with a rail station and usually with a baggage check-in facility. Buses or trains then get you to the airport. There will be a recommended check-in time for the terminal (as distinct from the airport check-in time) which may appear on your ticket; if not, the airline clerks will inform you.

If you are leaving your own vehicle at the airport there will probably be a long-term car park, costing a fraction of the short-term rates, where space may be booked in advance.

Although car parks are guarded, do not make things easy for thieves by leaving your parking ticket in a prominent place; hide it in the car or take it with you. Without the ticket, the car can only be removed when ownership has been proved.

Car rental companies have bases at all major airports.

Checking in

If you have had only telephone confirmation of your reservation, go to the airline ticket sales desk for your ticket before checking in. The check-in desk will have the name of the airline, and possibly your flight number, over it. Here baggage intended for the hold will be weighed and passed to the baggage handlers, while your ticket is checked and you are given a boarding pass.

There are good reasons for checking in earlier than the time shown on a ticket. Since scheduled passengers have great feeedom to change or cancel bookings, airlines routinely overbook their flights; sometimes passengers with confirmed reservation are denied boarding, or "bumped". Latecomers are most likely, and members of family groups and handicapped passengers least likely, to be "bumped". The assertive and persistent passenger with a convincing argument will have a better chance of boarding too.

Any IATA airline is obliged to make alternative arrangements to get you to your destination as soon as possible, by another carrier if necessary. Stay at the check-in desk and argue until satisfactory arrangements have been made for you. In some countries, notably the USA, the civil aviation authorities require carriers to compensate passengers when denied boarding. Payments are made only when the delay is substantial, when the passenger has confirmed his reservation and checked in by the required time, and if the flight was not delayed or cancelled. The amount paid depends on length of delay.

If a passenger is required to travel economy (coach class) when he booked first class, he is entitled to a refund equal to the difference in fares; he cannot be charged extra if he is upgraded.

When your baggage is checked, the carrier becomes liable for loss or damage up to limits specified by the Warsaw Convention. A baggage check attached to your ticket records the weight of the baggage; make sure you get the check, and that the weight is not understated: compensation is paid by weight. If the baggage contents are worth more than the compensation rates printed on the back of your ticket, you can make a declaration of excess value, pay an extra charge and gain entitlement to greater compensation. Better still, take your valuables in your cabin baggage and arrange your own insurance beforehand.

If your flight is delayed, do not be in too much of a hurry to pass through security, passport and Customs control to the airside: on a fog-hit day the departure lounge is likely to become more crowded than the main concourse, and will have fewer facilities.

Airport facilities

The permanent facilities offered to passengers are usually signposted on terminal concourses in visual symbols. Various attempts have been made to design a set of symbols that will be immediately intelligible to people from any part of the world, but a successful Esperanto of symbols has yet to be established.

Flight announcements
Continually changing information, such as lists of flight arrivals and departures, is displayed on electronically controlled flipboards and TV monitors. In the most advanced system, the boards and monitors are linked to a central minicomputer so that they are always up to date and consistent. The character generators that inscribe the information on the screens can often handle Arabic or Cyrillic alphabets. A parallel system of monitors, unseen by the public, displays the information throughout the working areas of the terminal. The computer can also provide a print-out of flight statistics based on its own announcements.

There is almost nowhere in the terminal where you can find yourself out of range of announcements in several languages from the public address speakers. These may not come from a living announcer, but may be computer-assembled from pre-recorded snippets, like the announcements of a speaking clock. If the concourse becomes noisier, the volume of the announcements is automatically boosted.

At some airports, personnel are alerted to emergencies by coded messages which sound to passengers like routine announcements. Thus alerted, airport staff can begin to take any necessary action without alarming the public.

Passengers who find no announcements in their own language can enlist help from the desk of their national airline; there will probably also be a general enquiry desk administered by the airport authorities, and major tour operators may have their own desks as well.

Meeting and greeting
Newly arrived passengers can usually be met at the exit from which they appear when they have claimed their baggage, and perhaps also passed through Customs. But there are also designated meeting points. Lost friends can be paged over the public address system.

Messages and telegrams can usually be left at a central message desk. If you telephone any such message through to the airline desk, specify not only the passenger's name, but also his point of origin, expected time of arrival and, if possible, his flight number. The staff who take the message can page the person for whom it is intended as he passes through the arrivals section.

Although airlines communicate with their flight crews in flight on a special company frequency, it is not possible to pass a personal message to a passenger on board. In an emergency, an urgent message can be sent to the destination airport by telephone, cable or telex.

Post and telecommunications
A large airport may have its own post office, and philatelic acquaintances may appreciate letters or cards that have been franked with its date stamp. If there is a post office there will also be a telegraphic serivce, and perhaps telex offices.

Although telephones will be plentiful on the concourse, they cannot always be found on the airside of the terminal. But at some airports, notably in the USA, telephones are provided in the departure lounges and at points all the way to the embarkation gates.

Business facilities

Air terminals and hotels in and around large international airports may offer conference and secretarial facilities for executive travellers.

Animals

Airlines usually insist that pets be carried in the aircraft cargo holds, so it is advisable to search for an airline that is permissive in this respect if you want to carry a pet in the cabin. All pets should be carried in special pet carriers, available from vets and pet shops, and some animals may need to be tranquillized for the trip.

Animals are usually subject to quarantine regulations in force in the destination country. In the UK these are exceptionally strict, in an attempt to keep rabies out of the country. A dog taken out of the UK would be quarantined for six months on its return, at a cost of £2 to £4 ($4 to $8) a day, depending upon its size, dietary and exercise requirements. Other creatures will cost more or less, depending upon the kind of care they will need.

Children

Many airports are equipped with mothers' rooms where babies can be changed and fed, and others have staffed nurseries where older children can be left for short periods, or entertained during long delays. London's Heathrow Airport, for example, has trained nurses on duty in a nursery area where children up to eight years old can play. Frankfurt Airport's nursery handles up to 100 children a day.

Very young children — usually below six years old, although the age varies from airline to airline — will not be accepted on an airline flight unless accompanied by an adult, but older children can fly unaccompanied. Many airlines offer a child escort service. If notified in advance, they will arrange for ground staff to escort young passengers through Customs, passport and security checks, and hand them over to the care of the cabin staff at boarding time. Each child is provided with special documents advising all staff along the route that they are dealing with unaccompanied minors. In-flight they may be given special childrens' meals, and supervised (and entertained if necessary) by the cabin staff. At the destination they are escorted from the plane and through the airport formalities, to be handed over to an accredited collector.

Although airlines generally provide in-flight supervision free of charge, they may levy a charge for their special child escort services. Such services can also be provided for groups of children.

Welfare

Some very large airports — notably Amsterdam's Schiphol and London's Heathrow — have aid centres for receiving passengers who are destitute on arrival, who are emotionally disturbed, unable to contact relatives or friends, or who are lost. Heathrow Airport's "Wel-care" office is staffed by welfare officers who will counsel staff and passengers on any type of personal problem, from financial difficulties and lost passports or tickets to marriage guidance.

Rest rooms

All airports have lounges, often with bars serving drinks or snacks, but some airports now have rest rooms where passengers can sleep during short stopovers, or during delays. A small charge may be levied.

Chapels

Many large international airports have chapels, usually interdenominational, with regular services, for the use of both passengerss and the airport staff.

Airport facilities/2

Airport medical facilities

If it is not immediately obvious where to get medical aid at an airport, ask any member of the airline or airport staff. If there is no doctor permanently employed on the airport, there will certainly be one on call from the surrounding district, and many members of the airport staff have paramedical or first-aid training; at a small airport, the fire or police chief or the ground attendants may be the most likely people to approach for initial help. Asthma, coronaries, the effects of overindulgence in flight and unusual tropical diseases are some of the problems that airport medical services have to be ready for. The largest airports have medical centres as fully equipped as small hospitals. Many charge for their services.

Vaccination services

Some countries demand valid international certificates of vaccination before admitting foreigners and many international airports offer emergency immunization and vaccination services for passengers and staff. Because it takes eight days for a smallpox vaccination to become effective, and ten days for a yellow fever vaccination, and because there are often side-effects from vaccinations for cholera and some tropical diseases, it is advisable to have all vaccinations well in advance of a journey. But revaccinations are valid immediately, and have reduced side-effects. Countries may refuse to admit travellers with new vaccinations, or they may keep them under surveillance for a while.

Travellers should remember to take into account the health requirements of the country to which they are returning. The port health authorities may demand certificates of vaccination against diseases prevalent not only in countries visited, but also where stopovers have been made.

Fitness to travel

Few people are so badly disabled, or enfeebled by age, that they cannot travel by air. Scores of thousands of handicapped passengers are transported routinely by every major airline each year. Only people with infectious diseases, the severely mentally unstable and those whose indisposition (such as a bronchial condition) might be worsened by flying, will be refused a ticket.

A traveller with restricted mobility or other health problem, such as heart complaint, should find out from the travel agent or airline whether a medical certificate of fitness to fly is required. It is the passenger's responsibility to obtain it from a doctor, and it is wise to obtain several copies. Pregnant women should ask for a certificate stating the number of weeks they have been pregnant, and confirming their fitness to travel. Airlines will not usually permit women to fly in the later stages of pregnancy — usually after about 7 months.

Air travellers with health problems should always discuss the medical aspects of flying with their doctor.

Facilities for the disabled

There is usually a limit to the number of disabled people an airline will carry on one flight (governed by a ratio to available escorts) in case of emergency, so book early. It is the disabled passenger's responsibility to arrange for an ambulance or other transport to the airport terminal. He should arrive half an hour or more before the recommended check-in time to allow for delays, especially in negotiating the often long distances between car parks and terminals. Some airports have special parking spaces for disabled travellers, often near to the air terminal and under cover and wider than usual.

Special facilities for disabled travellers vary considerably between airports, but most air terminals are designed with automatic doors, wide corridors and concourses, and a maximum number of elevators and moving walkways. These are a boon to the disabled traveller. There may also be ramps and extra-wide walkways with non-slip surfaces and handrails, special toilets, drinking fountains, high dining tables, telephone booths and vending machines, and car rental agencies that hire out hand-controlled cars.

All disabled people can ask for an escort through the terminal formalities and onto the plane. Blind passengers *should* do so. They may take their guide dogs, but these will usually have to be carried with other pets in the cargo hold, and will not be exempt from quarantine laws. Deaf passengers can request written instructions and announcements to be provided for them on the ground and in the air.

Airline and airport staff are usually well drilled in assisting disabled travellers, especially those in wheelchairs. Help with baggage is as important a consideration as personal help; through his carrier, a disabled passenger can book a cart and porter at the points of departure, stopover and arrival. Collapsible wheelchairs will be carried in the cargo hold free of charge, and the airline will provide its own wheelchairs to take disabled passengers to the aircraft while their own are being loaded. Battery-operated wheelchairs can be carried only if the wet-cell batteries are packed separately in the correct way. Some airline or airport authorities operate ambulance services to convey disabled passengers from the terminal airside to the aircraft.

Airlines may also be able to provide special loading devices to lift disabled passengers from the ground to the aircraft. These usually consist of an enclosed room-like unit that protects its occupant from the weather. It is mounted on a crane resembling a fork-lift truck, and can lift a person in a wheelchair, or on a stretcher, to the aircraft door. Because airline aisles are narrow, the passenger will have to transfer to a special chair to be installed in the cabin seat, and because of the time involved in installing a handicapped person in his seat, he will be expected to check in ahead of the other passengers.

Airlines often require handicapped people to be attended, and their attendants will usually be required to pay full fare. Stretcher cases will usually need — and have to pay for — four seats and an attendant, usually at the first-class rate or higher; ambulance services are costly in many countries. Before undertaking any journey by air, handicapped travellers should make enquiries to find out how much the necessary extra services en route are likely to cost.

Booking special facilities

Airlines and airports can arrange and provide all sorts of special services, not only those listed here, but also special meals and other services in-flight (pages 64–65), but only if passengers give prior notification of their needs. The airline must know at least two days in advance, and preferably earlier, when the booking is made. The longer they have to prepare, the better the service they can provide. Having informed the airline or a travel agent of your requirements, check again shortly before the date of your flight.

Most airports publish publicity sheets detailing the special services they offer, and airlines and travel agents may also be able to provide information. In the Gazetteer (page 210) the various special facilities offered to passengers by most of the world's major airports are listed for quick and easy reference.

Duty-free goods

Duty-free goods began as a concession to sailors and travellers who needed to stock up on food for long voyages. Alcoholic drinks and tobacco products, highly taxed in many countries, are the fastest-selling items, but, depending on the country and the size of the airport, a wide variety of goods normally subject to duty and taxes may be sold: souvenirs, clothing, cameras, watches and electrical goods *can* be bargains. In Japan, for example, electronic equipment, televisions and cameras are particularly cheap. At the duty-free shop at Amsterdam's Schiphol Airport (the largest in the world, and the cheapest in Europe) antiques (which usually carry no duty) and even cars are sold.

Duty-free goods may perhaps be more accurately termed "duty-reduced" goods. Although the stock sold may be free of excise duty, it is not always free of local taxes, so it is essential to calculate the cost of a prospective buy in your own currency, to ensure that the goods will be cheaper than at home. At Frankfurt Airport's duty-free shop, where VAT is chargeable on sales to EEC passengers, prices are higher than at other duty-free shops; wine can be bought more cheaply at a landside shop.

Profits from duty-free sales play a large part in the revenue of some airports, and this can affect the prices of the goods sold there. Heathrow Airport is thought to take a cut of 35 to 45 per cent of the gross takings and this, supplemented by income from other concessionaires, accounts for a high proportion of the airport's income. The alternative to this practice would be higher landing fees, or airport taxes, both of which would be passed on to passengers. Schiphol's duty-free shop, on the other hand, runs at a considerable loss, the management having assumed that this will encourage future trade.

Seemingly cheap foreign goods may prove expensive once Customs duty and sales tax or VAT is paid in the home country. Check with your national Customs office for details of duty and other taxes on goods you may want to buy abroad. Rules in the USA are complex, so if in doubt, check with the US authorities, the airline, or a travel agent.

Check, also, on what you are allowed to take *into* foreign countries; citizens of the USA frequently have guns confiscated at the UK Customs. Keep receipts for all purchases, and also for any new items you may take abroad, as proof of origin.

The duty-free shop is located on the airside of the air terminal; only passengers who have passed through Customs may shop there, and, once purchased, the goods are put into sealed bags which should not be opened until after you have left the country. If you want to open your duty-free drinks in flight, ask the cabin staff for permission. Some airlines may object, and in some countries, such as the USA, it is illegal. A smaller selection of duty-free goods — usually drinks, perfume and tobacco — may be sold in flight.

Other shops on the airport landside sell a range of goods, generally more expensive than in town: fruit and souvenirs tend to be particularly highly priced. There are sometimes special duty-free shops on the airport landside; in Germany all tourists are entitled to an export discount, and many shops in London will charge tax-discounted prices on goods sent directly out of the country.

Despite the commercial character of duty-free shops, few countries are prepared to let homecoming travellers shop duty-free on arrival. Goods sold free of the country's excise duty are technically for export — you may bring back an allowance, but may not purchase that allowance at home.

Enplaning

Before boarding an international flight passengers must have passed through Customs, passport control and sometimes security checks; there may be a last-minute security check at the boarding gate.

There are restrictions on the amount of currency travellers can take out of some countries, notably some Eastern bloc countries. Convert any excess before leaving for the airport; if there are no exchange facilities on the airport, any currency you have may be confiscated before you leave the country. Receipts for travellers' cheques cashed may be demanded.

Not all airports conduct security checks, and the checks vary considerably in nature and thoroughness. At some, bags are passed through X-ray viewers, and must be opened if unidentifiable objects are seen. At others, all bags are searched by hand. The X-rays used in baggage checks are weak, but they can fog photographic film if the film is subjected to several checks in the course of a journey. They may also present some slight risk to equipment containing electronic circuitry, such as calculators, radios and cameras. Carry such items in the cabin bags or clear plastic bags, and ask the security staff to hand check it. Cameras should not be loaded: they may be opened by security staff.

At many airports, passengers are examined with a metal-detector. This may be a loop that is run over the body, or a walk-through metal frame. It emits no radiation and cannot cause any damage. In particular, it will not damage heart pacemakers or magnetic credit cards.

Flight announcements are usually broadcast all over the terminal — even in the toilets, coffee bars and restaurants and duty-free shops. Listen for the flight number, which will precede every announcement.

In flight

The amount of baggage passengers may carry aboard an airliner is limited, not because it may weigh too much but because excessive amounts of baggage in the cabin could make it uncomfortable and possibly dangerous in an emergency. Generally, passengers are allowed one bag, a handbag, a coat and umbrella, a camera or binoculars, reading matter, baby food and a baby-carrier. Stow baggage as quickly and thoroughly as possible after boarding. There are overhead racks, and space beneath the seat in front. Some US planes, catering for hurried executives, have a baggage compartment in the cabin for overnight bags.

Cigarette lighters are permitted in the cabin, but do not take a filled liquid-fuel lighter on board: it may leak at the reduced pressure of the cabin at altitude. Do not carry cans of spare lighter fuel or try to recharge a gas lighter in flight; boxed matches are safer than book matches.

An old cabin staff trick for preventing ears from "popping" during takeoff consists of yawning and swallowing, following by pinching the nostrils, then closing the mouth and blowing. Sucking the sweets distributed by the cabin staff may help.

In-flight entertainment

Newspapers and magazines, including the airline's in-flight magazine, stationery, toys and children's books are likely to be available on request. If you want to write letters, be choosy about the kind of pen you use: fountain pens can leak at the pressures at high altitudes.

Portable radios may not be switched on in flight; it is often said they could interfere with the aircraft's radio. A personal stereo for playing tapes of your choice causes no such problems. Electronic calculators can also be used.

On one domestic US service, the in-flight entertainment begins on the ground where passengers can watch flight-deck activity until after take-off on short-circuit TV. Movies are usually shown on long flights; family and mature films may be shown in different parts of the cabin. The sound track is heard over headsets plugged into consoles on the seat armrests, and these can also be used to listen to music and other entertainment from a choice of around ten recorded channels. Popular and classical music, country and western, children's songs and comedy can all be dialled up. Lufthansa offer a channel giving isometric exercises which the passenger can do without moving from the seat. Some airlines have tapes that give basic lessons in the language of the destination country.

Children

Baby-care equipment up to about 26 pounds can be carried in addition to the normal baggage allowance. Mothers with small babies or more than one child will be given seats, on request, at the back of the cabin or near the emergency exits, where there is more leg room than in other parts of the cabin. Many airliners have special fold-down tables, and supplies of nappies (diapers) and talcum powder in the toilets for baby-changing. Certain baby foods can be supplied by the airline, or they will prepare those you have brought yourself if you give ample warning.

Unaccompanied minors will be entertained — and given special meals if a request is made in advance — and the cabin crew always will keep an eye on them to make sure that they are not lonely, nervous or bored. Some airlines have clubs for junior travellers, with badges, membership cards and magazines. They may provide log books in which the members have their mileages on each flight recorded by the captain. And there is a chance that on some airlines (other than on US airlines, where it is forbidden) visitors, including children, will be allowed onto the flight deck for short periods.

Caring for the disabled

Wheelchairs are usually carried free of charge, and are stowed in the hold. The airlines provide wheelchairs for deplaning as they do for enplaning; disabled passengers enplane first but deplane last.

Toilet facilities on board the aircraft are the greatest problem for the disabled person. The cabin crew will not take responsibility for assisting passengers with toilet equipment, so that use of the toilet may be impossible for an immobile, unaccompanied person. Medical advice may succeed in mitigating discomfort, by modifying eating patterns, or prescribing medicines. People who can move around should ask when booking for seats positioned near a toilet. Passengers are rarely permitted to use crutches on board the aircraft. They have to be carried in the hold, as they could be dangerous in turbulence.

Diabetics and people with heart complaints should notify the airline of their condition, and carry their medicines in their hand-baggage where it is accessible. Oxygen must be ordered at least 24 hours in advance; private oxygen supplies can travel as cargo only if properly packed and labelled.

If there is the slightest doubt about a passenger flying, the final decision rests with the captain. Although cabin crews always have emergency and first-aid training, it is standard procedure to ask if there is a doctor among the passengers if any person becomes ill en route.

Catering and service

Special diets (which can include salt-free, diabetic and dietetic ulcer as well as vegetarian, Moslem, kosher, kedassia, Hindu and slimming meals) should be ordered when booking, or at least 24 hours before departure. Some airlines carry a few special diets in case a passenger may have forgotten or did not have time to make a request.

Do not be tempted to eat too much, because pressure changes can cause indigestion in flight. First and business passengers will have more spacious and more comfortable seats than economy (coach) class. On some of the wide-bodied jets there are bar-lounges up or down stairs; on some, first class passengers leave their seats to eat in a dining area. The extra cost of the first-class ticket is reflected in the comfort, service and menu (see pages 64–65). Most airlines offer free drinks and more service in the first-class cabin. Members of airline clubs will benefit from reduced boarding problems and excess baggage fees, but are entitled to no special benefits in flight.

At the other extreme is the "no frills" service offered by many charter operators and on Richard Branson's Virgin Atlantic. Passengers pay extra for meals on these flights, and often choose to take their own. It is wise to avoid taking sticky, crumbly or smelly foods, and plastic bags should be taken for remains.

Overnight

Blankets and pillows are available for passengers who wish to sleep, and the seats can be tilted back far enough for tolerably comfortable sleep. If the aircraft is flying into the dawn, blinds can be drawn down.

Soap, talcum powder and cologne are provided for use in the morning. Cabin staff will supply electric shavers. Before the aircraft lands the passengers may be given hot towels to help them wake up, unstiffen and face the outside air.

Transit passengers changing planes between stages of an international journey do not always pass through a baggage claim, Customs or passport control, but they may be subjected to a security check before boarding the next flight.

If your bags are damaged or lost in transit, act immediately. Get a property irregularity report (PIR) from the airline that handled the latest stage of your journey, fill it in, return it to them and keep a copy for yourself. That carrier is responsible for carrying your claim through to its conclusion, even if another carrier is responsible for the damage or loss.

The PIR is not a claim. You must make a claim for damage within seven days, and for loss within 21 days. The airline must provide you with the necessary claim forms; if they fail to do so, write them a detailed letter, specifying the contents of your baggage.

Immigration control may demand evidence that your visit is really for its declared purpose (holiday, business or study), and that you have the financial means to support yourself during your stay. Return air bookings, hotel reservations and invitations to stay with friends are all useful. The landing cards filled in by foreign arrivals to many countries are collated with the records of departing passengers, so there is a record of those who overstay.

Customs officials have the right to search your baggage, and to require you to unpack and repack your bags. Goods on which duty must be paid are impounded until they are paid for. If you are returning to your home country, you should have receipts available for anything you have bought abroad, as well as any valuables you took with you, to prove they were not purchased abroad. Before you leave the air terminal, reconfirm any return or onward booking.

Health hints

Air travel today is more comfortable and more streamlined than ever before. But even the most experienced traveller can fall prey to various disorders. These range from air sickness or fatigue to the now renowned executive bugbear known as jet-lag. All these problems can, however, be either prevented or at least greatly eased.

Fatigue
During or after a flight fatigue is common. It is caused by the length of the journey and also frequently by pre-flight anxiety or excitement. Rest and relax before flying. See to pre-flight preparations such as immunization and vaccination well in advance, and avoid too hectic a schedule on the day before the flight.

Air sickness
Caused by a bumpy ride (and by anxiety and excitement) sickness is sometimes experienced in aircraft, just as it is in cars and boats. Because modern aircraft fly above bad weather, it is now an infrequent ailment, affecting probably not more than one in a thousand travellers.

But turbulence can upset the labyrinth mechanism of the inner ear — part of the organ of balance — and cause sickness. Keep the head as still as possible on the headrest. Avoid fried and fatty foods, excess alcohol and smoking. Ask a doctor's advice on sickness tablets, particularly in pregnancy. The effective drugs include hyoscine, cyclizine, diphenhydramine, meclozine and promethazine.

Pressurization problems
An aircraft cabin is a communal space suit; air is pumped in to keep the pressure at the outside equivalent of 8,000 feet altitude. For technical reasons it is not possible to achieve ground-level pressure in the aircraft, and the difference can cause discomfort when gases in the body, especially in the intestines, expand.

Palliatives are not to overeat, to avoid carbonated drinks and to wear loose clothing and shoes. Change of pressure during takeoff or landing can affect the ears. A popping sensation is common, or earache or even temporary deafness. These can all be overcome by constant yawning or swallowing. Babies achieve the same end by crying noisily. Anyone with a heavy cold or sinus trouble is prone to sinus pain or earache during a flight, particularly during the descent. Nose drops help but, if possible, avoid flying. Smokers in particular may be affected by the cabin atmosphere as they have a small amount of carbon monoxide in their blood. As the oxygen decreases so this amount increases, sometimes causing a headache or a feeling of being "one degree under". The remedy is to cut down smoking.

Dehydration
The aircraft's pumped-in atmosphere is slightly dry. As a result dehydration can occur. Combat this by drinking as much fluid as possible. Alcohol increases dehydration, so avoid it in flight and be particularly abstemious on long flights to hot countries; dehydration is a serious problem in hot climates.

Swollen ankles
Sitting in the same seat on a long flight puts continuous pressure on the veins in the thighs. People with varicose veins are most affected and their feet and ankles may swell slightly. Wear loose roomy shoes, preferably lace-ups, and walk up and down the cabin periodically.

Jet-lag
This affects travellers flying east-west or west-east journeys in which they change time zones. Biological

rhythms have a programme of around 24 hours, and jet-lag is the failure of the body to adjust its own routine to a clock that may, for instance, bring darkness — and bedtime — ten hours earlier or later than usual. Eating, sleeping and excreting may all be uncomfortably affected and mental reactions may also slow down considerably. The effects of jet-lag seem to be greater on eastbound flights than on westbound. Reactions can be slowed for two days following a ten-zone trip westward, and for three days after a similar eastward trip.

Some companies ban their executives from taking major decisions within 24 hours of a five-hour time change. At least one airline instructs its crews to keep their watches on home time regardless of what time zone they are in. The most cautious medical advice is that one full day of recovery is needed for each five-hour time change. Travellers should try to go to bed as near as possible to their usual bedtime on the first night after arriving; quick-acting aperient pills can allay constipation until the bowels become accustomed to a new daily routine.

The short-stay traveller, such as the businessman continually on the move, is most at risk from jet-lag; the long-stay traveller on holiday has enough time to acclimatize. Babies of up to three months are the most fortunate — their eating and sleeping cycles seem to be unaffected.

Medical problems

All the previous forms of discomfort can temporarily affect the healthy traveller but can be prevented or overcome easily. Diabetics should eat their flight meals at the same time as meals at home; the elderly and anyone with heart trouble should avoid smoking. Above all anyone who is in doubt about his state of health should consult a doctor before flying.

The air traveller's commandments
1. Plan the flight well in advance, taking a day flight if possible, and/or arriving when it is bedtime in the zone of origin; adapt gradually.
2. Lead as quiet a life as possible during the 24 hours before the flight.
3. Cut smoking before and while flying.
4. Drink little alcohol in flight.
5. Avoid the temptation to overeat during the flight.
6. Drink plenty of non-alcoholic, non-sparkling fluids during the flight.
7. Wear loose-fitting, comfortable clothes and shoes.
8. Have a 24-hour rest period after a five-hour time change.
9. Never attend important functions, nor take important decisions, after an east/west or west/east flight.
10. Consider taking a mild aperient and mild, quick-acting sedative if crossing time zones.

Buley's formula
ICAO calculate the number of days of rest needed to overcome jet-lag as:

$$\frac{T/2 + (Z-4) + C_d + C_a}{10}$$

T = hours in transit
Z = number of time-zones crossed*
(take this as 0 if Z is 4 or less)
C_d and C_a are the departure and arrival coefficients listed in the table blow.

Time of day	Departure coefficient	Arrival coefficient
0800–1157	0 = good	4 = bad
1200–1759	1 = fair	2 = fair
1800–2159	3 = poor	0 = good
2200–0059	4 = bad	1 = fair
0100–0759	3 = poor	3 = poor

Example
A traveller leaves Montreal at 1800 hours local time ($C_d = 3$), spends nine hours travelling, and arrives in Paris at 0800 hours ($C_a = 4$) having crossed five time zones. The number of days' rest he needs is:

$$\frac{\frac{9}{2} + 1 + 3 + 4}{10} = 1.25 \text{ days}$$

Rounded up to the nearest half-day = 1.5 days.

*See page 209 for time-zone map.

Fighting the fear of flying

Twenty-five million Americans are afraid to fly — one in six of the adult population. Some are not only fearful, but phobic. One difference between a fear and a phobia is in the intensity; a phobia is a disproportionate fear, an exaggerated or irrational feeling, beyond mere anxiety or discomfiture. Phobic air travellers see themselves losing control, suffocating, panicking, falling, crashing or (at the very least) making a fool of themselves.

For both the phobic flier and the merely fearful there are three ways of confronting the ghost. The first is education, or enlightenment. The second is relaxation; and thirdly, there are some techniques and tips that can work well for everyone.

Education

"Nothing is to be feared. It is only to be understood." Understand, then, that every year throughout the world more than 11,000 aircraft carry nearly 1,000 million people from 1,000 airports without incident or accident. According to Lloyd's of London it is 25 times safer to travel by air than by car.

Relaxation

A completely relaxed passenger cannot be fearful. Fear and relaxation are opposite states. Tension and fear adversely affect every muscle, organ, gland, nerve and cell in the body. Relaxation shifts the body motor to idle and all the components throttle back. Learning a simple breathing relaxation procedure helps to curb overwhelming anxiety. It also enables fearful travellers to prepare for comfortable flights.

At home, find a quiet place and settle into a comfortable chair with an arm and head rest. People who are frightened of flying try not to put their full weight down, but for the purposes of this exercise it is essential to do this, with feet uncrossed flat on the floor or supported on some kind of stool. Wriggle as far back into the seat as possible. Make sure jaw muscles are loose, teeth are not touching and lips are slightly parted. Nudge intruding thoughts aside.

Begin the first of three deep breaths by inhaling through the nose, mouth, or both. Inhale fully and hold that inhalation while silently counting to three. Then exhale, silently counting to three. Then exhale completely, saying aloud, "Relax, let go". Breathe normally for a few moments and luxuriate in a refreshing feeling of passivity. Take the second deep breath, repeating the same procedure, but inhaling and exhaling more fully. Relax and let go even more. Then breathe normally.

On the third and final inhalation-exhalation, consider increasing the volume of air by consciously extending the diaphragm. On exhaling, contract the diaphragm muscles so that more air is expelled. Exhale tension, stress and fear. Let go.

Practise the exercise several times before going on to desensitize past feelings about flying. If muscular tension persists, try counting from ten to one and slowly letting go of that tension. Think of a pleasant, peaceful place and fantasize being there, unworried and unafraid.

To learn to be comfortable when flying it is essential to confront fear. Relax with the breathing exercises and review a previous frightening experience or an anticipated one as rationally as possible. Stop any time fear begins to reassert itself. The next day it will be possible to recall the experience with less emotional involvement. From a relaxed position, keep examining your feelings about flying until familiarity dispels fear.

Projection

Once past fears have been confronted, conditioning and programming for a future flight can begin. Go to a deep level of relaxation with the breathing exercise and select some city or area that has a strong appeal for you. Maybe there is someone you would particularly like to visit there. Recall all previous happy, warm thoughts about being there and imagine enjoying the place and the people.

The next conditioning step is to envisage boarding the plane to make the trip and experiencing a mixture of excitement and fear; it will be difficult to differentiate between them. Choose excitement! Remember it is quite normal to be nervous.

Imagine that someone dear to you, who knows you well, is on board. The seat belt sign comes on and the flight becomes slightly choppy. Pretend that the plane is travelling over a cobbled road in the sky. Any feeling of being distraught or overly disturbed, experienced on past flights, will be reduced. It is quite normal to feel uncomfortable, but not unsafe.

Tips

Visit airports. Observe the different makes of aircraft. Park on the perimeter and watch the planes take off and land. Find out what kind you will be travelling on and learn to recognize it. All are safe.

Some people prefer morning flights so they can get up and go without spending the whole day uneasily. Allow a *minimum* of one hour for parking, buying a ticket or checking in, and security screening. Rushing exaggerates anxiety. Buy a magazine as a distraction.

On stepping aboard, tell the flight attendant that you are fearful, uncomfortable or terrified of flying and that you would like to take a peek into the flight deck. Generally, anyone who makes this request is welcomed by a relaxed crew.

After settling into the seat, do the deep breathing exercises. This singular procedure has worked effectively even for the most sceptical. Do it with your eyes closed. Turn inward for the strength that is waiting to be tapped. Some vestige of anxiety and fear is bound to remain but the important thing is that the previously fearful flier will find that his or her perception of flying has been updated.

In the air, listen for the sound of the landing-gears retracting; then the no-smoking sign will be turned off, the engine power will decrease, and the flaps will be retracted, usually in that order. As soon as possible stand up and stretch. Move about the cabin. Experience the triumph: you have conquered the fear of flying.

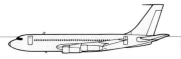

Aircraft noises
Today's jets are quiet. Modern turbofan engines are hardly audible in the sound-proofed cabin, but the bumps, bangs and changes in pitch that can be heard on takeoff and landing should be reassuring.

● **The first movement** may be under the control of a tug which pushes the aircraft back from the gate. There are bound to be mild thumps as this is first coupled to the nose landing gear and then disconnected.

● **To start taxiing** the pilot opens up the engines a little, making them audible for the first time. As the aircraft rolls — perhaps at over 60 mph, though in a 747 it will seem quite slow — there will be small noises, especially if the taxiway is not very smooth.

● **For takeoff** the engines are opened up to near full power, and this will be very obvious. Acceleration should be rapid. It is not unknown for odd sounds to be caused by a falling plate or other object in one of the galleys! After rotation the climb may seem very steep, and seconds later the landing gears may make thumping noises as they are retracted.

● **After landing** a jet may suddenly open up the engines to full power in reverse thrust, to help slow down the aircraft.

Air cargo

In contrast with passengers, who utilize far more space than is economic for their weight, freight containers require little more space than their own volume. Specially shaped to the contours of modern aircraft, they can be handled quickly, reducing pilferage and insurance rates and easing Customs clearance. They can be packed with all kinds of cargo, which is generally despatched in small consignments.

The organization and operation of air cargo services is now a highly specialized business. Except in remote areas, the days of throwing a mail bag or two in the back of the cabin or baggage compartment are long past. Due to the increase in the size and range of aircraft and the standardization of containers, air cargo carriage worldwide has expanded from a negligible total load in the 1950s to around 30 million ton miles in the 1980s. Although the price per ton mile of carrying goods by air is higher than that for any other form of transport, users of air cargo services value the reliability, frequency, security and particularly the speed of delivery offered by the air carrier. A fast delivery may permit a valuable piece of equipment to commence production earlier, reduce the length of time capital is tied up in stock in transit, and the perishable goods industries dealing in food and flowers depend on it.

Airport cargo terminals are similar to Post Office sorting offices. Full

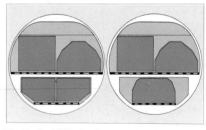

The Boeing 747F, the all-cargo version of the wide-bodied jet, has a hinged nose to permit containerized cargo to be loaded straight in. Standard rectangular containers (**1**) come in lengths up to 40 ft; pallets (**2**) are metal sheets on which loads are assembled and hold in place by nets; igloos (**3**) are pallets with rigid sides contoured, like LD3 containers (**4**) to the fuselage.

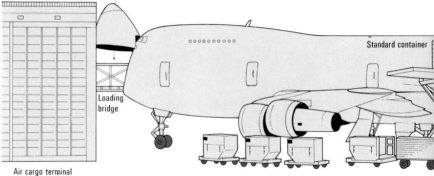

Standard container

Loading bridge

Air cargo terminal

automation in the huge cargo centre operated by Lufthansa at Frankfurt Airport means that over 4,500 items can be handled per hour by only 24 men. Goods and mail in a steady stream pass through import and export sections, each overseen by a separate Customs department. The processes along the way: receiving, routeing, stacking while awaiting shipment, recalling and despatching for loading, are controlled with minimum human supervision, by electronics. Computers keep automatic track of every packet that enters the terminal complex. The London Airport Cargo Electronic Data Processing scheme monitors the 800,000 or more tons of cargo handled annually at Heathrow, so that shippers and consignees alike can plan well ahead.

Air cargo terminals provide special facilities for the storage of many different types of cargo, including cages for animals and surveillance vaults for valuables. Vast amounts of valuable cargo such as jewels, travellers' cheques, precious metals, bullion, cigarettes and alcoholic drinks pass through air cargo terminals in small parcels, an easy target for pilferage. Radioactive chemicals are kept in lead-lined inner rooms, fragile cargo is stored on separate racks, and food and perishable goods in cold or refrigerated stores. Dangerous goods such as explosives, corrosives, flammable and toxic materials are carried regularly, but are subject to rigorous controls.

The enormous capacity of the 747F has revolutionized the air cargo industry. It can carry a maximum payload of about 260,000 pounds 4,000 miles, well beyond transatlantic range, without a refuelling stop.

Both freighter and convertible 747s have a mechanized cargo-handling system on the main deck. Pallets or containers can be loaded straight in on a motor-driven roller by two men, one at the nose and one inside, who can load and unload the aircraft in as little as 30 minutes.

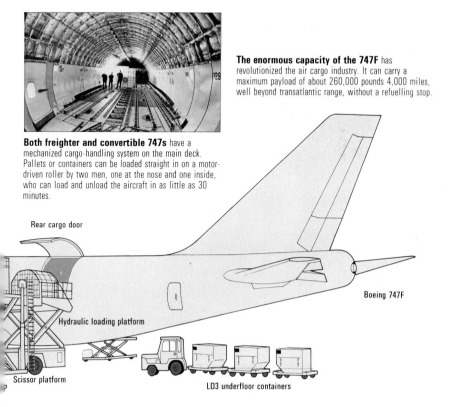

Rear cargo door

Hydraulic loading platform

Scissor platform

LD3 underfloor containers

Boeing 747F

Cargo consignments are assembled on large pallets — metal sheets ten feet by seven feet, sometimes covered by security "igloos". The whole assembly is bound by stout netting to prevent internal movement in transit. Bulky consignments are loaded in large containers. Mechanized rollers carry the containers from the make-up floor into the aircraft via a truck with a mechanized roller platform.

The airliner will carry as much cargo as the passenger and fuel load will allow. A narrow-bodied Boeing 707 can carry up to 40 tons of freight; the wide-bodied 747 has more space in its lower holds than the entire 707 and can take 16 tomes of cargo plus a full passenger load. An all-cargo 747 can carry nearly 140 tons.

The interchangeable passenger/freighter aircraft, sometimes called a "combi", is designed so that whole blocks of seats mounted on pallets, plus galleys, can be removed, and roller-equipped freight floors fitted in less than an hour. This flexibility makes such an aircraft an attractive proposition. Wide-bodied aircraft are costly to buy, but relatively cheap to operate, and a properly integrated fleet of these and the older all-freight aircraft can be profitable.

Scheduled services are frequently underbooked, and cargo provides the profit. Provided that adequate terminal facilities for rapid unloading, clearance and despatch can be provided at airports in developing countries, air cargo will multiply.

The BAe-200QT (Quiet Trader) is a side-loading freighter version of the BAe-200 airliner, which is itself an 8-ft longer "stretched" version of the BaA-100.

Just like the fish from which its name is taken, the Aero Spacelines Super Guppy ingests its cargo whole. This super-freighter has a hold 111 ft 6 in long, 25 ft 1 in wide, and 25 ft 6 in high, making a volume of 39,000 cu ft of usable space as compared with 23,630 in the Boeing 747. It can carry whole wings and fuselage sections of Airbus aircraft to the assembly plant. Developed from the 1940s Boeing Stratofreighter, it is powered by four turbo-prop engines, and has a 500-mile range fully loaded.

Maintenance and servicing

The rate at which streams of aircraft check in and out of the world's airports is little short of miraculous. Each departure is only the tip of an iceberg of organization designed to ready an airliner for takeoff.

Maintenance is the most important pre-flight activity. The present systems are the result of some 70 years' experience which began with the flimsy, fabric-covered, wire-braced wooden structures in which men first taught themselves to fly. Frequently they were wrecked in the process, to be rebuilt and fly again, perhaps the same day. From these fragile beginnings a system of repair and mantenance has evolved, carried out by aircraft maintenance engineers licensed by aviation authorities. They are trained to overhaul airframes, engines and systems.

Satisfactory maintenance of any advanced machinery originates with the manufacturer. To convince potential customers of the safety of a new aircraft he must satisfy both himself and them that it will be granted a Certificate of Airworthiness by the relevant national authorities. Manufacturers compile maintenance manuals and Service Bulletins to advise on the maintenance of aircraft and their engines when in service, and these are updated from reports from the airline pilots that fly them.

The manufacturer's maintenance schedule lays down the periods in which each part of an aircraft must be inspected, the type and degree of

Giant docks are needed for maintenance access to large jets. The one above, for DC-10s, is 78 ft high and built outside the hangar to enclose the tail and centre engine. The similar dock on the left is for TriStars. Such docks incorporate electric, hydraulic and compressed-air power. It has five working levels set at different heights to give access to various parts of the plane, and each level has floor sections which fit close to the aircraft.

Maintenance and servicing/2

inspection necessary, and it also rules on the replacement of individual items according to the number of landings, flying hours, and other criteria. It forms a basis for the proposals for maintaining his fleet which the airline operator must in turn submit to the airworthiness authority. Approval depends on his making satisfactory provision for such matters as suitable hangarage and workshops, tools and test equipment, quality and reliability control, and materials and training.

Enormous hangars are needed to house the wide-bodied airliners. The docks, huge stagings built around the aircraft so that every part is accessible for inspection and repair, are equipped with working platforms at many levels, built-in lighting, and lifts and conveyors for personnel, tools and spares.

The time needed to inspect and overhaul an airliner varies with its size and complexity. Aircraft usually have light checks at 50-60 flying hours, overnight checks at 300-600 hours, and full overhauls every 3,600 flying hours.

Components which will eventually need replacement, particularly the moving parts, must be easy to remove and replace. The BAe One-Eleven's tailplane (stabilizer), for example, is the aircraft's largest moving component and even this can be changed during an eight-hour overnight stop. Condition-monitoring is a system under which an aircraft, its components and systems, are analysed from pilots' reports of technical delays and

The quick turnaround is essential to airline profitability: an airliner is a vastly expensive piece of capital equipment which must be kept flying for as many hours as possible to earn its keep. Between landing and takeoff it must be unloaded, cleaned, loaded up with passengers, baggage, food, water, duty-free goods and cargo, and refuelled in the shortest possible time.

The Lockheed TriStar is designed so that 273 passengers and their baggage can be unloaded, and the plane refuelled, serviced and reloaded, within a normal turnaround time of 30 minutes. To do this, 14 or more vehicles may be assembled around the plane at once. Routine maintenance checks of the airframe, engines, tyre pressures, lights, brakes and other essentials take about 25 minutes; minor faults reported by the flight crew are corrected. Refuelling at a rate of about 20 gals a second takes 21 minutes. All the other servicing goes on simultaneously. Auxiliary power units ease congestion on the apron by replacing ground power units, air-conditioning trucks and units for starting up the engines.

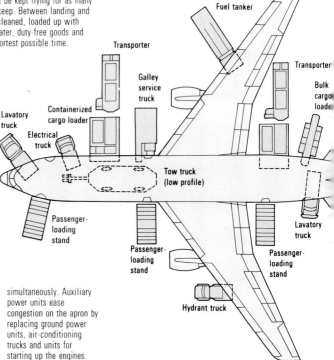

Fuel tanker

Transporter

Transporter

Galley service truck

Bulk cargo loader

Lavatory truck

Containerized cargo loader

Electrical truck

Tow truck (low profile)

Passenger-loading stand

Lavatory truck

Passenger-loading stand

Passenger-loading stand

Hydrant truck

unscheduled engine shut-downs, and inspected at predetermined intervals to establish "alert levels" for the future repair and replacement of parts, eliminating all unnecessary removal and dismantling. Non-destructive testing of vital components using X-rays, ultrasonic and magnetic particle methods detects fatigue-induced cracks before they become serious.

Maintenance programmes for older aircraft especially are dominated by numbers of "lifted" items, each having a "never exceed" time between overhauls. These items are highly stressed and critically important components which may be subjected to corrosion or severe vibration, or both. In all cases fatigue is a major consideration. Wing spars need inspecting at 3,500 flying-hour intervals, and cabin windows and other openings in the fuselage must be inspected every 300 flying hours.

Modern aircraft are less troublesome. All functioning items are linked to on-board computers. They are ignored unless a problem arises, and this in itself promotes reliability. In 1988 an RB.211 engine on the right wing of a TWA TriStar had flown over 10,000,000 miles since new in 1982 without being disturbed for maintenance.

Aircraft performance is affected by dirt deposited on the outer skin in polluted airspace above industrial areas, which raises fuel consumption, so aircraft are washed in giant hangar bays like car washes.

Servicing connections are designed to international standards and are positioned to ensure a practical distribution of servicing vehicles around the plane. The TriStar was designed for a *fast* turnaround time of 20 minutes, or even less on a short through-stop. A pre-flight inspection, carried out by the crew of all aircraft before a flight, takes the form of a walk-round external check for fuel, oil and hydraulic fluid leaks, and to ensure the security of all removable panels, controls, flaps, landing-gears and so on. Away from the maintenance base, minor repairs can be undertaken on the spot. Even an engine may be changed, and passengers may, occasionally, see an extra engine carried beneath the wing in a pod, for delivery to an overseas maintenance point. Some service points on the Lockheed TriStar **right** are as follows:

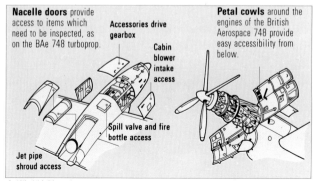

Nacelle doors provide access to items which need to be inspected, as on the BAe 748 turboprop.

Accessories drive gearbox

Cabin blower intake access

Spill valve and fire bottle access

Jet pipe shroud access

Petal cowls around the engines of the British Aerospace 748 provide easy accessibility from below.

1 Windshield washer system

2, 3 Oil fillers for air cycle turbine

4 Potable water filling point

5 Pneumatic power units

6 Pressure fuelling points

7 Hydraulic service panel

8 Gravity-fuelling points

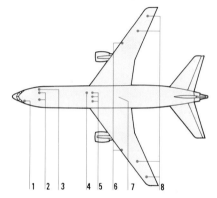

Airport vehicles

A fascinating range of vehicles can be seen at any airport. Some, such as the trucks with conspicuous "Follow me" signs to guide aircraft to their bays, are standard commercial vehicles. Many other special vehicles are harder to identify.

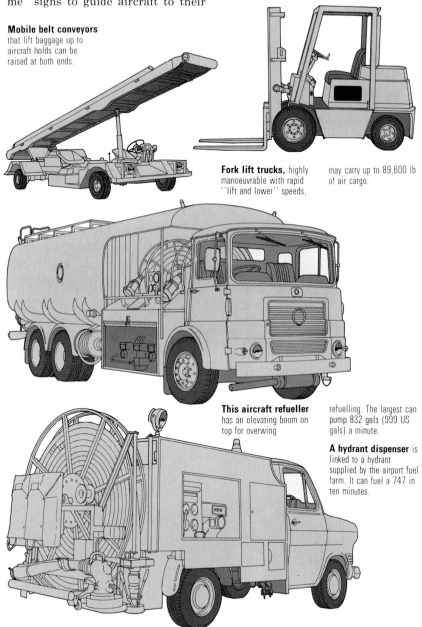

Mobile belt conveyors that lift baggage up to aircraft holds can be raised at both ends.

Fork lift trucks, highly manoeuvrable with rapid "lift and lower" speeds, may carry up to 89,600 lb of air cargo.

This aircraft refueller has an elevating boom on top for overwing refuelling. The largest can pump 832 gals (999 US gals) a minute.

A hydrant dispenser is linked to a hydrant supplied by the airport fuel farm. It can fuel a 747 in ten minutes.

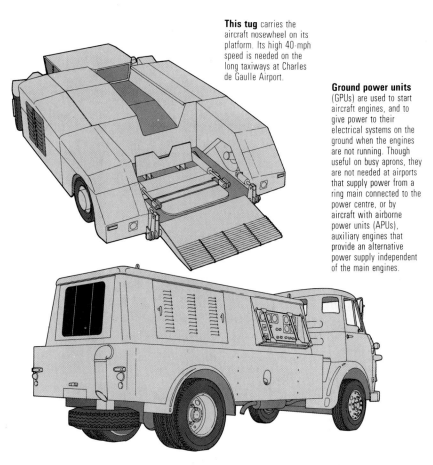

This tug carries the aircraft nosewheel on its platform. Its high 40-mph speed is needed on the long taxiways at Charles de Gaulle Airport.

Ground power units (GPUs) are used to start aircraft engines, and to give power to their electrical systems on the ground when the engines are not running. Though useful on busy aprons, they are not needed at airports that supply power from a ring main connected to the power centre, or by aircraft with airborne power units (APUs), auxiliary engines that provide an alternative power supply independent of the main engines.

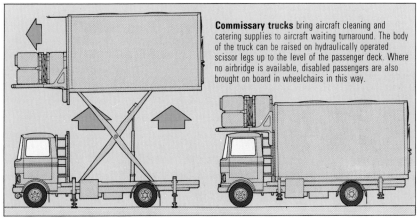

Commissary trucks bring aircraft cleaning and catering supplies to aircraft waiting turnaround. The body of the truck can be raised on hydraulically operated scissor legs up to the level of the passenger deck. Where no airbridge is available, disabled passengers are also brought on board in wheelchairs in this way.

Airport vehicles/2

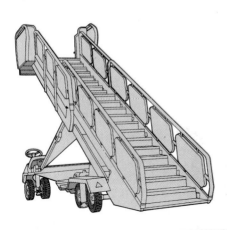

Self-propelled passenger steps adapt telescopically to any aircraft door height.

Self-propelled aerial platforms give easy access for aircraft maintenance.

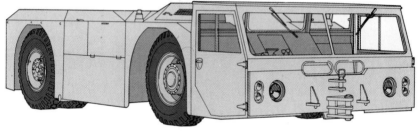

Heavy tugs, weighing an eighth of the 747s they pull, can have a single cab or one at each end. These can be raised and lowered to fit beneath different aircraft fuselages.

Push-out tugs are used to manoeuvre aircraft backward into and out of parking bays by attaching to the nosewheel and pushing it.

Drinking-water supply trucks holding 650 gals (780 US gals) or more can refill an aircraft tank at 20 gals (24 US gals) a minute.

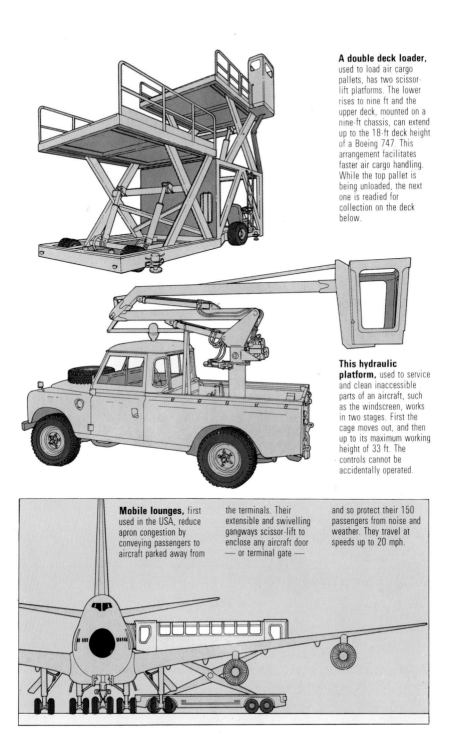

A double deck loader, used to load air cargo pallets, has two scissor-lift platforms. The lower rises to nine ft and the upper deck, mounted on a nine-ft chassis, can extend up to the 18-ft deck height of a Boeing 747. This arrangement facilitates faster air cargo handling. While the top pallet is being unloaded, the next one is readied for collection on the deck below.

This hydraulic platform, used to service and clean inaccessible parts of an aircraft, such as the windscreen, works in two stages. First the cage moves out, and then up to its maximum working height of 33 ft. The controls cannot be accidentally operated.

Mobile lounges, first used in the USA, reduce apron congestion by conveying passengers to aircraft parked away from the terminals. Their extensible and swivelling gangways scissor-lift to enclose any aircraft door — or terminal gate — and so protect their 150 passengers from noise and weather. They travel at speeds up to 20 mph.

Airport fire services

Seventy-five per cent of all aircraft accidents occur within half a mile of an airport. Aircraft fires are rare, but an airport is not permitted to operate without an efficient fire service.

Airport fire services will turn out on full emergency stand-by on the slightest indication that something is wrong with a landing plane: a deflated tyre, a circuit-breaker out in any important system, a warning light in the flight deck. They turn out on average once a day at a major airport, and are always on stand-by in bad weather or fog. During an emergency the fire service provides general emergency help, carrying stretchers (litters) and aiding disabled people.

Aircraft burn quickly, giving fire fighters under three minutes to reach them and carry out control and rescue operations. Until the 1960s, airport fire-fighting equipment consisted of little more than modified versions of that used by municipal fire services. Now, every major airport is equipped with rapid intervention vehicles (RIVs) able to reach the runways within two minutes of an alarm. Heavy duty vehicles are designed to cross rough round to reach a distant runway (usually by a circuitous route, because they cannot drive across runways in use) or the overshoot and undershoot areas where most fatalities occur.

No airport is awarded a licence unless it conforms to national standards based on ICAO recommendations, but each airport is equipped according to its own needs. Some Indian airports have tank-tracked tenders, and Auckland Airport in New Zealand uses hovercraft to negotiate mud flats at low tide.

This heavy-duty fire tender can discharge 9,000 gals (10,800 US gals) of water or foam a minute through its monitor, and 900 gals (1,080 US gals) through each of its two hand-lines, while moving forward or backward.

The light rescue unit carries 330 lb of dry powder sodium bicarbonate in two units pressurized by carbon dioxide. Each discharge pistol can eject powder at the rate of 3.3 lb per second over a range of 39 ft.

This heavy-duty airfield crash truck can be operated by one man, or carry a crew of five. It holds over 3,000 gals of water and over 360 gals of foam, and travels at 60 mph. It throws a 300 ft jet.

The tank holds 200 gals of foam concentrate and is designed so that the base slopes down to a sump.

Two 120-ft hoses of rubberized cloth are folded flat in open trays on each side.

RIVs are fast trucks that carry foam, water, medical and rescue equipment, and lights for use in fog and darkness. Their crews begin holding operations to contain the fire and clear escape routes. Heavy-duty foam tenders follow. They are large, but fast and manoeuvrable, and carry about ten times more foam than the RIVs. Turret-mounted foam guns ("blabbermouths") swivel to project the foam up to 300 feet.

Foam smothers the flames and cools the area around to prevent further outbreak of fire. Water is only really effective as a coolant. Spraying a blanket of foam on the runway to prevent a malfunctioning plane from catching fire on landing is now thought to be a waste of time, but foam is useful for fires that break out during refuelling, when a build-up of static electricity in the tank sparks the fuel. Kerosene is less inflammable than the fuels used by many airlines, but more expensive.

Powder is most effective on localized fires in wheels or tyres, or in electrical apparatus, but it produces toxic fumes on contact with foam. Inert vaporizing gases, such as Halon 1200, attack oxygen and are particularly useful for engine fires.

The emergency services are stationed at various points around the airfield, and are in radio contact with each other, the central station and the control tower.

Airport fire-fighters wear flame-resistant aluminized clothing and are equipped with breathing apparatus against smoke and the toxic fumes produced by burning furnishings in old aircraft. They train daily, and practise their craft on old fuselages in remote parts of the airfield.

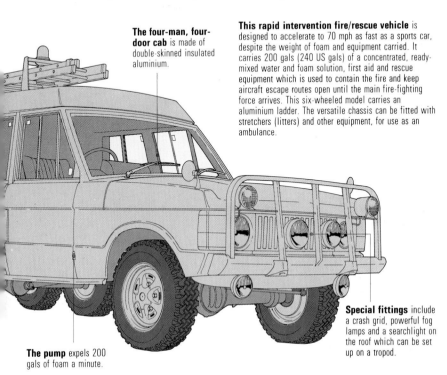

The four-man, four-door cab is made of double-skinned insulated aluminium.

This rapid intervention fire/rescue vehicle is designed to accelerate to 70 mph as fast as a sports car, despite the weight of foam and equipment carried. It carries 200 gals (240 US gals) of a concentrated, ready-mixed water and foam solution, first aid and rescue equipment which is used to contain the fire and keep aircraft escape routes open until the main fire-fighting force arrives. This six-wheeled model carries an aluminium ladder. The versatile chassis can be fitted with stretchers (litters) and other equipment, for use as an ambulance.

Special fittings include a crash grid, powerful fog lamps and a searchlight on the roof which can be set up on a tropod.

The pump expels 200 gals of foam a minute.

Keeping runways clear

Two millimetres of snow can affect the braking action of a runway so adversely as to make landing unsafe. Airport authorities in Switzerland and Austria have researched into surface heating to melt the snow as it falls but, using 200 watts of electricity per square yard, this method would be too costly for large areas.

Flush runway lights are easily obliterated by snow, but increasing their intensity may, initially, melt it. The French use the hot blast from a jet engine at Orly Airport to clear a 130-foot-wide path through fresh snow, but compacted snow and slush take much longer to clear. The system can also be used for de-icing and drying wet runways.

Powdery snow can be compacted and spread with hot sand or gravel to make a runway safe, but one inch of damp, heavy snow covering the runway of London's Gatwick Airport weighs 5,000 tons. This kind of snow freezes rock-hard when temperatures fall, and has to be cleared at once.

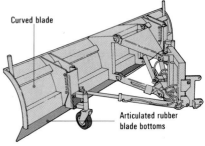

Curved blade

Articulated rubber blade bottoms

A runway snow-brush, below, can clear a heavy snowfall in one operation. Angled up to 45°, the 14-ft-long brush scatters snow up to 50 yds to either side. Variable speed control can be set to slow speeds for sweeping surface dirt, up to 550 rpm to clear heavy slush. By means of an air deflector, snow is thrown high to be carried away by the wind, or low to avoid blowback.

Snow cutters, top, clear snow drifts using rotating blades. Snow chips are directed into an ejection outlet in each drum, swept into the chutes by centrifugal force, and discharged to one side.

Snow ploughs, above, are specially shaped, and adjustable to left or right, to roll the snow and throw it to either side. The articulated rubber blades are designed to clear runway lights.

174

Mechanical clearance is the only solution to persistent heavy snowfall.

Snow clearance operations are carried out by chains or "congas" of vehicles. First, a high-speed runway sweeper makes swathes through the snow. Snow ploughs follow, moving the loose snow aside, and finally, snow blowers blow it clear.

Some airports have ice-alert systems to give visual and aural warning of the onset of freezing conditions. Anti-icing is carried out using polyglycol fluid dispensed from a vehicle with booms extending some 50 feet. About 500 gallons (600 US gallons) of fluid are needed to cover Gatwick's runway, at a cost of £2 ($4) a gallon, and the treatment takes about half an hour. Some runways are slightly cambered so that icemelt or rain can flow away, and flanked by loose gravel shoulders for complete drainage. Others have porous friction surface courses, or are banded with quarter-inch-deep grooves to break the surface film of water.

Snow-clearance machines are costly, but losses in revenue sustained by an airport closed by snow for one day would almost pay for the equipment needed to clear it. Snow sweepers have a dual role in clearing runways of debris that may be ingested into engines, or puncture tyres. Tyre rubber sticks to the lenses of flush runway lights, and these have to be cleaned by specialized machines with high-pressure water jets, or semi-automatic suction machines. The blast of jets at takeoff blows runway dust away, but at desert airports keeping the runways clear of sand is a major problem.

City street-cleaning trucks are sometimes used to clear runways and apron areas, and magnetic sweepers pick up stray pieces of metal around aircraft servicing bays.

Bird strike

A flock of birds sucked into a jet engine at takeoff can cause a dangerous loss of power, while a single large bird, hitting an engine with the force of a bullet, may smash a fan blade that can cause further severe engine damage. A tailplane hit by a bird at speed may be weakened initially, and torn off by resulting aerodynamic forces. Airframe and engine manufacturers test the resistance of fuselages and fan blades, and aircraft windshields are built to resist a four-pound chicken carcass fired at a velocity of over 400 mph.

Amplified bird distress calls, as well as dead and decoy birds, are only partially effective. Flares, loud noises and shellcrackers are a more successful harassment.

The use of falcons and other birds of prey is proving a strong deterrent in tests in the UK, but the long-term answer seems to be starvation. Rubbish dumps are covered up, insects and earthworms controlled and small mammals discouraged.

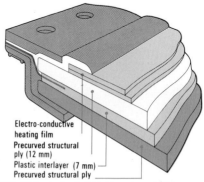

Electro-conductive
heating film
Precurved structural
ply (12 mm)
Plastic interlayer (7 mm)
Precurved structural ply

This flight-deck windshield, made specially for a Boeing 747, is one and a half inches thick. Made of special laminated glass, interfaced with plastic, it can withstand an impact of over 50 tons. This type of windshield was the first to exceed 10,000 hours service.

Airport medical services

Tense, nervous passengers become accident-prone at airports. They shut their fingers in doors, fall down stairs, walk into plate glass doors, drink too much, develop toothache and migraine and produce babies while waiting for their flights.

Airport medical staff deal with a surprising variety of cases. At Heathrow Airport they handle an average of 40 fatal coronaries, and a few strokes, every year, and they may also have to deal with inbound passengers suffering from overindulgence in flight. Many airports provide last-minute vaccinations for out-bound passengers, and airline services based at large airports treat airline flight crews.

Medical services provided at airports differ enormously. The smallest airports may not have so much as a first aid kit, and may be entirely unmanned until the local first-aid-trained fire service comes out from town to meet the daily flight. In contrast, large airports will have round-the-clock stand-by emergency services. John F. Kennedy Airport in the USA has two operating rooms and a medical centre that can handle up to 1,000 cases. Frankfurt's medical centre has operating facilities and a remedial pool.

No international body compels airports to provide medical services. Although London's Heathrow Airport has a fully-staffed 24-hour emergency service, and free facilities for airport users, the CAA stipulates only that to be granted a licence, an airport must arrange for local doctors and hospitals to be on 24-hour call, ready to meet an emergency.

Airline facilities alone are not intended to handle major disasters, so community fire, hospital and police services are necessary and even, sometimes, the military. An operation of disaster scale has to be planned — a plan is drawn up by the chiefs of the services involved — and rehearsed.

A disaster drill takes place on a site away from the main airport operations. A real aircraft is used, with flight and cabin crews and passengers. Casualities wear realistic make-up. The drill begins with notification

Flight data recorders, introduced in 1965, were dubbed ''black boxes'' (a nickname for any electronic ''box of tricks'') by the media. But they are usually egg-shaped, and painted bright red so that they are easily seen from a distance. The earliest versions recorded only altitude, airspeed, pitch attitude, acceleration and magnetic heading, but current models can record information from up to 60 different sources.

The black box **left** was recovered from a Vanguard which crashed in a snowstorm near Basle, Switzerland, in 1973. The pilot seemed to have lost his bearings while flying on instruments, but the black box contained no voice recorder, so what really happened was never made clear. Modern cockpit voice recorders tape all flight-deck conversation. The tape is ''wiped'' continuously, so that at any moment the tape stores the previous 12 hours.

from the aircraft to the control tower, from where all emergency services are alerted.

The captain and crew are in command until the fire services take over. Fire crews position their vehicles while passengers are evacuating the aircraft and casualties are lying on the ground. They begin fire control and rescue operations, while medical personnel stabilize the casualties, mark the deceased, and give treatments in inflatable hospital tents until the ambulances arrive.

Police are needed to clear the access roads, and the highways leading to the airport, for ambulances and fire and supply trucks. People descend on major disasters once they have been reported in the media. The influx of people and their cars can seriously hamper operations.

Fire fighters – both on the airport and those employed by neighbouring community fire services – need special training to deal with aircraft fires. They may attend periodic courses, where the cabin section of an old aircraft is set on fire for them to rehearse the use of equipment such as foam generators and breathing apparatus.

An enormous amount of equipment is needed at a disaster. In one disaster drill at a major international airport, eight converted cargo trailers were used to transport supplies. The first truck brought electrical equipment for lighting, folding desks for command personnel and a platform for the officer in charge of operations to supervise the action. Telephones and communications equipment were in a second, and others brought medical supplies and stretchers, wheelchairs, water supplies and backboards (narrower than stretchers, used to carry injured passengers along aircraft aisles) which, when laid on wooden horses, also make examination tables.

A disaster drill ends when the last casualty has been released from hospital. Photographing, recording and clearing-up operations ensure that the lessons learned are made available to other airports so that passengers receive the same fire and rescue attention at any airport.

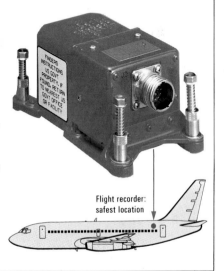

A modern flight recorder **right,** built to resist an impact of 5,000 lb, an acceleration of 1,000 times the force of gravity, and temperatures of 2,012 degrees Fahrenheit (1,100 degrees Celsius) for 30 minutes, may be the only part of a wrecked aircraft to remain intact. This recorder can be immersed in sea water for a month; an audio recorder inside enables it to be detected by sonar. Digital information is recorded magnetically, from up to 60 sources, onto fine stainless steel wire. This can be played back through an analog computer to build up a series of graphs giving a complete picture of the aircraft's flightpath. Data are simultaneously recorded on a non-accident-proofed tape, to be monitored after routine flights.

Used to provide airlines with information on all aspects of flight performance, the flight data recorder helps to solve aircraft design problems, a welcome bonus since it can cost over £100,000 ($180,000) to install a complete data and voice-recording system on a large airliner.

The recorder is usually installed high up in the base of the aircraft's fin since this part of the aircraft, behind the centre of gravity and away from the fuel tanks, is most likely to survive an impact.

Flight recorder: safest location

Airport security

When smuggling was the major airport crime, the passenger was rarely subjected to the indignity of personal search. The scourge of hijackings by politically-motivated terrorists has changed that. And airports — large, complex and richly-stocked, and vulnerable international frontiers — are prey to thieves and pilferers, illegal immigrants, drug traffickers and smugglers of all kinds.

Airport security starts at the perimeter fence, which will ideally have a ten-foot clear area on either side. Microwave fences, which flash a warning of intruders still some distance away are used for remote boundaries. But because fences have gates, identity cards are issued to airport workers and checked by security guards.

Isolated, as a rule, from the main airport buildings, cargo terminals are targets for thieves and pilferers. Few cargo terminals are as secure as the new one at Singapore Airport, which has armed security guards, closed-circuit TV with zoom lens cameras, videotape recording, and a twin-lock system for high value articles, with one key held by guards and the other by a document acceptance officer. At most airports, bonded stores for duty-free goods, and surveillance cages for valuable cargo, may reduce all but organized pilferage, but will not prevent theft during delivery or loading, or determined armed robbery. Airports have been the scenes of some spectacular thefts. Both London's Heathrow and New York's John F. Kennedy have recorded annual losses in excess of £5 million ($10 million). Heathrow has been dubbed "Thief-row" by the national press.

Terrorism is the worst threat, and airports and airlines at risk may have air cargo X-rayed or, as at the Lufthansa terminals, containerized cargo is routinely decompressed for 12 hours in remotely-sited chambers, to reduce the possibility of bombs exploding in aircraft cargo holds. At major airports containers and other cargo is checked in seconds by equipment such as the BAe Condor, which can detect drugs or explosives.

Ever since a Peruvian Airlines plane was hijacked in 1930, there has been piracy in the sky. Now, this

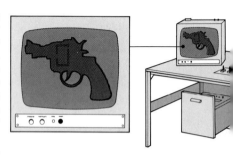

The camera has a zoom control to allow close-up inspection of any suspicious object on the X-ray monitor. Full pan and tilt control ensure that a suitcase can be minutely examined. Metal shows up densely, other materials as shadows. X-rays can fog film in cameras or baggage.

This metal-detection gateway has an electromagnetic field between doorframe-sized metal columns. Ferrous or non-ferrous metal carried through by a passenger disturbs the magnetic field, the disturbance registers on a control panel and an alarm sounds. Sensitivity can be reduced so as not to pick up the metal fastenings on clothes. The machine can be controlled by one person stationed away from the gateway and will not affect heart pacemakers, magnetic recording tape or magnetically-coded credit cards.

crime has reached epidemic proportions. Yet several ICAO members have not yet accepted the introduction of world-wide extradition agreements which would eliminate havens.

Because manual searches are undignified, time-consuming and ultimately inefficient, most airports screen passengers through electro-magnetic metal-detectors. Hand baggage is visually searched, using low dosage X-ray equipment. At some airports, "sniffer" dogs are used to detect explosives or drugs.

Security depends, eventually, on the observation of well-trained detection-equipment operators, and on experienced security guards.

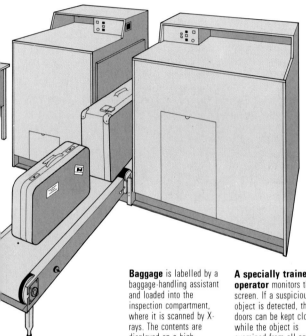

A combined check-in desk, electronic weigh unit with digital readout and X-ray security screening point could replace the airline check-in desk. One monitor can cover several desk points. The system is designed to handle large volumes of passenger baggage rapidly — it takes only eight seconds to clear a passenger's hand-baggage while he is screened by a magnetic metal detector so that frisking and hand-searches are unnecessary.

Baggage is labelled by a baggage-handling assistant and loaded into the inspection compartment, where it is scanned by X-rays. The contents are displayed on a high-definition TV screen.

A specially trained operator monitors the TV screen. If a suspicious object is detected, the doors can be kept closed while the object is examined from all angles and from close up.

If the contents are passed, the operator opens the doors to release the baggage. At the press of a button, it is fed, via a small conveyor belt, into the airport's main baggage conveyor system.

A portable explosives detector gives an audible alarm within four seconds of detecting explosive vapour. The probe, inserted into a handbag or suitcase, or passed over hands, clothing or containers, takes a sample of air. This is fed into the briefcase, which contains an electronic sensor unit, a rechargeable nickel-cadmium battery and a bottle containing argon gas, to detect and register the contents. The detector can respond to explosive vapour concentrations of one part per several million parts of air, and can detect traces of explosive on any material hours after contact, but it will ignore vapours from lighter fuel and cleaning fluid.

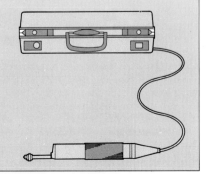

Economics of air travel

Commercial aviation is big business. The world's airline operators on all scheduled flights (except internal ones in the Soviet Union) had an operating result of £2,500 million ($4,500 million) in 1986. The 169 companies belonging to IATA have a total of 1,017,000 employees. Many thousands more people work for air charter and taxi companies or at airports, or in building, servicing and supplying the aircraft. Around a quarter of Amsterdam's one million inhabitants depend directly or indirectly on work generated by Schiphol Airport.

Investment
The capital investment is impressive. A short-haul airliner such as the Fokker 100, carrying only 100 passengers, costs over £25 million ($45 million). A 400-seater Boeing 747 can cost about £75–80 million (£135 million). Modern airliners have service lifetimes of around 25 years, during which they are repeatedly overhauled and rebuilt. When the machine is retired, there may be little of its original fabric left in it. Large airlines sell many old, but perfectly airworthy, airliners to smaller operators; at present, over half of the world's jet airliners are more than ten years old.

Costs
Short-haul routes are considerably more expensive to fly than intercontinental routes. The short-range airliner has to spend nearly as long on the ground during turnaround as the long-distance jet, as long in the stack waiting to land, and often has to pay the same landing charges per ton and per passenger. It is subject to the bans on night-time flying operated by many airports, while intercontinental flying continues day and night. Over the year, aircraft on routes in Europe are used for about 2,500 hours, or about seven hours per day. Intercontinental jets are used 14 hours a day or more. For all these reasons, roughly half of Europe's air traffic goes by charter (which can be cheaper than scheduled services).

A Boeing 747 uses about 3,100 gallons (3,700 US gallons) an hour when cruising. But because it flies so fast and carries so many passengers it is as economical to run as a family car. Modern jet airliners use about 7.7 gallons (9.25 US gallons) per flying hour per seat. After allowing for empty seats and the plane's cruising speed, on short-haul European flights scheduled services fly about 20 passenger-miles per gallon (17 per US gallon). Charter planes, which fly only if they are full, achieve about 31 passenger-miles per gallon (26 per US gallon).

On intercontinental flights, because of the greater average speed, the scheduled services achieve about 36.5 passenger-miles per gallon (30 per US gallon); charter flights achieve 45 per gallon (38 per US gallon).

Profit
The load factor, the percentage of total capacity that is actually sold, is crucial to the profitability of a service. An aircraft with 150 seats that takes off with 90 passengers has a seat load factor of 60 per cent. The overall load factor is the percentage of passengers and cargo combined. Standard weights for passengers and baggage are used in the calculation. At the break-even load factor total cost equals revenue.

The load factor in aviation has been around 55 per cent for the past few years. Few routes can rival the load factors of over 90 per cent on the Concorde's Europe-USA routes.

Aviation load factors compare well with those for mass transport on the ground. Trains and inter-city bus services have load factors under 40 per cent in many countries. Increasingly, airliners are being designed as "convertibles" so that the passenger space can quickly be turned into cargo space, and vice versa.

Expenditure

The airliner incurs large charges every time it lands and takes off. It is charged by its weight, by the number of passengers it is carrying, sometimes by the distance it has flown, and according to the time of day. The charges vary widely according to the size of the airport and are usually revised every six months. But typical charges for an international TriStar flight at peak times at a major airport could include: a £300 (over $500) landing charge (with no separate charge for takeoff); a £2.50 ($5) charge for each passenger arriving — which can total £1,000 (about $2,000) or more for a fully loaded 747; and passenger fees, which are paid on departures as well. A runway movement charge can be over £100 (nearly $200), and must be paid both on landing and takeoff. Charges for security checks must be paid for each passenger, and parking charges for excess time spent by the aircraft on the stand. At off-peak times these charges may be halved, and they are also reduced for domestic flights. Light planes carrying a few passengers may pay well under £100 ($200), even at peak times.

In one survey of large US airports it was found that landing charges and services provided to airliners on the airfield represented about a third of the total revenue, another third came from services provided to airlines in the terminal, and the rest came from concessions, such as restaurants.

Revenue

In the end the user pays — whether he sends a letter, a package or a piece of equipment, or travels himself. The pricing of air tickets is a complex matter, decided internationally and agreed to by governments. In general, the air traveller pays more the more flexible his arrangements are. The standard first-class and economy fares offer the passenger the most freedom: he can buy an open-date ticket, or he can make a firm reservation that guarantees him a seat on a certain flight, while retaining the ability to change his travel plans many times; he can change to another airline, make stopovers at intermediate airports, or divert to other destinations within a certain total distance from his starting point. He can even fail to show up at all. Tickets remain valid for one year, and the changes are without charge. All these uncertainties help to push up fares.

In addition, a large variety of reduced fares are available on many routes. By booking a long way ahead and limiting the period during which he can return, a passenger can make substantial savings. Some of the cheapest scheduled fares are only a little more expensive than charter fares. But the cheapest way of flying is still by charter, with or without accommodation and ground travel arrangements included. The passenger is then committed to fixed travel dates. If not enough passengers book on a particular charter, the flight may be cancelled.

Years when airlines lose money often alternate with those when they are profitable. Airline travel and profits slumped temporarily after the oil price rises of 1973, but manufacturers and operators are confident air travel will boom through the 1990s.

Commercial aviation is said to be a marginal industry, always working close to the borderline between profit and loss. Yet in 1986–87 Singapore Airlines earned more than £250 million ($450 million) on revenues of £1,950 ($3,500 million), an increase of nearly 60 per cent over 1985–86.

The flight crew

The captain

A 747 lifts off from runway 09 Right at Miami International en route to Chicago O'Hare. Suddenly there is a power drop on number three engine, the inboard flaps refuse to retract, and as the main gear rise, fire erupts in the nose-gear bay. This will be a long and arduous flight. The cabin pressurization will fail; so will a VHF receiver and the gear hydraulics. Fire will disable number one engine and an oil pressure drop on the troublesome number three will force its shutdown as well. Thus the already hard-pressed crew must make an instrument approach and landing into the world's most congested airport with two of their aircraft's four engines inoperative. They will do a fine job; if not, they will just have to do it all over again – but this was just a test on a flight simulator.

Pilots sometimes leave the simulators which stage such dramas shaking and soaked in perspiration. But they may be required to go through the experience twice a year so that their reactions to a set of catastrophes, more than they are likely to meet in their whole flying career, can be measured. A pilot can lose his licence if he fails a simulator test but, in practice, his three years' basic training even before being accepted by an airline ensures that this is rare. Licences are more likely to be lost for medical reasons. A senior pilot undergoes a rigorous medical every six months and a commercial pilot's licence holder, every 12, and twice as often over the age of 40. Half the applicants to training colleges for airline pilots are rejected for eyesight reasons alone.

No pilot can become a captain on a large airliner until he has flown many years as a co-pilot. Promotion usually depends on seniority. In Britain, there is enough flexibility to take into

account a pilot's ability and qualifications as well as experience but, in the USA, the system is more rigid and a pilot may fly for years before becoming a captain. Only the pilot in command may wear a cap with "scrambled egg" on the peak. A 747 captain is usually fiftyish with 30 years of flying behind him, often partly in the air force. Not many pilots are women—there are fewer than a dozen working for major British airlines, for example.

The bigger the aircraft the higher the captain's pay. Captains of widebodied jets can earn up to £50,000 a year in Britain and around $200,000 in the United States. Such salaries reflect the responsibility of the job and the risk of losing it at the six-monthly checks. But it may not be the money that makes him endure 150 pre-flight checks a year and endure the frustrations of passing through Customs three times a week; it may be a love of flying. And, once the doors are closed on the last passenger, the captain's authority is absolute. Any troublesome person, regardless of rank, can be strapped to the floor with no right of redress until touchdown.

An average crew will work between 900 and 1,200 hours a year, including layovers and rest periods. Many pilots use their considerable free time to run other businesses.

Some older aircraft may carry a flight engineer. He is answerable to the captain for the performance of all the aircraft's systems, from engines to galley ovens. He goes out to the aircraft ahead of the rest of the flight crew, and checks the exterior: tyres, control surfaces, skin condition and so on, and makes sure that the necessary maintenance and refuelling has

been completed to his satisfaction. A large plane may have 600 circuit breakers in its electric systems, and these, and any backup systems necessary to the aircraft's safety — the second, third and fourth hydraulic systems — for instance, must be in working order. But a flight crew may choose to fly a short haul with a non-essential system, like the air-conditioning, in less than perfect order.

In flight, the engineer's territory is a control panel, on the side wall behind the co-pilot, of up to 500 gauges, lights and switches; about 18 alarm bells, buzzers and sirens supplement the visual systems failure warnings. On some aircraft an electric motor on his seat can power it along a railway to the space between the pilots so he can help them in emergencies. He monitors the aircraft's progress, keeping track of its speeds, altitudes and fuel consumption, and listens out for weather broadcasts. At takeoff he has a particularly vital role, calculating the takeoff speeds and adjusting the engine settings if necessary.

It is even harder to become a flight engineer than a pilot: only four per cent of applicants are accepted for training because fewer airlines are still employing them. Besides, only one engineer is needed for every two pilots, and some airlines make do with another pilot in the third seat. This is unpopular with pilots, who dislike being tied to an instrument panel, and may turn out to be expensive on the long-haul flights, because pilots do not have an engineer's Inspection Approval, the all-important licence enabling him to sign out an aircraft for continued flight after a diversion to an airfield which does not have the normal ground maintenance cover.

The flight deck of an Airbus A320 has modern instruments that employ coloured displays on square television-type screens. Major instruments are duplicated for the pilot and co-pilot.

Cabin crews/Ground staff

Cabin crews

The opportunity to travel gives a flight attendant's job an aura of glamour, but it is also plain hard work. On a six- to twelve-week training course, the male and female flight attendants learn how to comfort nervous passengers, assist mothers with (and deliver) babies, and cope with belligerent passengers. They are taught how to cope with heart attacks and diabetic comas, and how to recognize the outward signs of cholera (which would cause a captain to radio ahead to warn the health authorities). They will be taught some first aid, the theory of flight, and be drilled in emergency procedure. They serve meals efficiently, mix cocktails, and check sales of duty-free goods so the stocks can be renewed. Their uniforms may be designed by distinguished couturiers and the airline will advise, at least, on grooming and sometimes rule on make-up, hair length and on the wearing of jewellery and other accessories.

Educational qualifications may not be high, but candidates are expected to be alert and articulate. Foreign languages are required by many airlines, and they are always an advantage on overseas routes. Flight attendants do not have to be gourmet cooks; aircraft meals are pre-cooked and merely reheated on board. They are judged for qualities which cannot be tested in examinations: confidence, self-reliance, appearance and the capacity to react coolly in tense situations.

The most important part of cabin crew training is toward a skill that most passengers never see: the ability to evacuate up to 500 passengers from a wide-bodied jet in an emergency landing. Cabin simulators, as realistic as flight-deck simulators, are used to train the crew to empty a plane in 90 seconds, knowing that a few

The cabin crew consists of the flight attendants, usually headed by a chief steward or purser (the senior cabin officer), who liaises with the flight crew.

Before the flight, the whole crew report to the airline's staff office, where they are briefed for the flight and allocated any special tasks.

wasted seconds may turn a minor incident into a major disaster. The "passengers" must be representative.

A flight attendant on a transatlantic flight can expect to walk up to 13 miles during the crossing. If the attendant works for Pan Am, he or she will have been chosen for the job out of 10,000 applicants a year. Over the years, a female attendant's average flying life has increased from 18 months to five or six years, largely because she no longer has to remain single or retire at 30. A few go on to retirement age. The pay is comparable with that of a top secretary, but there are travel allowances and expenses, and a great deal of time off, amounting to the equivalent of every other day.

A senior flight attendant will be in charge of the cabin crew and will assign responsibilities (the most critical job is in the galley, where expertise with the ovens is vital to good cabin service). On a big jet a purser will direct the staff, and on some airlines there may be a cabin service officer, the most senior rank.

Ground staff

A single passenger out of the tens of thousands who pass through a major airport every day will meet very few of the 30,000 or so people employed to see him safely, comfortably and legally on and off the plane. About five per cent of the people who work at an airport are employed by its management; another five per cent will be civil servants — immigration and Customs officers, health unit officers and air traffic controllers. The rest are largely airline staff.

Passenger service begins with the ticket sales and reservation staff. As front-line personnel, they are trained to do more than just write out tickets and hand out boarding passes. They have to master one of up to 20,000 computer terminals the airline may

have around the world, all linked to a central computer which not only processes seating information but handles all the airline planning and control, from aircraft scheduling to payrolls. They will also check passports, visas and vaccination certificates, and are trained to defuse aggressive or agitated latecomers, and remain steadfastly cool-headed in the face of nervous air travellers. As the ground equivalent of cabin crew, they may become attendants responsible for liaising with passengers at airports or city terminals, escorting them to the right places at the right times, manning information desks, looking after luggage and making special arrangements for VIPs or invalids. Every large airport has a stand-by medical service, usually consisting of teams of nurses and doctors. These are backed up by airline medical services, primarily for the crew, but they may check on anyone with a condition likely to be aggravated by flying, such as pregnancy. Airlines usually refuse to carry women past their seventh month of pregnancy.

While outbound passengers are processed on the first floor of the terminal, airside crews on the ground-level aprons turn round newly arrived aircraft, refuelling and checking tyres with the urgency of a pit-stop team, beginning as the inbound passengers are still disembarking. The Customs inspectors are the first on the plane, closely followed by the cleaners ("groomers") who spruce up the inside for the next flight. Catering staff load and unload meals. Maintenance engineers correct any faults reported from the flight deck and perform routine checks on landing-gears, engines, avionics and systems. These engineers have served apprenticeships in the aircraft industry and are experienced specialists in electrical systems, hydraulics, engines, airframes or other fields.

Tips for air passengers

Throughout this book there is information and advice about various aspects of air travel. The next few pages summarize some of the ways flying can be made as painless and enjoyable as possible.

Before you go

Tip number one has to be: plan your trip as far in advance as possible. This will enable you to do the best deal in terms of fares, and let you sort out any difficulties while there is still time. It is too late after you have checked in at the airport to discover that there are no facilities for getting your disabled grandmother's wheelchair onto the aircraft.

You can buy your ticket direct from the an airline, through a travel agent or from a discount ticket agent. You must know exactly what you want when booking with an airline, whereas a good travel agent should be able to advise you about cheap fare options, stop-overs, and so on. Again, the earlier you make such enquiries, the better will be the terms you get.

CHECKLIST

Make sure that you have:

★ An up-to-date passport.

★ Any necessary visas.

★ Any required vaccinations and vaccination certificates. Remember that a course of anti-malaria tablets has to be started before you leave.

★ Foreign currency and/or traveller's cheques (or Eurocheques). Check the expiry date of your credit cards.

★ Insurance cover for personal effects (loss or damage); make a note of the serial numbers of cameras and so on. You can also insure against ticket cancellation charges.

★ Medical insurance.

★ Air tickets. Check the name, date, destination, flight time and airport terminal.

TICKETS AND BOOKING

★ Discount ticket agents – popularly called bucket shops – sell tickets at much less than the official fares.

★ Unoccupied seats are sold by airlines at a large discount – often through a middleman – to bucket shops, which in turn offer bargain fares.

★ Check the conditions attached to tickets obtained in this way – there may be heavy penalties for cancellation.

★ Any particular requirements, such as special diets (or disabilities), should be made known to the airline at the time of booking, and in any case at least 24 hours before departure time.

★ If you are pregnant, check with your doctor that it is safe for you to fly (and with the airline that it will take you).

★ If you take regular medication, make sure you have an adequate supply for the whole trip.

★ If you wear spectacles or contact lenses, take a spare pair with you.

Bonus miles

In some countries, particularly the United States, people who travel regularly by air can collect "bonus miles". Each trip entitles them to a certain number of miles of free travel or class up-grades. As a result somebody taking a business trip from, say, New York to Los Angeles may deliberertely take a series of short flights – each segment of the journey will have a bonus rating – rather than fly non-stop from coast to coast. Bonus miles are also given as premiums with certain purchases or credit card transactions.

The idea does not apply in some other countries because their tax authorities consider bonus miles to be personal income and therefore liable to taxation.

Airline privileges

Regular fliers can benefit by joining one or more of the clubs run by the major international airlines. For an annual membership fee of about £25 ($50), you get various privileges at the airport. For example, you may be able to drive up to the entrance of the departure section of a terminal and hand over your car keys for an airline agent to park your car for you. On your return, the car will be brought to you at the exit of the arrivals section of the terminal.

Baggage allowances may be less rigorously enforced for club members. Inside the airport terminal, frequent traveller's clubs usually have their own comfortable departure lounges, with facilities such as free beverages and free local telephone calls. And if seats are unfilled in first-class, you may be up-graded.

BAGGAGE TIPS

★ Do not carry that versatile Swiss penknife – it may be confiscated.

★ Do not attach a baggage label with your home address visible – it is an invitation to professional thieves to rob your home while you are away. Use instead baggage labels on which your address is securely concealed behind a tab.

★ Remember that each passenger is allowed to take only one item of hand baggage inside the aircraft. This must be small enough to fit under the seat in front.

★ A carrying basket for a baby is permitted above the free baggage allowance, but may have to be put in the hold.

★ Assume that your baggage will be thrown around. If there is any doubt about the strength of locks or zips, secure straps around your bags.

★ If you wish to take a particularly valuable, fragile, bulky package with you – such as large musical instrument – book a separate seat for it. The security and peace-of-mind will be worth the cost.

★ Golf bags, skiing and scuba equipment, bicycles, etc., are not usually included in the baggage allowances. But if you have only one piece of baggage, golf clubs may be treated as part of the free allowance.

Tips for air passengers/2

Baggage regulations

When you have packed your bags, weigh them to make sure that they are within the baggage allowance, if that is the form of control (some airlines stipulate the numbers of bags – usually two). Excess baggage is expensive. But if you are travelling with somebody else, remember that any excess weight of your baggage can be offset by any underweight of his or hers. And the new baggage-handling systems, which use lasers to scan bar codes attached to the items of luggage, should make lost baggage a thing of the past – although 98 per cent of it does turn up eventually.

Packing

You are not permitted to pack certain kinds of items in baggage to be carried on an aircraft. These include:

Corrosive substances (e.g. acids, alkalis, wet accumulators/batteries)

Compressed gasses (e.g. aqualung cylinders, camping gas, gas lighter fuel)

Explosives (e.g. amunition, flares, fireworks)

Flammable substances (e.g. lighter fuel, lacquers, matches, paint, solvents)

Oxidixing substances (e.g. bleach, chlorates, fibreglass kits)

Poisons (e.g. insecticides)

The check-in

The latest check-in-time – usually an hour before flight time – will be stated on your ticket. But do not leave it that late. Allow plenty of time to travel to the airport, particularly if you have to park a car. A traffic jam or public transport breakdown could result in a ruined trip or a wait for hours even days for the next available flight. And remember that rush-hour traffic can double the time it takes.

CHECK-IN TIPS

★ Remember that lines at the check-in desk and passport control are longest nearer the departure time.

★ On Intercontinental flights you may need to check-in two hours before departure time. For other flights check-in is usually one hour before departure.

★ Many airports have special check-in desks for passengers with hand-baggage only. These help to avoid delays if you are travelling light.

★ Early arrivals also have time to browse around duty-free shops or have a drink.

★ Do not drink too much alcohol before checking in – the airline would have a legal right to refuse to take you.

★ It is often possible to reserve a seat when you buy your ticket, or by telephone days ahead of the flight. On the day checkers-in have the choice of available seats. It is no use asking for a seat in the non-smoking part of the cabin if they are already taken (except on American airlines which are required to create non-smoking areas for all passengers who insist).

★ If you are a woman travelling alone and are nervous about who you might have as a companion on a long trip, ask to be seated next to another woman passenger.

★ Aisle seats allow the most freedom, but you may be frequently disturbed by occupants of the adjacent seats. In addition, their food and drinks – and leftovers – will be passed across your lap at each meal service.

★ Aisle seats can also be unpleasant near the toilets, especially when there is a waiting line of jostling passengers.

★ The greatest leg-room is obtained in seats immediately behind a cabin bulkhead or next to an emergency exit.

★ Remember that, even on the same type of aircraft, seating configurations vary from airline to airline – and may change from time to time with a single airline. So do not assume that a particular seat number will always offer the same convenience. Check each time.

★ Keep an eye on your baggage at all times – your confusion or hesitancy makes it easy for thieves and pickpockets.

★ As you part with your bags at the check-in, make sure that the correct destination airport code is on the tags attached to them. (See the Airports section, pp. 210–233, for a list of codes.)

★ If you have not obtained foreign currency before going to the airport, get it *before* going through passport control. Few international airports have airside banking facilities.

ON THE AIRCRAFT

★ Follow exactly instructions about fastening your seat belt and extinguishing cigarettes. Keep your seat belt loosely fastened all through the flight; no pilot flies into turbulence deliberately, but unexpected turbulence can take everybody by surprise.

★ Put your hand-baggage under the seat in front, and put coats and lightweight articles in the overhead lockers. Do not put bottles of duty-free drinks in the overhead lockers.

★ Listen to announcements made on the aircraft – they may affect your landing arrangements or transfer flight.

★ On a long trip, try to get some sleep if possible (earplugs and an eye-mask sometimes help).

★ Even if you never take sleeping pills, one taken on a long flight will not hurt and could ensure that you arrive refreshed and relaxed.

★ Many people find that sleep helps to diminish the effects of jet-lag; it certainly combats boredom.

★ Reading also reduces boredom, although you should be aware that your attention span is likely to be limited because of interruptions.

★ If you cannot sleep, you can watch the in-flight movie or plug into the aircraft's sound system (there is usually a small charge for earphones).

Tips for air passengers/3

ON THE AIRCRAFT

★ Take your own favourite music with a personal stereo casette player – but make sure that it *is* personal and that the volume is not loud enough to annoy others.

★ The low cost of duty-free drinks – or even free drinks – tempts some people into drinking too much alcohol, which can cause unpleasant symptoms in pressurized cabins at high altitudes. Alcohol produces dehydration, is a diuretic (increasing urine production) and makes jet-lag worse.

★ Fizzy drinks can also have unpleasant consequences. Fruit juices or non-gassy mineral water are best.

★ If you wear contact lenses, remove them on a long flight. The effects of dry air and pressurization can make them uncomfortable.

★ Another medical tip is to remove your shoes, to combat the swollen ankles suffered by some air travellers. But if you wear tight shoes, take a shoe-horn to help to get them on again.

★ Pressurization of the air in the cabin can make toothache flare – and make fountain pens or felt-tip pens leak in your pocket or handbag.

★ If you need a landing card, fill it in before you reach your destination to save time at customs or immigration.

Smoking in aircraft has become a highly-charged issue, particularly in the United States where travelling smokers are being allotted fewer seats farther back in the cabin, often alongside toilets or busy galleys. Some routes or trips that take less than an hour are smoke free. Airline policy in other countries varies. Japanese airlines permit smoking in 56 per cent of their business seats, Middle East airlines allow it in 50 per cent, whereas on a British airline it varies between 45 and 25 per cent, depending on class.

SMOKING

★ Do not smoke when the "No Smoking" light is lit.

★ Do not smoke in the toilets or when walking along the aisles.

★ Use the ashtrays, not the floor.

★ The effects of smoking are worsened in a pressurized cabin, increasing discomfort to the eyes and throat.

★ Even if you have a supply of cheaper, duty-free cigarettes, try not to smoke more than usual.

When you arrive
On arrival in another country, the usual procedure is to go through passport control (and immigration if necessary) before collecting your baggage. So make sure all your paper work is in order and ready.

At the baggage collection point, decide whether you need help before picking up your bags. There may be porters or baggage trolleys, but at some airports you need local currency to "hire" a trolley from a machine.

You should have familiarized yourself with local customs regulations, particularly with regard to duty-free goods and the amount of currency and the value of other goods that you are allowed to take in without declaring them. Some of these regulations can be quite subtle. For example, a ban on the taking-in of plants may include fresh fruit, seeds and even herbs and spices. In case a customs official wants to search your baggage, have the keys handy.

Coping with jet-lag

When the local time changes because you have travelled across several time zones, your body rhythms may take several days or even weeks to adjust. This gives rise to the unpleasant symptoms of jet-lag. It should not be ignored in the hope that it can be overcome by sheer effort or with sleeping pills after you arrive. Rather you should adopt the approach that you will either keep to home time or train yourself for the new local time before you travel. If neither of these is possible or practicable, you should try to arrive at the best possible compromise.

It is possible to schedule your flight times to minimize the effects of jet-lag. For instance, a late afternoon or evening flight from Europe will arrive in the American West Coast in the evening. Your body clock will tell you to sleep on the aircraft and, if you do, you will arrive less tired and ready for an evening meal before going to bed.

Business people who do arrive at their destinations jet-lagged should try to avoid meetings or decision-making until they have at least partly recovered.

AVOIDING JET-LAG

★ Plan ahead so that events will fit in best with your own home rhythm, whether these are for business or pleasure.

★ Plan your flight so that you make life easy for yourself.

★ Calculate the time difference between your home and your destination.

★ For a few days before your journey, start going to bed an hour earlier or later each night (depending on whether you are travelling east or west).

★ Rise an hour earlier or later each morning.

★ Adjust your meal times to the new schedule.

DECISION-MAKING

★ Do not make decisions when you body clock tells you that it is time to sleep.

★ Schedule important decisions to fit in with your body clock.

★ Make no important decisions until you have had at least one good night's sleep after your arrival.

★ Do not make decisions if you have recently arrived from a different time zone and eaten a big meal or had alcohol to drink.

★ Even after a good night's sleep, try to postpone decision-making until the afternoon.

Painting an aircraft

Inside the cathedral-sized spray-painting hall at Toulouse, Airbus Industrie painters on movable staging swing their spray guns back and forth over the sides of a huge A300 Airbus or a Concorde. It can take more than two weeks to paint an aircraft; a BAe 1-11 needs 25 gallons of top coat alone (which adds more than 250 lb to its weight).

Paint on an aircraft is not just an expensive cosmetic. Applied to a properly prepared aircraft skin it is a protective, guarding against corrosion and metal fatigue, which can start from a slight scratch in the surface.

Sometimes aircraft skins are polished. Normally aluminium has a microscopically thin surface layer of corrosion-resistant oxide. But if this is enthusiastically buffed away during polishing, the metal beneath can become corroded. The affected parts of the aircraft then have to be re-skinned, an expensive remedy. A similar problem can occur with internal metal parts which, if poorly protected, also become corroded. Each piece of metal, down to the smallest nut, has to be given the appropriate priming coat or be electroplated before assembly, and a proper paint finish applied afterward.

Painting an aircraft has not changed much over the years except in the chemical composition of the paint and the evolution of airline liveries into almost an art form. Brushes are still used for small jobs, but a spray gun is the only practical way of covering an aircraft such as a Boeing 747, with a surface area bigger than the size of six tennis courts.

Until the 1940s, the use of paint was restricted to sombre camouflage colours; from about 1948 the use of colour brought a dazzling profusion of airline liveries. And in the last few years, since deregulation, liveries change almost monthly as smaller airlines come and go or are absorbed by their bigger brothers.

Most aircraft now have white tops to the fuselage, largely to reflect sunlight and keep down cabin temperatures. But the high speeds of high-flying jet aircraft make the early synthetic paints crack, peel and even strip. Synthetic and epoxy paints have been to a great extent superseded by polyurethane products for top coats and liveries on modern aircraft. Epoxy paints for external finishes become dull and chalky and need to be stripped off and renewed after about two years. Polyurethane finishes, applied over properly prepared surfaces, may last three times as long — as long as the airline does not change its livery.

The weight of the paint added to a large aircraft in a single trip to the paint-shop can equal the weight of two passengers. But unpainted, the surface can become scratched, and scratches can sow the seeds of dangerous metal fatigue.

Airline insignia

Aer Lingus is the Republic of Ireland's national airline, with regular scheduled flights between Ireland, Britain and the rest of Europe and the United States.

Aeroflot, the Soviet Union's national airline, is the biggest in the world, carrying 110 million passengers each year over a total of 620,000 route-miles.

Aeronica, the national airline of Nicaragua, was founded in 1981 and today serves much of Central America and Miami in addition to its domestic services.

AeroPeru, a transcontinental airline founded in Lima in 1973, flies a wide range of modern aircraft, mainly to cater for the country's extensive tourist industry.

Air Afrique, founded in 1961 by 11 former French colonies in Africa, now links 22 African states with destinations throughout Europe and the United States.

Air Algérie operates scheduled passenger and cargo flights in North Africa, with links to West Africa, Europe, the Middle East and the Soviet Union.

Airline insignia

Air Canada provides extensive internal services as well as international flights to the United States and the Caribbean, and transatlantic flights to Europe.

Air France, with British Airways the only airline to fly Concorde, is Europe's second largest airline with extensive services worldwide.

Air-India, founded at the time of India's independence in 1948, flies from four major Indian cities to 40 other destinations throughout the world.

Air Jamaica operates from Jamaica's capital Kingston to the other Caribbean Islands, and has international flights to North America and Europe.

Air Malta, founded in 1973 with the help of PIA (Pakistan International Airways), links Malta with various destinations in Europe and North Africa.

Air Manitoba is a newly-named Canadian airline with internal scheduled flights and charter and cargo operations throughout much of North America.

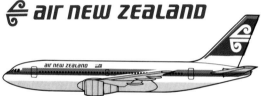

Air New Zealand, with a distinctive Maori emblem on its aircrafts' tails, provides inter-island flights and serves 15 international destinations.

Air UK was formed in 1980 from four older British airlines, and currently flies scheduled services to Amsterdam, Brussels and the Channel Islands.

Air Vendee is a commuter airline which connects various French cities. It has scheduled international flights to Amsterdam, Brussels and London.

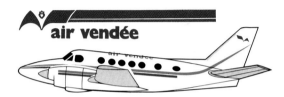

Air Zimbabwe, the state airline, operates short-haul domestic flights and provides services to destinations in various other southern African countries.

Alaska airlines, with its unique Eskimo logo on the tails of its aircraft, currently serves 30 cities in Alaska and along the west coast of the United States.

Alitalia, Italy's national airline, has a fleet of more than 100 aircraft flying internal routes and around the Mediterranean, as well as providing a worldwide international service.

Airline insignia

American Airlines, given its present name in 1930, is one of the world's largest airlines, serving more than 80 destinations throughout the world.

Ansett Airlines has been operating internal flights in Australia for more than 30 years and now has a fleet consisting almost entirely of Boeing aircraft.

Austrian Airlines, formed in 1957, flies nearly 30,000 route-miles, serving 30 countries throughout Europe, the Middle East and North Africa.

Balair is a Swiss charter airline which flies passengers and cargo to destinations in the Mediterranean, Far East, Africa and North and South America.

British Airways flies over more route-miles (more than 350,000) than any other international airline, serving more than 80 cities throughout the world.

British Midland, founded in 1939 as a domestic airline, now flies scheduled services to various destinations in Europe and the Channel Islands.

BWIA (British West Indian Airlines), owned since 1967 by the Trinidad Government, flies routes throughout the Caribbean and North, Central and South America.

Brymon, originally a British domestic airline, now also flies short take-off Dash-8s from London's new Docklands Airport to various European destinations.

CAAC (Civil Aviation Administration in China) flies more than 160 domestic routes and has international services to 17 countries throughout the world.

Canadian Airlines International flies an extensive network of scheduled passenger and cargo services to more than 90 destinations in 16 countries on 5 continents.

Cargolux Airlines International, founded in Luxembourg in 1970, is an all-cargo carrier with services to the Middle East, Asia and North America.

Cathay Pacific, based in Hong Kong, flies passengers and cargo throughout south-eastern Asia and has services to Australia, Bombay, Frankfurt and London.

Airline insignia

Chalks International, one of the few airlines still operating flying boats, provides services from three places in Florida to islands in the Bahamas.

Challenge Air Cargo, formed only in 1986, offers cargo charter and flies all-cargo schedules from Miami to various Central American countries.

China Airlines (CAL), operating from Taiwan, provides a domestic service and international flights to Asia, the Middle East and North America.

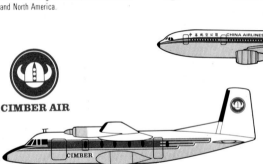

Cimber Air, based in Denmark, is mainly a charter airline, although it does operate some domestic scheduled flights and a service to Humberside, England.

Comair is a South African domestic airline with inter-city scheduled flights (some for South African Airways) and popular safari flights for tourists.

Continental Airlines, based in California, flies domestic routes throughout the United States, with services also to Mexico, Australia and New Zealand.

Crossair, based in Switzerland, is a charter airline wholly owned by Swissair. It carries mainly tourist traffic on similar routes to the parent company.

CSA (Ceskoslovenske Aerolinie), the national airline of Czechoslovakia, provides domestic services and also operates an extensive international network.

Dan-Air is a British airline with scheduled services to many destinations in Europe and flies many holiday charter flights from Britain and Berlin.

Delta Air Lines is one of the major operators in the United States, serving more than 80 American cities and six international destinations.

Eastern Air Lines, an American operator which has been flying since 1928, has a vast route network encompassing more than 120 destinations in 17 countries.

El Al Israel Airlines, formed in 1948, is the state airline, based in Tel Aviv. Its scheduled flights serve most European capitals, the United States and Canada.

Airline insignia

Emirates Airlines, flying since 1985, carries the flag of the United Arab Emirates from Dubai to the Middle East, India and south-eastern Asia.

Finnair, founded as long ago as 1924, operates an intensive domestic service in Finland and international flights as far as Thailand and the United States.

GB Airways, based in Gibraltar, flies a Vickers Viscount on its Tangier route and a Boeing 737 on its daily flights to London–Gatwick.

Gulf Air is the national carrier of the Persian Gulf states of Bahrain, Oman, Qatar and the United Arab Emirates, serving mainly the Middle East and Asia.

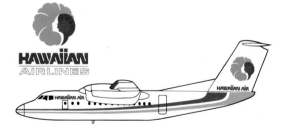

Hawaiian Airlines flies its de Havilland Dash 7s on its inter-island routes, with Tri-Stars for services to the North American mainland, American Samoa and Tonga.

Iberia, the Spanish state airline, can trace its origins back to 1927, and today provides an estensive domestic service and international flights worldwide.

ICELANDAIR

Icelandair has operated internal flights for more than 50 years, and now offers scheduled and charter services to destinations in more than 10 countries.

IRAN AIR

Iran Air flies passengers or cargo on its scheduled flights throughout Iran and the Middle East. It also flies to Europe, Afghanistan and India.

الخطوط الجوية العراقية

Iraqi airways

Iraqi Airways, with its mixed fleet of Boeing and Soviet-built aircraft, operates a domestic service and international flights to Africa, Asia and Europe.

JAPAN AIR·LINES

JAL (Japan Air Lines) flies to more than 40 destinations in Asia, Australasia, Europe, the Middle East, and North, Central and South America.

YUGOSLAV AIRLINES

JAT (Jugoslovenski Aerotransport) runs domestic and international flights to Europe, the Far East, the Middle East, North Africa and North America.

KLM ROYAL DUTCH AIRLINES

KLM (Royal Dutch Airlines) is the world's oldest airline, which began the Amsterdam–London route in 1920. Today it flies 225,000 route-miles.

Airline insignia

Lauda Air, a charter airline based in Vienna and carrying mainly holidaymakers to Mediterranean resorts, was founded by Austrian racing driver Nikki Lauda.

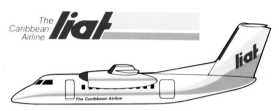

LIAT, advertised as the Caribbean Airline, is based in Antigua and owned by the governments of the dozen islands it serves for passengers and cargo.

Lufthansa, the West German airline, is one of Europe's largest with many internal flights and a worldwide network of routes serving more than 70 countries.

Malaysian Airline System, the national carrier based in Kuala Lumpur, provides domestic services and international flights to Asia, Australia and Europe.

Malév (Magyar Légikozlekedési Vallalat) is the national airline of Hungary, flying Soviet-built aircraft on various domestic and international routes.

Martinair Holland is a specialist cargo airline, carrying freight in its wide-bodied jets on scheduled flights to destinations in Asia, Europe and the Middle East.

Minerve, a privately-owned French Airline based in Paris, operates to French Overseas Territories, Africa, Asia and North and South America.

NFD (Nurenberger Flugdienst) is a West German commuter airline linking various German cities, and has international flights to many European capitals.

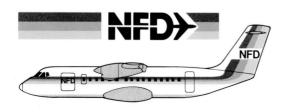

Nigeria Airways, one of the fastest-growing airlines in Africa, has a large domestic network and international services to major European cities and New York.

Northwest, one of the largest airlines in the United States, has a fleet of more than 300 aircraft with scheduled services to more than 20 countries.

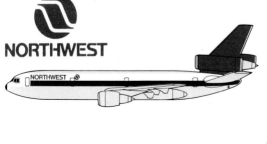

Norving provides domestic passenger and cargo flights within Norway and to Finland and Sweden, as well as operating a Scandinavian air ambulance service.

Olympic Airways, a Greek airline with the Olympic Movement's symbol on the tails of its aircraft, has flights to Africa, Asia, Europe and North America.

Airline insignia

Pakistan International Airlines (PIA) provides passenger and cargo services domestically and to Africa, Europe, the Far and Middle East, and North America.

Pan American World Airways (Pan Am), with a route-mileage in excess of 85,000, flies over the Atlantic and Pacific to destinations in more than 40 countries.

Philippine Airlines uses a mixed fleet of aircraft on its extensive domestic network and international flights to Australia, Europe and North America.

Piedmont, originally a domestic airline in the eastern United States, now provides commuter flights throughout the country, with links to Europe.

Polynesian Airlines is Western Samoa's national airline, with scheduled passenger and cargo services to Australia, New Zealand and many Pacific islands.

Presidential Airways was formed in 1985 as a north-south regional carrier based in Washington D.C., to which it provides feeder services for United Airlines.

Qantas Airways, its Australian origin represented by a kangaroo symbol on its aircrafts' tails, has a worldwide network of passenger and cargo services.

Royal Air Maroc, the national airline of Morocco, flies from Casablanca and Tangier to destinations in Europe, North Africa, the Middle East and the Americas.

Royal Jordanian, founded by King Hussein's royal decree in 1963, flies to destinations throughout the Middle East, with other routes to Europe and North America.

Sabena Belgian World Airlines has a wide network of scheduled routes within Europe and to Africa, Asia, the Middle East and North America.

SAS (Scandinavian Airlines System) is the national airline of Denmark, Norway and Sweden, with flights to 100 destinations in more than 45 countries.

Saudia (Saudi Arabian Airlines) is the largest regional airline in the Middle East, with additional international flights to more than 40 other destinations.

Airline insignia

Singapore Airlines, the state-owned national airline since 1972, flies mainly big jets to link Asia with Australasia and various European destinations.

South African Airways, with its distinctive springbok symbol on its aircrafts' tails, serves African countries and has routes to Asia, the Americas and Europe.

Southwest Airlines, based in Dallas, Texas, has over the last 20 years become one of the largest domestic operators in the United States.

Sudan Airways, the national airline of the Sudan, operates domestic flights and international routes from East Africa to Europe and the Middle East.

Syriannair (Syrian Arab Airlines), the government-owned airline based in Damascus, has scheduled flights to Europe, the Middle East and North Africa.

TAP (Transportes Aéros Portugueses), Portugal's national airline for more than 40 years, flies to destinations in Africa, Europe, and North and South America.

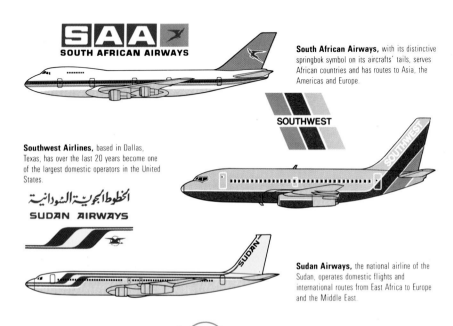

Tarom (Transporturile Aeriene Romane) is the state airline of Romania, with American and Soviet aircraft serving mainly Europe and the Middle East.

Thai Airways International, Thailand's government-owned flag-carrier, based in Bangkok, flies big jets to Europe, the United States and most major Asian cities.

Trans World Airlines (TWA) is one of the world's largest airlines, with domestic and international routes serving more than 60 cities throughout the world.

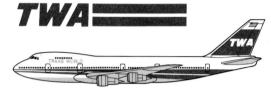

Turk Hava Yollari (THY), Turkey's national airline, connects Ankara and Istanbul with various destinations in the Middle East, Pakistan and European countries.

United Airlines, a domestic operator with a history dating back more than 60 years, flies passengers and cargo in more than 350 aircraft to 100 American cities.

USAir is a domestic and commuter airline with an extensive network of routes that serve 25 states in the north-eastern and mid-western United States.

Airline insignia

Varig (Viação Aérea Rio Grandense), the Brazilian national airline, serves more than 60 destinations worldwide in addition to its domestic network.

VASP (Vigção Aérea São Paulo), the domestic airline of Brazil for more than 50 years, has a vast network of routes throughout that country and charter flights to the United States.

VIASA (Venezolana Internacional de Aviación) operates services from Caracas and Maracaibo in Venezuela to the rest of the Americas and to destinations in Europe.

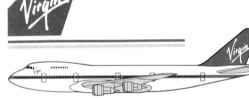

Virgin Atlantic Airways, founded by Richard Branson in 1984, flies Boeing 747s on the transatlantic route between London Gatwick and New York and Miami.

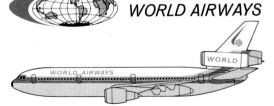

World Airways, formed 50 years ago and based in California, is one of the largest airlines that concentrates on charter flights for both passengers and cargo.

Zambia Airways, founded soon after Zambia achieved independence in 1964, serves Central and East Africa, with links to India, Sri Lanka and many European countries.

Airports of the world

How many airports are there in the world? If you count the airports served by international flights, the number is just over 800, but if you count as well all those with scheduled domestic and international flights, there are well over 4,000. And if you include airports used by business and private aircraft, there are around 4,000 in the USA alone. The USA, which accounts for more than a third of the world's airline activity, and about 90 per cent of its business and private flying, can muster the impressive total of 122,500 landing places. These range from big, international airports to privately-owned grass strips, from heliports to seaplane bases.

Of the world's 25 busiest airports, 16 are in the United States. O'Hare International Airport in Chicago continues to top the list. In the late 1980s, it handled over 55 million passengers each year, involving more than 800,000 aircraft movements (equivalent to one landing or take-off every 40 seconds). At the peak of the 1987 holiday charter season, London's Gatwick Airport had a daily throughput greater even than that of O'Hare.

In the following pages, nearly 400 of the world's major airports are listed, in alphabetical order, country by country (state by state in the USA).

Within each country or state the airports with a substantial international traffic, or an annual throughput of not less than 100,000 passengers, are listed under their cities.

Each entry gives the approximate travelling distance to the airport from the centre of the nearest town or city; the airport's IATA code (so the passengers may check that their baggage is correctly coded at the point of departure, and thus reduce the possibility that it may be lost) and the telephone number.

The entries have been compiled largely from information sent in by the various national airport authorities. Where the relevant authority did not respond fully to our enquiries, the information has been drawn from other authoritative sources. Airport facilities are constantly being extended and phone numbers changed, but airlines and travel agents are kept up to date.

The world is divided into 24 time zones, within each of which all clocks should be set to the same time. In general each zone is one hour ahead of the next zone to the west (except at the International Date Line in the Pacific, where a westbound traveller will go forward by 24 hours). The zones are based on 15-degree divisions of longitude, but have been modified for political convenience. Certain countries introduce daylight saving time; during the summer they put clocks one or two hours ahead of the appropriate setting for their time zone.

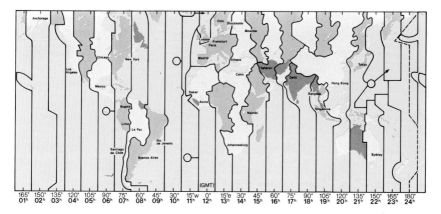

Airport facilities

Most major airports that handle international flights provide a wide range of facilities and services for air travellers. But in some smaller airports, which claim international status only because of occasional overseas flights (often to only a few destinations), facilities can be much more spartan.

For this reason, it is a wise precaution for a traveller who may require a particular service — such as conference facilities — to check ahead with the airline, travel agent or airport itself. And even a basic facility may be unavailable at certain airports. For example, for security reasons, some airport authorities do not allow passengers to post letters once they have gone through passport control — that is, once they are officially airside.

Similarly, there may be banking facilities near the check-in desks, but none airside. The following pages list the world's major airports, with their official name and international three-letter code (as it should appear on your baggage label), with their telephone numbers and information about the distance from the airport to the town or city centre.

Most airports have bus and taxi services into the centre, and a few of the major ones — such as Amsterdam (Schiphol), Boston (Logan International), Frankfurt, London (Heathrow) and Baltimore (Washington International) — also have a rail link, indicated by the letter **R** following the city-centre distance.

In general, the bus is the cheapest, then the train (if available). Taxi fares can be expensive, especially if there is no official licensing system, although they are more convenient than public transport if you are carrying a lot of baggage.

The symbols below itemize the many airport facilities that are available. They should be used as a checklist *before* you make a trip.

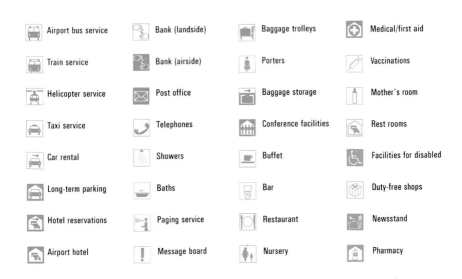

Airport bus service	Bank (landside)	Baggage trolleys	Medical/first aid
Train service	Bank (airside)	Porters	Vaccinations
Helicopter service	Post office	Baggage storage	Mother's room
Taxi service	Telephones	Conference facilities	Rest rooms
Car rental	Showers	Buffet	Facilities for disabled
Long-term parking	Baths	Bar	Duty-free shops
Hotel reservations	Paging service	Restaurant	Newsstand
Airport hotel	Message board	Nursery	Pharmacy

Airports gazetteer

AFGHANISTAN

Kabul
Kabul Airport   `KBL`
Tel: 26341
City centre: 10 miles (16 km)

ALGERIA

Algiers
Dar-el-Beida Airport   `ALG`
Tel: 76 10 18
City centre 12 miles (19 km)

ANGOLA

Luanda
Bellas Airport   `LAD`
Tel: 24141
City centre: 2.5 miles (4 km)

ARGENTINA

Buenos Aires
Aeroparque Airport   `AEP`
Tel: 773 2066
City centre: 2 miles (3 km)

AUSTRALIA

Adelaide
Adelaide Airport   `ADL`
Tel: 084 32211
City centre: 5 miles (8 km)

Brisbane
Brisbane International Airport   `BNE`
Tel: 268 9511
City centre: 7 miles (11 km)

Melbourne
Melbourne International Airport   `MEL`
Tel: 338 2211
City centre: 15 miles (24 km)

Perth
Perth International Airport   `PER`
Tel: 277 2466
City centre: 7 miles (11 km)

Sydney
Kingsford Smith International Airport   `SYD`
Tel: 667 0544
City centre: 6 miles (10 km)

Tasmania/Hobart
Hobart Airport   `HBA`
Tel: 48 50 01
City centre: 12.5 miles (19.5 km)

AUSTRIA

Graz
Graz/Thalerhof Airport   `GRZ`
Tel: 291 541/3
(also 291 406, 291 324)
City centre: 7.5 miles (11.5 km)

Klagenfurt
Flagenfurt Airport   `KLU`
Tel: 41500
City centre: 2.5 miles (3.5 km)

Innsbruck
Innsbruck/Kranebitter Airport   `INN`
Tel: 82325
City centre: 3 miles (5 km)

Linz
Linz/Hörsching Airport   `LNZ`
Tel: 2700-0
City centre: 9 miles (15 km) **R**

Salzburg
Salzburg Airport   `SZG`
Tel: 45323
City centre: 4 miles (6.6 km)

Vienna
Schwechat Airport   `VIE`
Tel: 77 700
City centre: 10 miles (16 km)

Kingsford Smith International Airport, Sydney

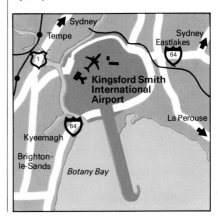

BAHAMAS, THE

Freeport
Freeport International Airport **FPO**
Tel: 6020
City centre: 2 miles (3 km)

Nassau
Nassau International Airport **NAS**
Tel: 77281
City centre: 12 miles (19 km)

BAHRAIN

Bahrain
Bahrain International Airport,
Nuharraq **BAH**
Tel: 21540
City centre: 5 miles (8 km)

BANGLADESH

Dacca (Dhaka)
Tezgoan Airport **DAC**
Tel: 310151
City centre: 5 miles (8 km)

BELGIUM

Brussels
Brussels National Airport **BRU**
Tel: 511 18 60
City centre: 7.5 miles (11.5 km) **R**

Ostend (Oostende)
Ostend Airport **OST**
Tel: 70 08 01/05
City centre: 3 miles (5 km)

BERMUDA

Hamilton
Finchley Field (U.S. Naval Air
Station) **BDA**
Tel: 3 8111
City centre: 9 miles (14 km)

BOLIVIA

La Paz
Kennedy International Airport **LPB**
Tel: 59310
City centre: 5 miles (8 km)

BRAZIL

Brasilia
Brasilia International Airport **BSB**
Tel: 242 6889
City centre: 8 miles (13 km) **R**

Rio de Janeiro
Galeâo Airport **RIO**
Tel: 398 4132
City centre: 12.5 miles (19.5 km)

São Paulo
Congomás Airport **SAO**
Tel: 61 666
City centre: 6 miles (10 km)

BULGARIA

Sofia
Vrajdebna Airport **SOF**
Tel: 45 11 21
City centre: 6 miles (10 km)

Varna
Varna Airport **VAR**
Tel: 4 18 11 or 4 8 12
City centre: 4.5 miles (7 km)

BURMA

Rangoon
Mingaladon Airport **RGN**
Tel: 40111
City centre: 12 miles (19 km)

CAMEROON

Douala
Douala Airport **DLA**
Tel: 42 46 93
City centre: 3 miles (5 km)

CANADA

Montreal
Dorval International Airport `YUL`
Tel: 636 3221
City centre: 12 miles (19 km)

Mirabel Airport `YMX`
Tel: 514 476 3010
City centre: 33 miles (53 km)

Quebec
Foy Airport (Aéroport de
Québec) `YQB`
Tel: 418 872 2304
City centre: 12 miles (19 km)

Toronto
Toronto International Airport
(Lester B. Pearson International
Airport `YYZ`
Tel: 969 5551
City centre: 18 miles (29 km)

Vancouver
Vancouver International
Airport `YVR`
Tel: 666 7321
City centre: 11 miles (18 km)

Winnipeg
Winninpeg International
Airport `YWG`
Tel: 786 4105
City centre: 4 miles (6.5 km)

CHANNEL ISLANDS

see UNITED KINGDOM, CHANNEL
ISLANDS

CHILE

Santiago
Pudahuel Airport `SCL`
Tel: 733968
City centre: 10 miles (16 km)

CHINA, PEOPLE'S REPUBLIC

Peking (Beijing)
Peking Airport `PEK`
Tel: 555531
City centre: 16 miles (25.5 km)

COLOMBIA

Bogotà
El Dorado Airport `BOG`
Tel: 66 92 100
City centre: 8.5 miles (14 km)

CORSICA

see FRANCE, CORSICA

CUBA

Havana
Jose Marti Airport `HAV`
City centre: 14 miles (22.5 km)

CYPRUS

Larnaca
Larnaca Airport `LCA`
Tel: 041 55 323
City centre: 3 miles (5 km)

CZECHOSLOVAKIA

Prague (Praha)
Ruzyne Airport `PRG`
Tel: 334
City centre: 11 miles (17 km)

DENMARK

Copenhagen (København)
Kastrup Airport `CPH`
Tel: 45 01 509333
City centre: 6 miles (10 km)

DOMINICAN REPUBLIC

Santo Domingo
Las Americas Airport `SDQ`
Tel: 687 0421
City centre: 17 miles (27 km)

ECUADOR

Quito
Mariscal Sucre Airport | UIO |
Tel: 241977
City centre: 5 miles (8 km)

EGYPT

Cairo (Al Qahirah)
Cairo Airport | CAI |
Tel: 968866
City centre: 9 miles (15 km)

EIRE see IRELAND, REPUBLIC OF

EL SALVADOR

San Salvador
Ilopango Airport | SAL |
Tel: 27 0025
City centre: 5 miles (8 km)

ENGLAND see UNITED KINGDOM

ETHIOPIA

Addis Ababa
Bole Airport | ADD |
Tel: 447330
City centre: 5 miles (8 km)

FIJI

Nandi
Nandi International Airport | NAN |
Tel: 72500
City centre: 6 miles (10 km)

FINLAND

Helsinki
Vantaa Airport | HEL |
Tel: 82921
City centre: 12 miles (19 km)

FRANCE

Bordeaux
Mérignac Airport | BOD |
Tel: 47 14 47
City centre: 8 miles (13 km)

Lyon(s)
Satolas Airport | LYS |
Tel: 71 92 21
City centre: 15.5 miles (25 km)

Marseille(s)
Mérignane Airport (Aéroport
Marseille Provence) | MRS |
Tel: 89 90 10
City centre: 17 miles (28 km)

Mulhouse (see also Basel,
Switzerland)
Basel/Mulhouse Airport | MLH |
Tel: 44 32 40
City centre: 15.5 miles (24 km)

Nice
Côte d'Azur Airport | NCE |
Tel: 83 19 40
City centre: 4 miles (7 km)

Paris
Charles de Gaulle Airport | CDG |
Tel: 862 12 12
City centre: 15 miles (25 km) **R**

Orly Airport | ORY |
Tel: 587 51 41
City centre: 12 miles (19 km) **R**

Strasbourg
Strasbourg/Entzheim Airport | SXB |
Tel: 78 40 99
City centre: 7 miles (12 km) **R**

Toulouse
Blagnac Airport | TLS |
Tel: 49 30 21
City centre: 6 miles (10 km)

FRANCE, CORSICA

Ajaccio
Ajaccio/Compo dell'Oro Airport AJA
Tel: 21-13-66/22-03-64
City centre: 4 miles (7 km)

GABON

Libreville
Libreville Airport LBV
Tel: 71 02 28
City centre: 4 miles (7 km)

GERMANY, EAST

Berlin, East
Schonefeld Airport SXF
Tel: 67 20
City centre: 12 miles (19 km) **R**

Dresden
Klotzsche Airport DRS
Tel: 58 941
City centre: 6.5 miles (10 km)

Leipzig
Leipzig Airport LEG
Tel: 41011
City centre: 7.5 miles (11.5 km)

GERMANY, WEST

Berlin, West
Tegel Airport TXL
Tel: 41011
City centre: 4 miles (7 km)

Bremen
Bremen/Neuenland Airport BRE
Tel: 55951
City centre: 2 miles (3.5 km) **R**

Cologne (Köln)
Cologne-Bonn (Wann) Airport CGN
Tel: 40 24 04
City centre: 9 miles (14 km)

Düsseldorf
Lohausen Airport DUS
Tel: 4211
City centre: 5 miles (8 km) **R**

Frankfurt
Frankfurt Airport FRA
Tel: 0611 690
City centre: 7 miles (12 km) **R**

Hamburg
Fuhlsbuttel Airport HAM
Tel: 5081
City centre: 5.5 miles (8 km)

Hanover (Hannover)
Langenhagen Airport HAJ
Tel: 73051
City centre: 7 miles (11 km)

Munich (München)
Riem Airport MUC
Tel: 92111
City centre: 6 miles (10 km) **R**

Nuremberg (Nürnberg)
Nuremberg Airport NUE
Tel: 375440
City centre: 4 miles (5.5 km)

Stuttgart
Echterdingen Airport STR
Tel: 79011
City centre: 9 miles (14 km)

GHANA

Accra
Kotoka Airport ACC
Tel: 76171
City centre: 6 miles (10 km)

GIBRALTAR

Gibraltar
Gibraltar Airport GIB
Tel: 5984
City centre: 0.5 miles (1 km)

GREAT BRITAIN
see UNITED KINGDOM

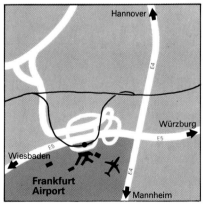

Frankfurt Airport

GREECE

Athens
Athens Airport `ATH`
Tel: 9811 211
City centre: 6.5 miles (11 km)

Corfu (Kerkyra)
Kerkyra Airport `CFU`
Tel: 34144
City centre: 2 miles (3 km)

Heraklion
Heraklion Airport `HER`
Tel: 081 221 401
City centre: 3 miles (5 km)

Rhodes (Rhodos)
Maritsa Airport `RHO`
Tel: 24302
City centre: 10 miles (16 km)

GUATEMALA

Guatemala City
La Aurora Airport `GUA`
Tel: 60311
City centre: 4 miles (5.5 km)

HOLLAND

see NETHERLANDS, THE

HONG KONG

Hong Kong
Hong Kong International
Airport `HKG`
Tel: 3 820211
City centre: 4 miles (6 km)

HUNGARY

Budapest
Ferihegy Airport `BUD`
Tel: 140 400
City centre: 10 miles (16 km)

ICELAND

Reykjavik
Keflavik International Airport `KEF`
Tel: 92 1442
City centre: 31 miles (50 km)

INDIA

Bombay
Santa Cruz Airport `BOM`
Tel: 535461
City centre: 19 miles (30 km)

Calcutta
Dum Dum Airport `CCU`
Tel: 572031
City Centre: 17 miles (27 km)

Delhi
Delhi Airport `DEL`
Tel: 391058
City centre: 8 miles (13 km)

Madras
Meenambakkar Airport `MAA`
Tel: 433168
City centre 10 miles (16 km)

INDONESIA

Jakarta
Halim International Airport `HLP`
Tel: 84071
City centre: 7 miles (11 km)

IRAN

Abadan
Abadan Airport `ABD`
Tel: 32145
City centre: 7.5 miles (11.5 km)

Tehran
Mehrabad Airport `THR`
Tel: 641171
City centre: 12 miles (19 km)

IRAQ

Baghdad
Baghdad International Airport `BGW`
Tel: 551 8888
City centre: 10.5 miles (16 km)

IRELAND, NORTHERN

see UNITED KINGDOM

IRELAND, REPUBLIC OF

Dublin
Dublin Airport `DUB`
Tel: 379900
City centre: 5.5 miles (8 km)

Cork/Corcaigh
Cork Airport `ORK`
Tel: 965388
City centre: 5 miles (8 km)

Shannon/Limerick
Shannon International Airport `SNN`
Tel: 61444
City centre: 15 miles (24 km)

ISRAEL

Tel Aviv
Ben Gurion International Airport | TLV |
Tel: 299333
City centre: 12.5 miles (8 km)

ITALY

Milan (Milano)
Linate Airport | LIN |
Tel: 710135
City centre: 4.5 miles (7 km)

Malpensa Airport | MXP |
Tel: 02 868029
City centre: 28 miles (45 km)

Naples (Napoli)
Capodichino Airport | NAP |
Tel: 7805 762/763/707
City centre: 4 miles (97 km)

Pisa
Galileo Galilei Airport | PSA |
Tel: 48219/28088
City centre: 1 mile (2 km) **R**

Rome (Roma)
Ciampino Airport | CIA |
Tel: 600021
City centre: 7.5 miles (11.5 km)

Leonardo da Vinci (Fiumicino) | FCO |
Airport
Tel: 601982
City centre: 20 miles (32 km)

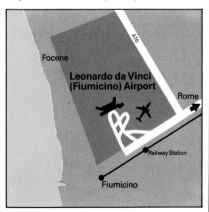

Sicily/Catania
Fontanarossa Airport | CTA |
Tel: 340290
City centre: 4.5 miles (6.5 km)

Turin (Torino)
Casselle Airport | TRN |
Tel: 57781
City centre: 10 miles (16 km)

Venice (Venezia)
Marco-Polo-Tessera Airport | VCE |
Tel: 757333
City centre: 8 miles (13 km)

IVORY COAST

Abidjan
Port-Bouet Airport | ABJ |
Tel: 368171
City centre: 10 miles (16 km)

JAMAICA

Kingston
Norman Marley Airport | KIN |
Tel: 938 7819
City centre: 12 miles (19 km)

Montego Bay
Sangster International Airport | MBJ |
Tel: 952 3124
City centre: 3 miles (5 km)

JAPAN

Kagoshima
Kagoshima Airport | KOJ |
Tel: 09995 8 2111
City centre: 21 miles (33.5 km)

Osaka
Osaka International Airport | OSA |
Tel: 06203 1212
City centre: 10 miles (16 km)

Tokyo
Narita Airport | NRT |
Tel: 03747 3131
City centre: 42 miles (67 km) **R**

Tokyo International Airport | TYO |
Tel: 03747 3131
City centre: 12 miles (19 km) **R**

JORDAN

Amman
Amman Airport | AMM |
Tel: 51401
City centre: 5 miles (8 km)

KENYA

Nairobi
Nairobi International Airport   `NBO`
Tel: 822111
City centre: 8.5 miles (14 km)

KUWAIT

Kuwait
Kuwait Airport   `KWI`
Tel: 710788
City centre: 10 miles (16 km)

LAOS

Vientiane
Vientiane Airport   `VTE`
City centre: 2.5 miles (3.5 km)

LIBYA

Benghazi
Benina International Airport   `BEN`
Tel: 3102
City centre: 18 miles (29 km)

Tripoli
Tripoli International Airport   `TIP`
Tel: 34840
City centre: 21 miles (33.5 km)

LUXEMBOURG

Luxembourg
Luxembourg (Findel) Airport   `LUX`
Tel: 47911
City centre: 4 miles (6.5 km)

MADAGASCAR

Tananarive
Ivato Airport   `TNR`
Tel: 44098
City centre: 11 miles (18 km)

MALAYSIA

Kuala Lumpur
Kuala Lumpur International
Airport   `KUL`
Tel: 03-760714
City centre: 14 miles (22.5 km)

Penang
Bayan Lepas Airport   `PEN`
Tel: Bayan Lepas 04 831411
City centre: 11 miles (17.5 km)

MALTA

Valletta
Luqa Airport   `MLA`
Tel: 622910
City centre: 4 miles (6 km)

MARIANA ISLANDS

Guam
Agana Field Air Terminal   `GUM`
Tel: 646 41481
City centre: 2 miles (3 km)

MAURITIUS

Port Louis
Plaisance Airport   `MRU`
Tel: 73531
City centre: 18 miles (29 km)

MEXICO

Acapulco
Acapulco Airport   `ACA`
Tel: 4-03-04
City centre: 12 miles (20 km)

Guadalajara
Miguel Hidalgo Airport   `GDL`
Tel: 18-27-13
City centre: 10.5 miles (17 km)

Mexico City
Mexico City International Airport   `MEX`
Tel: 5713478
City centre: 6 miles (10 km)

Monterrey
Monterrey Airport   `MTY`
Tel: 54-34-34
City centre: 12 miles (19 km)

MOROCCO

Casablanca
Nouasseur Airport   `CMN`
Tel: 339100
City centre: 22 miles (35 km)

NETHERLANDS, THE

Amsterdam
Schiphol Airport   `AMS`
Tel: 511-0432
City centre: 9 miles (15 km) **R**

Maastricht
Maastricht Airport   `MST`
Tel: 666444
City centre: 9 miles (15 km)

Rotterdam
Rotterdam Airport `RTM`
Tel: 3110-115-860
City centre: 5 miles (10 km)

NETHERLANDS ANTILLES

Aruba/Oranjestad
Prinses Beatrix Airport `AUA`
Tel: 4800
City centre: 2.5 miles (3.5 km)

Curaçao/Willemstad
Dr A. Plesman Airport `CUR`
Tel: 82288
City centre: 7 miles (11 km)

St Maarten/Philipsburg
Prinses Juliana Airport `SXM`
Tel: 2160
City centre: 9.5 miles (14.5 km)

NEW ZEALAND

Auckland
Auckland International Airport `AKL`
Tel: 50 789
City centre: 8.5 miles (14 km)

Christchurch
Christchurch International
Airport `CHC`
Tel: 585029
City centre: 7 miles (11 km)

Wellington
Wellington International
Airport `WLG`
Tel: 725659
City centre: 4 miles (6 km)

Schiphol Airport, Amsterdam

NICARAGUA

Managua
Las Mercedes Airport `MGA`
Tel: 31627
City centre: 5.5 miles (8 km)

NIGERIA

Kano
Kano Airport `KAN`
Tel: 3891
City centre: 5 miles (8 km)

Lagos
Murtala Muhammed Airport `LOS`
Tel: 31031
City centre: 13.5 miles (21 km)

NORWAY

Bergen
Flesland Airport `BGO`
Tel: 522-60-00
City centre: 11 miles (19 km)

Oslo
Fornebu Airport `OSL`
Tel: 2-12-13-40
City centre: 6 miles (10 km)

Stavanger
Sola Airport `SVG`
Tel: 45-50020
City centre: 8 miles (13 km)

OMAN

Muscat
Seeb International Airport `MCT`
Tel: 619223
City centre: 22 miles (35 km)

PAKISTAN

Islamabad
Chaklala Airport `RWP`
Tel: 62736
City centre: 1.5 miles (2 km)

Karachi
Karachi International Airport `KHI`
Tel: 512041
City centre: 10 miles (16 km)

Lahore
Lahore Airport `LHE`
Tel: 371090
City centre: 2 miles (3 km)

PAPUA NEW GUINEA

Port Moresby
Jackson Field Airport `POM`
Tel: 256611
City centre: 5 miles (8 km)

PARAGUAY

Asuncion
President General Stroessner
Airport `ASU`
Tel: 22012
City centre: 9.5 miles (14.5 km)

PERU

Lima
Jorge Chavaz International
Airport `LIM`
Tel: 52-9570
City centre: 4 miles (6.5 km)

PHILIPPINES, THE

Manila
Manila International Airport `MNL`
Tel: 831784
City centre: 7.5 miles (11.5 km)

POLAND

Warsaw (Warszawa)
Okecie Airport `WAW`
Tel: 469470
City centre: 6 miles (10 km)

PORTUGAL

Faro
Faro Airport `FAO`
Tel: 23081
City centre: 4.5 miles (6.5 km)

Lisbon (Lisboa)
Lisbon Airport `LIS`
Tel: 88-11-01
City centre: 4.5 miles (7 km)

Madeira/Funchal
Funchal Airport `FNC`
Tel: 52441
City centre: 14.5 miles (23 km)

Oporto
Oporto Airport `OPO`
Tel: 948-12-41
City centre: 10.5 miles (17 km)

QATAR

Doha
Doha International Airport `DOH`
City centre: 5 miles (8 km)

RHODESIA see ZIMBABWE

ROMANIA

Bucharest
Otopeni Airport `BUH`
Tel: 333137
City centre: 12 miles (19 km)

RUSSIA see SOVIET UNION

SAUDI ARABIA

Jeddah
Jeddah International Airport `JED`
Tel: 22111
City centre: 1.5 miles (2 km)

Riyadh
King Khaled International
Airport `RUH`
Tel: 61400
City centre: 17.5 miles (27.5 km)

SCOTLAND see UNITED KINGDOM

SENEGAL

Dakar
Yoff Airport `DKR`
Tel: 5118085
City centre: 10.5 miles (16 km)

SEYCHELLES

Mahé Island/Mahé
Mahé Airport `SEZ`
Tel: 76553
City centre: 6 miles (10 km)

SIERRA LEONE

Freetown
Lungi Airport `FNA`
Tel: Lungi 215
City centre: 18 miles (29 km)

SINGAPORE

Singapore
Singapore International Airport `SIN`
Tel: 888321
City centre: 12.5 miles (20 km)

SOUTH AFRICA

Capetown
D. F. Milan Airport   `CPT`
Tel: 932767
City centre: 15 miles (24 km)

Durban
Louis Botha Airport   `DUR`
Tel: 426111
City centre: 10 miles (16 km) **R**

Johannesburg
Jan Smuts Airport   `JBN`
Tel: 9751185
City centre: 14.5 miles (23 km)

SOVIET UNION

Kiev
Borispol Airport   `KBP`
Tel: 7744223
City centre: 24 miles (38 km)

Leningrad
Pulkovo Airport   `LED`
Tel: 2117980
City centre: 10.5 miles (17 km)

Moscow
Sheremtievo Airport   `SVO`
Tel: 155-5005
City centre: 16 miles (26 km)

SPAIN

Alicante
Alicante Airport   `ALC`
Tel: 285011
City centre: 8 miles (13 km)

Barcelona
Barcelona Airport   `BCN`
Tel: 317-00-08
City centre: 6 miles (10 km) **R**

Bilbao
Bilbao Airport   `BIO`
Tel: 453-1350
City centre: 6 miles (10 km)

Canary Islands/Las Palmas
Las Palmas Airport   `LPA`
Tel: 24-41-40
City centre: 12.5 miles (19.5 km)

Ibiza
Ibiza Airport   `IBZ`
Tel: 302200
City centre: 5 miles (8 km)

Madrid
Barajas Airport   `MAD`
Tel: 2-22-11-65
City centre: 7.5 miles (12 km)

Majorca/Palma
Palma Airport   `PMA`
Tel: 262600
City centre: 6 miles (10 km)

Malaga
Malaga Airport   `AGP`
Tel: 31-60-00
City centre: 5 miles (8 km) **R**

Santiago
Santiago Compostela Airport `SCQ`
Tel: 597 400
City centre: 6 miles (10 km)

Valencia
Valencia Airport   `VLC`
Tel: 325-63-90
City centre: 7.5 miles (11.5 km)

SRI LANKA

Colombo
Bandaranaike Airport   `CMB`
Tel: 0315 361
City centre: 20 miles (32 km) **R**

SUDAN

Khartoum
Khartoum Civil Airport   `KRT`
Tel: 73624
City centre: 2.5 miles (3.5 km)

SWEDEN

Gothenburg (Göteborg)
Landvetter Airport   `GOT`
Tel: 941100
City centre: 15.5 miles (25 km)

Malmo (Malmö)
Sturup Airport   `MMA`
Tel: 75040
City centre: 20 miles (32 km)

Stockholm
Arlanda Airport   `ARN`
Tel: 08-780-5000
City centre: 26 miles (42 km)

SWITZERLAND

Basel/Mulhouse
Basel/Mulhouse Airport   `BSL`
Tel: Basel 573111/Mulhouse
690000
City centre: 6 miles (10 km)

Geneva
Cointrin Airport   `GVA`
Tel: 98-11-22
City centre: 2.5 miles (4 km)

Zurich (Zürich)
Zurich Airport   `ZRH`
Tel: 8127111
City centre: 7.5 miles (12 km)

SYRIA

Damascus
Damascus International Airport   `DAM`
City centre: 18 miles (29 km)

TAIWAN

Taipei
Sungshan Airport   `TPE`
Tel: 7521212
City centre: 3 miles (5 km)

TANZANIA

Dar-es-Salaam
Dar-es-Salaam Airport   `DAR`
Tel: Wageni 221
City centre: 8 miles (13 km)

THAILAND

Bangkok
Bangkok International Airport   `BKK`
Tel: 5237258
City centre: 12 miles (20 km) **R**

TONGA

Tongatapu/Nukualofa
Fua'amotu International
Airports   `TBU`
City centre: 13 miles (21 km)

TRINIDAD AND TOBAGO

Port of Spain
Piarco Airport   `POS`
City centre: 16 miles (25.5 km)

TUNISIA

Djerba
Melita Airport   `DJE`
Tel: 03-50-223
City centre: 3.5 miles (5 km)

Monastir
Skanes Airport   `MIR`
Tel: 03-61-315
City centre: 5 miles (8 km)

Tunis
Carthage Airport   `TUN`
Tel: 01-289-000
City centre: 5 miles (8 km)

TURKEY

Ankara
Esenboga Airport   `ESB`
Tel: 241270
City centre: 18 miles (29 km)

Istanbul
Yesilkoy Airport   `IST`
Tel: 737240
City centre: 15 miles (24 km)

UNION OF SOVIET
SOCIALIST REPUBLICS

see SOVIET UNION

UNITED KINGDOM

Aberdeen
Aberdeen Airport   `ABZ`
Tel: 0224 722331
City centre: 5.5 miles (8 km)

Belfast
Aldergrove Airport **BFS**
Tel: 0232 29271
City centre: 14 miles (22 km)

Birmingham
Birmingham Airport **BHX**
Tel: 021-743 4272
City centre: 5 miles (8 km)

Darlington/Middlesborough
Tees-side Airport **MME**
Tel: 0325 332811
City centre: Darlington 6 miles
(9.5 km)
Middlesborough 13 miles
(22 km)

Derby
East Midlands Airport **EMA**
Tel: 0332 810621
City centre: 12 miles (19 km)

Edinburgh
Turnhouse Airport **EDI**
Tel: 031-334 2351
City centre: 7 miles (11 km)

Glasgow
Prestwick Airport **PIK**
Tel: 0292 79822
City centre: 32 miles (51 km) **R**

Leeds/Bradford
Leeds/Bradford Airport **LBA**
Tel: 0532 509696
City centre: Leeds 8 miles (13 km)
Bradford 6 miles (9km)

Liverpool
Liverpool Airport **LPL**
Tel: 051-494 0066
City centre: 6 miles (10 km) **R**

London
Gatwick Airport **LGW**
Tel: 0293 28822
City centre: 27 miles (43 km) **R**

Heathrow Airport **LHR**
Tel: 01-759 4321
City centre: 15 miles (25 km) **R**

Luton Airport **LTN**
Tel: 0582 405100
City centre: 30 miles (48 km) **R**

Stansted Airport **STN**
Tel: 0279 502380
City centre: 34 miles (55 km) **R**

Manchester
Manchester International
Airport **MAN**
Tel: 061-437 5233
City centre: 10 miles (16 km)

Newcastle upon Tyne
Newcastle Airport **NCL**
Tel: 0632 860966
City centre: 5 miles (8 km)

Southampton
Eastleigh Airport **SOU**
Tel: 0703 612341
City centre: 4 miles (6 km) **R**

Southend-on-Sea
Southend Airport **SEN**
Tel: 0702 40201/6
City centre: 2 miles (3 km)

UNITED KINGDOM, CHANNEL ISLANDS

Guernsey/St Peter Port
La Villiaze Airport **GCI**
Tel: 37682
City centre: 4 miles (6.5 km)

Jersey/St Helier
Jersey Airport **JER**
Tel: 41272
City centre: 5.5 miles (9 km)

Heathrow Airport, London

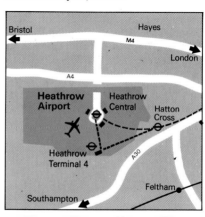

UNITED STATES OF AMERICA

ALABAMA
Birmingham
Birmingham Municipal Airport
Tel: (205) 595-0533
City centre: 5 miles (8 km)

`BHM`

Huntsville
Madison Airport
Tel: (205) 772-9395
City centre: 11 miles (18 km)

`HSV`

Mobile
Mobile Municipal Airport
Tel: (205) 342-0510
City centre: 15 miles (24 km)

`MOB`

Montgomery
Montgomery Municipal Airport
Tel: (205) 281-5040
City centre: 7 miles (11 km)

`MGM`

ALASKA
Anchorage
Anchorage International
Airport
Tel: (907) 279-3486
City centre: 5 miles (8 km)

`ANC`

Fairbanks
Fairbanks International Airport
Tel: (907) 452-2151
City centre: 5 miles (8 km) **R**

`FAI`

ARIZONA
Phoenix
Skyharbor International
Airport
Tel: (602) 262-6291
City centre: 4 miles (6.5 km)

`PHX`

Tucson
Tucson International Airport
Tel: (602) 294-3411
City centre: 10 miles (16 km)

`TUS`

ARKANSAS
Little Rock
Adams Field Airport
Tel: (501) 372-3439
City centre: 3 miles (5 km)

`LIT`

CALIFORNIA
Bakersfield
Meadowfield Airport
Tel: (805) 861-2218
City centre: 4 miles (6.5 km)

`BFL`

Burbank
Hollywood-Burbank Airport
Tel: (213) 847-6321
City centre: 4 miles (6.5 km)

`BUR`

Fresno
Fresno Air Terminal
Tel: (209) 251-6051
City centre: 7 miles (11 km)

`FAT`

Los Angeles
Los Angeles International
Airport
Tel: (213) 646-5252
City centre: 15 miles (24 km)

`LAX`

Monterey
Peninsula Airport
Tel: (408) 373-3731
City centre: 3 miles (5 km)

`MRY`

Oakland
Oakland International Airport
Tel: (714) 984-1207
City centre: Oakland 11 miles
(18 km)
San Francisco 19 miles (30.5 km)

`OAK`

Ontario
Ontario International Airport
Tel: (714) 984-1207
City centre: Ontario 3 miles
(5 km)
Los Angeles 14 miles (22.5 km)

`ONT`

Palm Springs
Palm Springs Municipal Airport
Tel: (714) 323-8161
City centre: 2 miles (3 km)

`PSP`

Sacramento
Sacramento Metropolitan
Airport $\boxed{\text{SMF}}$
Tel: (916) 929-5411
City centre: 11 miles (18 km)

San Diego
San Diego International
Airport $\boxed{\text{SAN}}$
Tel: (714) 291-3900
City centre: 3 miles (5 km)

San Francisco
San Francisco International
Airport $\boxed{\text{SFO}}$
Tel: (415) 761-0800
City centre: 14 miles (22.5 km)

San Jose
San Jose Municipal Airport $\boxed{\text{SJC}}$
Tel: (408) 277-4000
City centre: 3 miles (5 km)

Santa Barbara
Santa Barbara International
Airport $\boxed{\text{SBA}}$
Tel: (805) 967-7111
City centre: 6 miles (10 km)

COLORADO
Colorado Springs
Colorado Springs Airport $\boxed{\text{COS}}$
Tel: (303) 398-0188
City centre: 8 miles (13 km)

Denver
Stapleton International Airport $\boxed{\text{DEN}}$
Tel: (303) 398-3844
City centre: 7 miles (11 km)

Stapleton International Airport, Denver

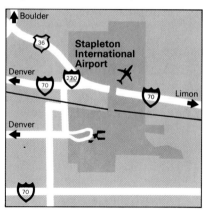

Grand Junction
Walker Field Airport $\boxed{\text{GJT}}$
Tel: (303) 243-3695
City centre: 6 miles (10 km)

CONNECTICUT
Windsor Locks
Bradley International Airport $\boxed{\text{BDL}}$
Tel: (203) 623-3940
City centre: 13 miles (21 km)

DISTRICT OF COLUMBIA
Washington
Dulles International Airport $\boxed{\text{IAD}}$
Tel: (703) 471-7596
City Centre: 26 miles (42 km)

Washington National Airport $\boxed{\text{DCA}}$
Tel: (703) 557-2045
City centre: 4 miles (6.5 km) **R**

FLORIDA
Daytona Beach
Daytona Beach Regional
Airport **DAB**
Tel: (904) 225-8441
City centre: 3 miles (5 km)

Fort Lauderdale/Hollywood
Fort Lauderdale-Hollywood
Airport **FLL**
Tel: (305) 765-5910
City centre: 4 miles (6.5 km)

Fort Myers
Page Field Airport **FMY**
Tel: (813) 936-3143
City centre: 4 miles (6.5 km)

Gainesville
Gainesville Regional Airport **GNV**
Tel: (904) 374-2176
City centre: 6 miles (10 km)

Jacksonville
Jacksonville International
Airport **JAX**
Tel: (904) 757-2261
City centre: 17 miles (27 km)

Miami
Miami International Airport **MIA**
Tel: (305) 526-2000
City centre: 7 miles (11 km)

Orlando
Orlando International Airport **MCO**
Tel: (305) 885-8841
City centre: 12 miles (19 km)
[Disney World 23 miles (36 km)]

Pensacola
Pensacola Regional Airport **PNS**
Tel: (904) 436-4315
City centre: 5 miles (8 km)

Sarasota
Bradenton Airport **SRQ**
Tel: (813) 355-2761
City centre: 4 miles (6.5 km)

Tampa
Tampa International Airport **TPA**
Tel: (813) 883-3400
City centre: 5 miles (8 km)

West Palm Beach
West Palm Beach International
Airport **PBI**
Tel: (305) 683-5722
City centre: 3 miles (5 km)

GEORGIA
Atlanta
Atlanta International Airport **ATL**
Tel: (404) 766-2772
City centre: 8 miles (13 km)

Augusta
Bushfield Airport **AGS**
Tel: (404) 798-3236
City centre: 7 miles (11 km)

Columbus
Columbus Metropolitan
Airport **CSG**
Tel: (404) 324-2449
City centre: 5 miles (8 km)

Savannah
Savannah Municipal Airport **SAV**
Tel: (912) 964-0517
City centre: 8 miles (13 km)

HAWAII
Hilo
Lyman Field Airport **ITO**
Tel: (808) 935-0809
City centre: 3 miles (5 km)

Honolulu
Honolulu International Airport **HNL**
Tel: (808) 847-9411
City centre: 4 miles (6.5 km)

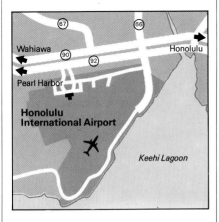

Kailua
Ke-Ahole Airport **KOA**
Tel: (808) 329-2984
City centre: 8 miles (13 km)

IDAHO
Boise
Gowen Field Airport **BOI**
Tel: (208) 344-3239
City centre: 4 miles (6.5 km) **R**

ILLINOIS
Alton
Civic Memorial Airport **ALN**
Tel: (618) 259-2531
City centre: 5 miles (8 km)

Champaign
University of Illinois Airport **CMI**
Tel: (217) 333-3204
City centre: 6 miles (10 km)

Chicago
Chicago Midway Airport **MDW**
Tel: (312) 767-0500
City centre: 10 miles (16 km)

O'Hare Airport **ORD**
Tel: (312) 686-1220
City centre: 18 miles (29 km)

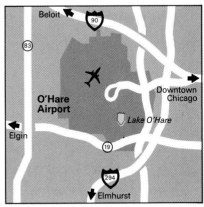

Merril C. Meigs Field **CGX**
Tel: (312) 744-4787
City centre: 1.5 miles (2 km)

Moline
Quad-Cities Airport **MLI**
Tel: (309) 764-9621
City centre: 4 miles (6.5 km)

Peoria
Greater Peoria Airport **PIA**
Tel: (309) 697-8272
City centre: 9 miles (14.5 km)

INDIANA
Evansville
Evansville Dress Regional
Airport **EVV**
Tel: (812) 424-5511
City centre: 3 miles (5 km)

Fort Wayne
Fort Wayne Municipal Airport **FWA**
Tel: (219) 747-6598
City centre: 9 miles (14.5 km)

Indianapolis
Indianapolis International
Airport **IND**
Tel: (317) 247-6271
City centre: 8 miles (13 km)

South Bend
Michiana Regional Airport `SBN`
Tel: (219) 233-2185
City centre: 4 miles (6.5 km)

IOWA
Cedar Rapids
Cedar Rapids Municipal Airport `CID`
Tel: (319) 362-3131
City centre: 8 miles (13 km)

Des Moines
Des Moines Municipal Airport `DSM`
Tel: (515) 283-4255
City centre: 3 miles (5 km)

KANSAS
Wichita
Mid-Continent Airport `ICT`
Tel: (316) 942-8101
City centre: 6 miles (10 km)

KENTUCKY
Lexington
Blue Grass Field Airport `LEX`
Tel: (606) 254-9336
City centre: 6 miles (10 km)

Louisville
Stundiford Field Airport `SDF`
Tel: (502) 368-6524
City centre: 5 miles (8 km)

LOUISIANA
Baton-Rouge
Ryan Airport `BTR`
Tel: (504) 355-0333
City centre: 8 miles (13 km)

New Orleans
New Orleans International
Airport `MSY`
Tel: (504) 729-2591
City centre: 14 miles (22.5 km)

MAINE
Bangor
Bangor International Airport `BGR`
Tel: (207) 942-4675
City centre: 3 miles (5 km)

Portland
Portland International Jetport `PWM`
Tel: (207) 774-7301
City centre: 2 miles (3 km)

MARYLAND
Baltimore
Washington International
Airport `BAL`
Tel: (301) 761-7100
City centre: 10 miles (16 km) **R**

MASSACHUSETTS
Bedford
Hanscom Field Airport `BCD`
Tel: (617) 274-7200
City centre: 3 miles (5 km)

Boston
Logan International Airport `BOS`
Tel: (617) 567-5400
City centre: 3 miles (5 km) **R**

MICHIGAN
Battle Creek
W. K. Kellogg Regional Airport `BTL`
Tel: (616) 966-3470
City centre: 3 miles (5 km)

Detroit
Detroit City Airport `DET`
Tel: (313) 224-1300
City centre: 6 miles (10 km)

Detroit Metro Wayne Airport `DTW`
Tel: (313) 278-3910
City centre: 19 miles (30.5 km)

Flint
Bishop Airport `FNT`
Tel: (313) 767-4232
City centre: 4 miles (6.5 km)

Grand Rapids
Kent County Airport `GRR`
Tel: (616) 949-4500
City centre: 11 miles (18 km)

Kalamazoo
Kalamazoo Municipal Airport `AZO`
Tel: (616) 385-8177
City centre: 4 miles (6.5 km)

Lansing
Capital City Airport `LAN`
Tel: (517) 371-2020
City centre: 4 miles (6.5 km)

Oakland
Oakland-Pontiac Airport `PTK`
Tel: (313) 666-3900
City centre: 5 miles (8 km)

Saginaw
Tri-City Airport `MBS`
Tel: (517) 695-5555
City centre: 10 miles (16 km)

MINNESOTA
Duluth
Duluth International Airport `DLH`
Tel: (218) 727-2968
City centre: 7.5 miles (11.5 km)

Minneapolis
St Paul Airport `MSP`
Tel: (612) 726-1717
City centre: 13 miles (21 km)

Rochester
Rochester Municipal Airport `RST`
Tel: (507) 282-2328
City centre: 8 miles (13 km)

St Paul
St Paul Downtown Airport `STP`
Tel: (612) 224-4306
City centre: 1 mile (2 km)

MISSISSIPPI
Jackson
Jackson Municipal Airport `JAN`
Tel: (601) 939-5631
City centre: 10 miles (16 km)

MISSOURI
Kansas City
Kansas City Municipal Airport `MCI`
Tel: (816) 243-5200
City centre: 17 miles (27 km)

St Louis
Lambert St Louis Int. Airport `STL`
Tel: (314) 426-7777
City centre: 13 miles (21 km)

Springfield
Springfield Municipal Airport `SGF`
Tel: (417) 869-7231
City centre: 8 miles (13 km)

MONTANA
Billings
Logan Field Airport `BIL`
Tel: (406) 245-3567
City centre: 2 miles (3 km)

NEBRASKA
Lincoln
Lincoln Municipal Airport `LNK`
Tel: (402) 435-2925
City centre: 5 miles (8 km)

Omaha
Eppley Field Airport `OMA`
Tel: (402) 422-6800
City centre: 5 miles (8 km)

NEVADA
Las Vegas
McCarran International
Airport `LAS`
Tel: (702) 739-5211
City centre: 7 miles (11 km)

Reno
Reno International Airport `RNO`
Tel: (702) 785-2375
City centre: 3 miles (5 km)

NEW JERSEY
Newark
Newark International Airport `EWR`
Tel: (201) 961-2000
City centre: 3 miles (5 km)
[New York 16 miles (25.5 km)]

NEW MEXICO
Albuquerque
Albuquerque International
Airport `ABQ`
Tel: (505) 766-7894
City centre: 5 miles (8 km)

Albany
Albany County Airport ALB
Tel: (578) 869-5312
City centre: 10 miles (16 km)

Buffalo
Greater Buffalo International
Airport BUF
Tel: (716) 842-5768
City centre: 8 miles (13 km)

New York
John F. Kennedy International
Airport JFK
Tel: (212) 656-4444
City centre: 15 miles (24 km)

La Guardia Airport LGA
Tel: (212) 476-5000
City centre: 8 miles (13 km)

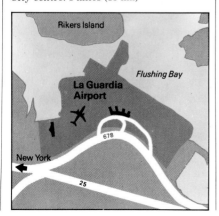

Rochester
Monroe Airport ROC
Tel: (716) 436-5624
City centre: 5 miles (8 km)

Syracuse
Hancock International Airport SYR
Tel: (315) 454-3263
City centre: 7 miles (11 km)

NORTH CAROLINA
Asheville
Asheville Municipal Airport AVL
Tel: (704) 684-2226
City centre: 12 miles (19 km)

Charlotte
Douglas Municipal Airport CLT
Tel: (704) 684-2226
City centre: 8 miles (13 km)

Fayetteville
Fayetteville Municipal Airport FAY
Tel: (919) 484-7314
City centre: 5 miles (8 km)

Greensboro
Greensboro-Highpoint Regional
Airport GSO
Tel: (919) 299-6896
City centre: 11 miles (18 km)

Raleigh
Durham Airport RDU
Tel: (919) 787-4580
City centre: 14 miles (22.5 km)

NORTH DAKOTA
Bismarck
Bismarck Municipal Airport BIS
Tel: (701) 223-5900
City centre: 3 miles (5 km) **R**

Fargo
Hector Field Airport FAR
Tel: (701) 235-4100
City centre: 3 miles (5 km)

OHIO
Akron
Canton Regional Airports CAK
Tel: (216) 986-2385
City centre: 15 miles (24 km)

Cincinnati
Greater Cincinnati Airport CVG
Tel: (606) 283-3151
City Centre: 12.5 miles (19.5 km)

Cleveland
Hopkins International Airport | CLE |
Tel: (216) 265-6000
City centre: 10 miles (16 km) **R**

Lakefront Airport | BKL |
Tel: (216) 781-6411
City centre: 12 miles (19 km)

Columbus
Port Columbus International
Airport | CMH |
Tel: (614) 422-1116
City centre: 7 miles (11 km)

Dayton
James M. Cox Airport | DAY |
Tel: (513) 898-4631
City centre: 12 miles (19 km)

Toledo
Toledo Express Airport | TOL |
Tel: (419) 865-2351
City centre: 17 miles (27 km)

Youngstown
Youngstown Municipal Airport | YNG |
City centre: 14 miles (22.5 km)

OKLAHOMA
Oklahoma City
Will Rogers Airport | OKC |
Tel: (405) 681-5311
City centre: 11 miles (18 km)

Tulsa
Tulsa International Airport | TUL |
Tel: (918) 835-8412
City centre: 9 miles (14.5 km)

OREGON
Portland
Portland International Airport | PDX |
Tel: (503) 233-8331
City centre: 9 miles (14.5 km)

PENNSYLVANIA
Allentown
Bethlehem-Eastern Airport | ABE |
Tel: (215) 264-2831
City centre: 3 miles (5 km)

Erie
Erie International Airport | ERI |
Tel: (814) 833-4258
City centre: 6 miles (10 km)

Harrisburg
Olmstead State Airport | MDT |
Tel: (717) 787-7702
City centre: 1 mile (2 km)

Philadelphia
Philadelphia International
Airport | PHL |
Tel: (215) 492-3000
City centre: 8 miles (13 km)

Pittsburgh
Greater Pittsburgh Airport | PIT |
Tel: (412) 771-2500
City centre: 16 miles (25.5 km) **R**

RHODE ISLAND
Providence
T. F. Green State Airport | PVD |
Tel: (401) 737-4000
City centre: 7 miles (11 km)

SOUTH CAROLINA
Charleston
Charleston International
Airport | CHS |
City centre: 11.5 miles (18 km)

Columbia
Columbia Metropolitan Airport | CAE |
Tel: (803) 794-3419
City centre: 6 miles (10 km)

Greenville
Greenville-Spartanburg Airport | GSP |
Tel: (803) 877-7426
City centre: 15 miles (24 km)

SOUTH DAKOTA
Rapid City
Rapid City Regional Airport | RAP |
Tel: (605) 394-4195
City centre: 7.5 miles (11.5 km)

Sioux Falls
Joe Foss Field Airport | FSD |
Tel: (605) 336-0762
City centre: 3 miles (5 km)

TENNESSEE
Bristol
Bristol Tri-City Airport | TRI |
Tel: (615) 323-6271
City centre: 16 miles (25.5 km)

Chattanooga
Lovell Field Airport | CHA |
Tel: (615) 892-1666
City centre: 10 miles (16 km)

Knoxville
Knoxville Municipal Airport | TYS |
Tel: (615) 577-6621
City centre: 13 miles (21 km)

Memphis
Memphis International Airport   MEM
Tel: (901) 345-7777
City centre: 9 miles (14.5 km)

Nashville
Nashville Metropolitan Airport   BNA
Tel: (615) 367-3012
City centre: 6.5 miles (10 km)

Amarillo
Amarillo International Airport   AMA
Tel: (806) 225-1671
City centre: 9 miles (14.5 km)

Austin
Robert Mueller Municipal
Airport   AUS
Tel: (512) 742-5439
City centre: 4 miles (6·5 km)

Corpus Christi
Corpus Christi International
Airport   CRP
Tel: (512) 882-5451
City centre: 10 miles (16 km)

Dallas
Dallas Fort Worth Airport   DFW
Tel: (214) 574-3112
City centre: 21 miles (33.5 km)

Love Field Airport   DAL
Tel: (214) 352-2663
City centre: 7 miles (11 km)

El Paso
El Paso International Airport   ELP
Tel: (915) 772-4271
City centre: 5 miles (8 km)

Houston
Houston International Airport   IAH
Tel: (713) 443-4731
City centre: 22 miles (35 km)

William P. Hobby Airport   HOU
Tel: (713) 643-4336
City centre: 10 miles (16 km)

Lubbock
Lubbock International Airport   LBB
Tel: (806) 762-6411
City centre: 6 miles (10 km)

Midland
Midland Regional Airport   MAF
Tel: (915) 563-1460
City centre: 10 miles (16 km)

San Antonio
San Antonio International
Airport   SAT
Tel: (512) 824-5335
City centre: 8 miles (13 km)

Salt Lake City
Salt Lake City International
Airport   SLC
Tel: (801) 355-6251
City centre: 6 miles (10 km)

Burlington
Burlington International
Airport   BTV
Tel: (802) 863-2874
City centre: 3 miles (5 km)

Newport News
Patrick Henry International
Airport   PHF
Tel: (804) 877-0221
City centre: 10 miles (16 km)

Norfolk
Norfolk International Airport   ORF
Tel: (804) 857-3351
City centre: 6 miles (10 km)

Richmond
Richard Evelyn Bird Airport   RIC
Tel: (804) 222-7361
City centre: 7 miles (11 km)

Roanoke
Roanoke Municipal Airport   ROA
Tel: (703) 981-2531
City centre: 4 miles (6.5 km)

WASHINGTON STATE
Seattle
Boeing Field International
Airport   BFI
Tel: (206) 344-7380
City centre: 5 miles (8 km)

Tacoma Airport   SEA
Tel: (206) 433-5385
City centre: 13 miles (21 km)

Spokane
Spokane International Airport   GEG
Tel: (509) 624-3218
City centre: 6 miles (10 km)

WEST VIRGINIA
Charleston
Kanawha Airport   CRW
Tel: (304) 346-0707
City centre: 4 miles (6.5 km)

Huntingdon
Tri-State Airport   HTS
Tel: (304) 453-3481
City centre: 9 miles (14.5 km)

WISCONSIN
Green Bay
Austin Straubel Airport   GRB
Tel: (414) 494-2900
City centre: 8.5 miles (13 km)

Madison
Dane County Airport   MSN
Tel: (608) 241-1251
City centre: 5 miles (8 km)

Milwaukee
General Mitchell Field Airport   MKE
Tel: (414) 747-5300
City centre: 7 miles (11 km)

URUGUAY

Montevideo
Carrasco Airport   MVD
Tel: 502261
City centre: 12 miles (19 km)

YUGOSLAVIA

Belgrade (Beograd)
Sucrin Airport   BEG
Tel: 601-555
City centre: 10 miles (16 km)

Dubrovnik
Dubrovnik Airport   DBV
Tel: 77-122/77-144
City centre: 13.5 miles (21 km)

Ljubljana
Ljubljana Airport   LJU
Tel: 25-761/2
City centre: 15.5 miles (26 km)

Zagreb
Pleso Airport   ZAG
Tel: 525-522/516-200
City centre: 10 miles (16 km)

ZAMBIA

Lusaka
Lusaka International Airport   LUN
Tel: 74331
City centre: 13 miles (21 km)

ZIMBABWE

Harare
Harare (Salisbury) Airport   SAY
Tel: 50422
City centre: 7 miles (11 km)

Glossary of terms

A

Abort To abandon a course of action; e.g., to cancel a takeoff already started.

Acceleration The rate of change of velocity — of speed, or direction, or both at once. (See: **Deceleration**.)

Aerodynamics The science dealing with air or other gas in motion and its effects on a moving body.

Aerofoil (airfoil) A suitably shaped structure that generates lift when propelled through the air, such as a wing, propeller, rotor blade or tailplane.

Afterburner (reheat) A system in which fuel is injected into the jet exhaust and ignited to give extra thrust to supersonic aircraft for short periods.

Aileron A movable control surface hinged to the trailing edge of each wing, usually near the tip.

Air brake A hinged surface that increases drag.

Aircraft surface movement indicator (ASMI) A radar screen in a control tower that shows all objects on the airfield.

Airspeed indicator (ASI) An instrument that measures the speed at which an aircraft is moving through the air (not generally equal to ground speed).

Airway A path for air traffic, defined by radio beacons such as VORs or NDBs (q.v.).

Alphanumeric display Computer "writing" in letter and number characters on a TV-type screen.

Altimeter An aircraft altitude indicator.

Angle of attack The angle at which an aerofoil meets oncoming air.

Annular Ring-shaped.

Aquaplaning Riding on a thin film of water on the runway.

Artificial horizon A gyro-stabilized flight instrument that shows the pitching and rolling movements of an aircraft.

Astro-navigation Traditional navigation using the positions of the sun and stars.

Autopilot Automatic pilot, a gyroscopically controlled device that keeps an aircraft in steady flight or puts it through pre-set manoeuvres, such as climbing to a chosen flight level.

B

Baffle A structure that impedes the flow of a fluid, such as fuel in a tank.

Barrette Closely spaced ground lights that from the air appear as a bar of light.

Bleed air High-pressure air "bled" from a main engine for cabin pressurization and other services.

Bogie Four-, six- or eight-wheel truck on a main landing leg.

Boom carpet The strip of ground along which sonic boom from supersonic aircraft is heard.

Bulkhead A transverse panel across a fuselage, such as those at the front and rear of pressure cabins.

By-pass engine A jet engine (q.v.) in which up to about half of the intake air is ducted around the combustion chamber by a fan. When the by-pass ratio is higher the engine is called a turbofan (q.v.).

C

Camber The curvature of an aerofoil surface.

Canard An aircraft with main wing at the rear, with a "foreplane" — a horizontal control surface — at the front.

Cantilever wing A wing supported at the root only, and lacking bracing wires or struts.

Centre of gravity (CG) The point at which the total weight of an aircraft is considered to act.

Chord The distance from the leading to the trailing edge of an aerofoil. The mean chord is the average chord of a tapered wing.

Clean (Describing an aircraft) having all extensible devices (landing-gears, flaps, etc) retracted — the normal en route configuration.

Clear air turbulence (CAT) High-level turbulence occurring in clear weather conditions.

Clearway The area of land or water over which an aircraft may begin its climb in the first few seconds after takeoff.

Collective-pitch control Control that varies the angle of attack of all the blades of a helicopter rotor simultaneously to make the craft rise or descend. (See: **Cyclic-pitch control**.)

Combi A transport plane in which the proportion of passengers to cargo can easily be varied by removing or adding seats in order to achieve the most economical combination.

Compressor A device that compresses (increases the density of) intake air in a piston engine, turboprop or jet engine.

Condition-monitoring Continuous monitoring of an aircraft's components and sysytems.

Control surface A movable aerofoil (such as a stabilizer) or section of an aerofoil (such as an aileron or elevator) that controls an aircraft's flight.

Cyclic-pitch control Control that varies a helicopter's direction of movement by tilting each blade according to its position in the circle of rotation. (See: **Collective-pitch control**.)

D

Deceleration The rate of reduction of speed, also called negative acceleration. (See: **Acceleration**.)

Delta wing A triangular or near-triangular wing; named after the Greek letter corresponding to "D".

Doppler radar Airborne equipment that determines speed and direction of movement by measuring the changes in frequency of several radar beams transmitted from the aircraft and reflected from the ground. (See: **Radar**.)

Drag The air's resistance to moving objects.

Drift The lateral movement of an aircraft away from its desired track; caused by the wind.

Duct A channel or tube through which fluid passes.

E

Elevator A horizontal control surface on the tailplane (stabilizer) that controls climb and descent. Many modern jets have pivoted tailplanes and no elevators. (See: **Elevon.**)

Elevon A control surface on the wing of a tailless craft, functioning as both elevator and aileron.

EPNdB Effective perceived noise decibel, a unit of noise that is intended to represent both its duration and its "annoyance value". (*See:* **PNdB.**)

F

Feather To turn the blades of a propeller edge-on to the slipstream when power has been cut off, so that they are not forced to rotate.

Fin (Vertical stabilizer) The fixed vertical surface at an aircraft's tail that helps to control roll and yaw.

Flame-out Extinction of combustion in a gas-turbine engine, resulting in total loss of power.

Flap A movable surface on an aircraft wing that increases lift, or both lift and drag. Most are fitted at the trailing edge, but one type (the Krüger) is on the leading edge. Flaps are extended before takeoff or landing.

Flight director A flight-deck instrument that tells the pilot whether he should guide the aircraft left or right, up or down, or stay level and on a pre-set heading.

Flight envelope The limiting accelerations and speeds that an aircraft may fly at. (See: **G-forces.**)

Flight recorder An airborne device, able to withstand accidents, that continuously records important features of an airliner's flight, such as height, speed, control-surface position, etc.

Floatplane An aircraft with floats, capable of landing on water, usually called a seaplane in the U.K. (See: **Flying boat.**)

Flutter An unstable air-induced oscillation of an aerofoil.

Flying boat An aircraft that can land and take off from water on its boatlike hull. (See: **Floatplane.**)

G

Gas turbine An engine driven by hot gases, formed by the burning of fuel, which escape through blades that are thereby forced to rotate. Most jet engines, including turbofans, as well as turboprops and turboshafts, are gas-turbine engines.

G-forces The crew of a plane in a turn or pulling out of a dive experience "centrifugal" forces (that is, forces directed away from the centre of the curved path). These "g-forces" (gravity-forces) give the crew a feeling of increased weight, can cause blackouts, and stress the aircraft.

Gimbals A mounting that permits an instrument such as a compass or gyroscope to move freely and so maintain a constant orientation regardless of an aircraft's movement.

Glidepath The path an aircraft follows as it comes in to land; also, the beam in an ILS system giving vertical guidance.

Ground effect Extra lift experienced by an aircraft very close to the ground. It is caused by the downwash of air striking the surface.

Gyrocompass A device incorporating gyroscopes that indicates true north.

H

Head-up display (HUD) Information projected onto an aircraft's windshield, focused at infinity, so that the pilot can see it without lowering his eyes.

Heat sink Any structure that can absorb a large amount of heat while undergoing only a small rise in temperature.

Horizontal situation indicator (HSI) Flight-deck instrument that indicates aircraft heading, the distance and bearing of radio beacons and other position information.

Hypersonic More than five times as fast as sound.

I

Inertial navigation system (INS) A system incorporating three sensitive accelerometers, which continuously measure changes in an aircraft's speed and direction, and a computer which works out the position from this information.

Instrument flight rules (IFR) The procedures a pilot must follow when flying without visual cues from the ground.

Instrument Landing System (ILS) A system that guides a pilot during landing by means of two sets of radio beams transmitted from the ground near the runway.

J

Jet engine An engine that takes in air, uses it to burn fuel, emits a stream of hot gas, and experiences a reaction thrust. (See: **Gas turbine, Turbofan, Turbojet.**)

Jet-lag The discrepancy between local time and the time to which an air traveller, recently arrived from another time zone, is adapted.

Jet stream Clearly defined streams of fast-moving air at high altitudes.

K

Knot A speed of 1 nautical mile per hour, equal to 1.15 statute miles per hour.

L

Leading edge The front edge of an aerofoil.

Lift The force generated on an aerofoil at right angles to the flow of air around it. Usually denotes the supporting force generated by a wing (including a helicopter rotor blade); but the

Glossary of terms

thrust created by a propeller is the same kind of force.

Lift dumper A surface extended from a wing upper surface immediately after landing in order to "spoil" the airflow and reduce lift.

Loran Long-Range Navigation, a radio navigation system in which signals from three linked ground stations are automatically compared by an onboard receiver.

M

Mach number The ratio of true airspeed to the local speed of sound. Since the latter varies with altitude, a given Mach number does not represent a fixed speed.

Magnetic compass An instrument containing a magnetized needle showing the direction of magnetic north.

Microwave Landing System A newly accepted radio landing aid that will replace the Instument Landing System (q.v.). Aircraft are guided to the runway from many directions by a microwave beam (a type of very short-wave radio beam) that scans a large area of sky. Since aircraft do not have to join a single glidepath, MLS can handle a greater volume of traffic than ILS.

N

Nautical mile The unit of distance used in air navigation, equal to approximately 1.15 statute miles.

Navaid Navigational aid.

NDB Non-directional beacon, radio navaid giving position, but not steering guidance.

O

Omega A nagivation system that employs a world-wide network of VLF (very low frequency) radio transmitters. Their precisely synchronized transmissions are compared by an airborne computer. The entire world is covered by eight transmitters.

P

Phonetic alphabet An alphabet that uses words instead of letters to prevent confusion over the radio:

A = Alpha	B = Bravo	C = Charlie
D = Delta	E = Echo	F = Foxtrot
G = Golf	H = Hotel	I = India
J = Juliet	K = Kilo	L = Lima
M = Mike	N = November	O = Oscar
P = Papa	Q = Quebec	R = Romeo
S = Sierra	T = Tango	U = Uniform
V = Victor	W = Whiskey	X = X-ray
Y = Yankee	Z = Zulu	

Pitch The angular setting of a propeller blade or helicopter rotor blade; or up-and-down movements of an aircraft's nose.

Pitot head Forward-facing, open-ended tube measuring dynamic air pressure (which increases with speed), surrounded by an outer tube with side perforations to measure "static" atmospheric pressure. (See: **Airspeed indicator**.)

PNdB Perceived noise decibel, a unit of noise that takes account of the annoying quality of the different frequencies present. (See: **EPNdB**.)

Q

QNH Air pressure at sea level. This figure, which varies, is supplied by air traffic control to aircraft captains so that they can set their altimeters correctly.

R

Radar Radio Direction and Ranging. *Primary* radar equipment, housed in ground stations, planes or ships, emits ultra-high-frequency radio pulses to determine the position of objects by measuring the time taken for the radio waves to return after being reflected from them, and displays them as glowing "blips" on a TV-type screen. Ground-based *secondary* radar also scans an areas with a radio beam, but triggers a transponder (transmitter-responder) in suitably equipped aircraft. The transponder sends a radio pulse to the interrogating station, carrying information about the aircraft's identity, heading, speed, altitude, etc. This information is "written" on the radar display next to the blip representing the aircraft. (See: **Doppler radar**.)

Radio compass An airborne instrument that indicates true north on the basis of radio signals from ground stations.

Radio direction finder (RDF) An airborne instrument that shows the direction of a ground radio station. (See: **VOR**)

Radio magnetic indicator (RMI) Flight-deck instrument that shows the magnetic heading of a VOR (q.v.) station and the magnetic heading of the aircraft.

Radome Streamlined protective covering for radar aerials, transparent to radar waves.

Refanned engine A turbofan (q.v.) that has had its fan blades replaced with larger ones.

Reverse pitch A setting of aircraft propeller blades at which they exert a backward thrust to slow the aircraft after touchdown.

Reverse thrust Rearward thrust from a jet engine, achieved by deflecting the jet forward, to slow aircraft after touchdown.

Roger "Message received and understood".

Roll Rotation of an aircraft about its nose-to-tail line (longitudinal axis).

Roll-out The distance an aircraft requires to come to a halt after touchdown.

Rotate To pull up the nose of an aircraft on the runway and take off.

Rotor An assembly of moving wings and their hub, usually turning in a horizontal plane, as on a helicopter; or the rotating part of the fan, compressor or turbine in a jet engine.

Rudder The vertical control surface at the rear edge of the fin.

Runway visual range (RVR) Visibility along a runway. At major airfields it is measured by automatic equipment.

S

Servomotor Motor controlled by small inputs, and delivering large outputs; an airliner's control surfaces are driven by servomoters guided by pilot movements or autopilot signals.

Shockwaves Pressure waves that trail from aircraft travelling at or beyond the speed of sound.

Slat A small auxiliary wing mounted on the leading edge of an aerofoil. It is extended to increase lift.

Slipstream Stream of air thrown back by a propeller.

Slot Gap between a leading edge and slat (q.v.).

Span The distance from wing-tip to wing-tip.

Spoilers Control surfaces on the wings of an aircraft that destroy lift by interfering with the airflow. Sometimes they are used as lift dumpers (q.v.) after landing.

Spool A rotating assembly in a turbine engine, consisting of a turbine, a drive shaft and a compressor or fan.

SST Supersonic transport aircraft.

Stability An aircraft's resistance to change in its condition of steady flight.

Stall Loss of lift due to excessive angle of attack (q.v.), often caused by insufficient speed.

Standard instrument departure (SID) A specified route from an airport, marked by radio beacons, that an airliner must follow.

Static dischargers Metal "prongs" or fine metal-impregnated wicks mounted on an aircraft's trailing edges which discharge static electricity into the air.

Stator The stationary part of a machine around, within or alongside which a rotor (q.v.) turns; in a gas turbine or its compressor, a set of fixed blades, interspersed with rotor blades, that guide the air or gas flow.

STOL Short takeoff and landing.

Stratosphere The upper atmosphere lying above the "region of weather", or troposphere.

Streamline The path of a particle in a moving fluid.

Supercharger An air compressor that increases the power output of a piston engine.

Supercritical wing A wing designed to delay the build-up of shockwaves (q.v.) at transonic Mach numbers. The top is flatter than a conventional wing's, and lift is more evenly distributed.

T

Tabs Small movable surfaces fitted to main control surfaces. The large force developed on them by the airstream moves the main control surface.

Tailplane (horizontal stabilizer) The horizontal aerofoil at the tail that can be fixed or pivoted.

Torque The twisting reaction force that a propeller or rotor exerts on the aircraft carrying it.

Trailing edge The rear edge of an aerofoil.

Transonic Close to the speed of sound.

Trim To adjust the tabs (q.v.) or other control surfaces of an aircraft so that it flies in the correct attitude without manual effort.

Turbofan A jet engine in which most of the intake air bypasses the combustion chamber and is discharged as a cold jet.

Turbojet A jet engine (q.v.) in which all the intake air goes through the combustion chamber; it is also called a straight jet.

Turboprop A gas-turbine engine that drives a propeller.

Turboshaft A gas-turbine engine that drives an output shaft — in, for example, a helicopter.

Turbulence Violent and irregular motion of air.

U

Undershoot area The unobstructed section of a runway before the threshold, in which a pilot should not land.

V

V_1 A critical speed during takeoff. Below V_1 the takeoff must be abandoned if an engine fails. Above V_1, the takeoff must be continued.

V_2 The speed required by an airliner to climb safely at the desired angle after takeoff.

V_R "Velocity-rotate," the speed at which an airliner must be travelling along the runway when its nose is pulled up to take off.

Variable-geometry wing A wing whose sweepback can be reduced for takeoff, landing or cruising, and increased for high-speed flight.

Vector A directional quantity, such as the distance and bearing of a landmark.

Vertex A "corner" of a geometric form; a triangle has three vertices, a cone one, and so on.

Visual approach slope indicator (VASI) A system of light beams projected from lamps near a runway, whose apparent colour indicates to the pilot whether he is on, below or above the correct glidepath.

Visual flight rules (VFR) The procedures a pilot follows when flying without radar guidance from Air Traffic Control.

VOR VHF omnidirectional range, a system of radio navigation employing a network of radio transmitters whose bearings are determined by receivers in the aircraft.

Vortex A region of a fluid in rotary motion; a smoke ring is an example. Vortices trail from aircraft wings, increasing drag; but they are deliberately generated on some wings to control airflow or increase lift.

VTOL Vertical takeoff and landing.

W

Wilco ("Will comply.") Message received and understood; I will obey your instructions.

Y

Yaw Movement of an aircraft's nose to left or right.

Yoke The control column of an aircraft.

Acknowledgements

The Publishers received invaluable help from the following people and organizations:
David P. Davies (Chief Test Pilot, the UK Civil Aviation Authority, Airworthiness Division); Captain Hugh Dibley (Training and Technical Management, British Airways); Phil Jarrett (Editor, *Aeroplane Monthly*); John W. R. Taylor (*Jane's All the World's Aircraft*); Anthony Vandyk (IATA); Captain B. O. Walpole (Flight Manager (Technical), British Airways Concorde)

George Anderson (Romana Air Travel); Hugh Cloudsley; Chris Cooper; Antonia Gaunt; Ann Kramer; Freda Parker; Penny Stapley; Ann Tilbury; Daphne Wood

Aeroflot Ltd Soviet Airlines; Aéroport de Paris; ACS Engineering Sales Ltd; Aérospatiale; Air Associates Ltd; Airbus Industrie; Aircraft Engineering; Aircraft Furnishing Ltd; Air France; Air-India; Airside Systems Division, Ludwig Honold Manufacturing Co; Air Transport and Travel Industry Training Board; Air Transport Users Committee; American Science and Engineering Inc; L'Armement Naval de la SNCF; Aviaexport USSR; Avions Marcel Dassault – Breguet Aviation; Avis Rent A Car; BBC "Tonight" Programme; B.P. Trading Ltd; Beaufort Air-Sea Equipment Ltd; Beech Aircraft Corp; Boeing Commercial Airplane Co; Bonser Engineering Ltd; British Aerospace Aircraft Group; British Aircraft Corp Ltd; British Airports Authority; British Airways; British Caledonian Airways Ltd; Bell Helicopter Co; British Hovercraft Corp; British Oxygen Co; Britten-Norman (Bembridge) Ltd; Bunce Ltd; CAA (Civil Aviation Authority); CFM International SA; Canadair Ltd; Canadian Pacific Ltd; Cessna Aircraft Corp; Chelton (Electrostatics) Ltd; Chubb Fire Vehicles Ltd; College of Air Training, Hamble; Thomas Cook & Son Ltd; Combs-Gates Denver, Inc; Davall & Sons Ltd; The Decca Navigator Co Ltd; Decca Radar Ltd; de Havilland Aircraft of Canada Ltd; Donne Security Group; F.L. Douglas (Equipment) Ltd; Dowty Group Services Ltd; Dowty Rotol Inc; The Dunlop Co Ltd; EECO; English Electric Ltd; Equipos Técnicos de Transporte SA; Fairey Britten-Norman Ltd; Fairey Hydraulics Ltd; F.F. Impulsphysics Corp Inc; US Federal Aviation Administration; Flight International; Flight Refuelling Ltd; Flughafen Hannover-Langenhagen GmbH; Fokker-VFW BV; GEC Overseas Services Ltd (Aviation Services Division); General Aviation Manufacturers & Traders Association; General Dynamics/Convair; Gloster Saro Ltd; Grumman American Aviation Corp; Hamburger Flugzenban GmbH; Harper & Row Publishing Inc (with whose permission Captain Cummings has contributed to this book); HCB-Angus Ltd; Hertz Rent A Car; Hestair Eagle Ltd; Houchin Ltd; Hoverlloyd Ltd; Infoplan Ltd; Institution of Civil Engineers; International Aeradio Ltd; International Air Transport Association; International Civil Airports Association; International Civil Aviation Administration, Canada; International Civil Aviation Organization; The International Paint Co Ltd; Israel Aircraft Industries Ltd; KLM Royal Dutch Airlines; Lockheed Aircraft Corp; Loganair Ltd; Lucas Aerospace Ltd; Lufthansa German Airlines; Manpower Services Commission, Employment Services Division – Heathrow; Marconi Avionics Ltd; McDonnell Douglas Corp; The Meteorological Office, Bracknell; Normalair-Garrett Ltd; Oshkosh; Palmer Aero Products Ltd; Pan American World Airways; Piper Aircraft Corp; Plessey Radar Ltd; Port Authority of New York and New Jersey; Power Lifts Ltd; Qantas Airways Ltd; RFD Inflatables Ltd; Racal-Amplivox Ltd; Rockwell International Sabreliner Division; Rolls-Royce Ltd (Aero Division); L.A. Rumbold Ltd; Sabena Belgian World Airlines; John Schneller & Associates; Secmafer SA; Shell Aviation News; Shell International Petroleum Co Ltd; Short Brothers and Harland Ltd; Singapore Airlines; Skihi Ltd; Smiths Industries Ltd; Southern Meals Supplies Ltd; Sundstrand Data Control Inc; Sweepster Inc; Swissair; C.F. Taylor Ltd; Taylor-Woodrow Construction Ltd; Thorn Lighting; Trans World Airlines Inc; Trepel Airport Equipment; Triplex Safety Glass Co Ltd; UBM Aero Docks; VFW-Fokker International; Vickers-Armstrong (BAC); Wadham Stringer Ltd; The Walter Kidde Co Ltd; Weldwork Cargo Systems Ltd; Westland Aircraft Ltd; Wollard Aircraft Equipment Inc.

Picture credits

Aerofilms; 68/69 all pictures
Aerophotos/Chris Brooks; 97T, 103, 114, 115, 132B
Aeroports de France; 138T
Airports International; 60, 64
Aviation Photographs International; 41B, 88T, 100, 106, 122, 124, 125, 127T, 127B, 129T, 131T, 133T
Aviation Picture Library; 19R, 101, 108, 116, 126B, 128T, 129B, 174, 177
Barnaby's Picture Library; 139CR
British Aerospace; 30/31 all pictures, 54T, 65, 72, 81, 83 all pictures, 84 all pictures, 98, 105 all pictures, 110, 111, 118, 164B, 182
British Aerospace/Hawker Siddeley; 61
British Airports Authority; 138B
British Airways; 87, 92
Boeing; 85
Camera Press; 15B, 18L, 139CL
Civil Aviation Authority; 18R, 19L
Colorific/Lee Battaglia; 15T
Costain International; 139B
Crown Copyright; 13
Paul Duffy; 86B, 88B, 91, 97B, 117, 119, 120, 126T, 131B

Embraer; 121
Exxon; 54B, 55
Flight International; 41T, 74
Flughafen Hanover/Langenhagen GmbH; 136/7
Fokker BV; 94, 95, 128B, 192
General Electric; 32
KLM Royal Dutch Airline; 67, Keystone Press Agency; 14, 176
Los Angeles Department of Airports; 139T
Lufthansa; 86T, 99, 162
McDonnell Douglas Corp; 93, 96, 102, 113, 132T
PanAm; 163
Plessey Radar Ltd; 71
Plessey Navaids (Parker PRA Associates Ltd); 76
Saab Scania; 123
Brian Service; 104
Shorts; 130 all pictures
UBM Engineering; 165
Virgin Atlantic Airways; 42, 107, 133B
Zefa Picture Library; 184 all pictures